THE PLOT AGAINST THE PRESIDENT

THE PLOT AGAINST THE PRESIDENT

The True Story of How Congressman
Devin Nunes Uncovered the Biggest
Political Scandal in US History

LEE SMITH

CENTER
STREET.

NEW YORK   NASHVILLE

To my wife Catherine

And to all the families put through this trial by ordeal

Center Street
Hachette Book Group
1290 Avenue of the Americas
New York, NY 10104

www.CenterStreet.com

Printed in the United States of America

First Edition: October 2019

Center Street is a division of Hachette Book Group, Inc.
The Center Street name and logo are trademarks of Hachette Book Group, Inc.

The publisher is not responsible for websites (or their content) that are not owned by the publisher.

The Hachette Speakers Bureau provides a wide range of authors for speaking events. To find out more, go to www.HachetteSpeakersBureau.com or call (866) 376-6591.

Library of Congress Cataloging-in-Publication Data has been applied for.

ISBNs: 978-1-5460-8502-7 (hardcover), 978-1-5460-8501-0 (ebook)

Printed in the United States of America

LSC-C

10 9 8 7 6 5 4 3 2 1

CONTENTS

ISA Dossier Subpoena Fusion GPS Clinton Special Counsel Hou

PART ONE

telligence Gongressman Nunes Russia Putin Conspiracy Muelle

THE OPERATION

Chapter 1

"OBJECTIVE MEDUSA"

"WELCOME," said Congressman Devin Nunes, "to the last gasp of the Russian collusion conspiracy theory."

It was July 24, 2019, the first time he'd come face to face with Special Counsel Robert Mueller III. And now their meeting was taking place in public, on Capitol Hill, in front of millions of people watching at home on television. At least half the audience had their hopes pinned on Mueller. The former director of the Federal Bureau of Investigation had been appointed in May 2017 to continue the Bureau's probe into Russian interference in the 2016 election. He represented what had once been the best chance of changing the outcome of the election by bringing down Trump.

What had stopped him was Nunes. The former chairman and now ranking member of the House Intelligence Committee had been studying the Russia-Trump collusion investigation for nearly two and a half years. Nunes had discovered, and produced evidence, that the FBI and Department of Justice had abused the resources of the federal government to spy on Donald J. Trump, his campaign, his transition team, and his presidency.

Nunes knew that the FBI had no collusion case against Trump. The FBI had no evidence, except for political dirt paid for by Hillary Clinton's campaign.

With Nunes closing off avenues, Mueller had to adjust. He turned it into an obstruction investigation, which had lasted nearly two years until Attorney General William Barr had shut that down, too. Like Nunes, Barr understood that Mueller was running an operation, not an investigation.

On March 22, 2019, Mueller produced his final report. After spending more than $30 million and employing dozens of attorneys and FBI agents, the special counsel found no evidence that Trump or his associates had colluded with Russia. Nonetheless, Mueller's devotees found hope in the report insinuating that the president might have obstructed justice. Democrats summoned him to testify before Congress in an effort to bring the report to life, a television reenactment that might with luck lead to Trump's impeachment. After a long career in public service, the seventy-four-year-old Mueller's last act was as a political mannequin.

He surely wasn't there to answer real questions about the investigation, the questions that Nunes had been asking since March 2017: When did the investigation start? Based on what evidence? Under whose authority? What other US agencies or departments were involved? Which US governmental personnel had a hand in the operation? How high did it go? How many spies were sent against Trump's presidential campaign?

Mueller brushed any probing questions aside. They weren't, as he said repeatedly, "in his purview." The special counsel stumbled over even friendly questions. He claimed ignorance of important investigative details. He appeared not to know much of what was in the report that carried his name.

Nunes read from a prepared statement:

In March 2017, Democrats on this committee said they had "more than circumstantial evidence" of collusion, but they couldn't reveal it yet. Mr. Mueller was soon appointed, and they said he would find the collusion.

Then when no collusion was found in Mr. Mueller's indictments, the Democrats said we'd find it in his final report.

Then when there was no collusion in the report, we were told Attorney General Barr was hiding it.

Then when it was clear Barr wasn't hiding anything, we were told it will be revealed through a hearing with Mr. Mueller himself.

And now that Mr. Mueller is here, they are claiming that the collusion has actually been in his report all along, hidden in plain sight.

Mueller started impassively at Nunes as the congressman concluded his speech. "It's time for the curtain to close on the Russia hoax," said Nunes. "The conspiracy theory is dead."

Nunes spoke the truth for those with ears to hear it. It was the American voter who chose Trump, not Putin. The efforts to undermine Trump's candidacy, destroy his presidency, and criminalize political differences were also attacks on American institutions and the American public. No one had risked more to tell the truth than Nunes. His strange odyssey had started precisely two years before Mueller filed his final report.

————————

On March 22, 2017, Nunes was on his way to the White House to tell Trump about what he'd seen. The chairman of the House Permanent Select Committee on Intelligence (HPSCI) looked alarmed. What concerned him that afternoon wasn't a hostile action taken by foreign adversaries, terrorists, or the intelligence services of a rogue nation-state; rather, it was something that American spies had done to Americans. Nunes had seen evidence of a plot against the president.

Earlier in the month, the recently inaugurated Trump had written on Twitter that his predecessor had spied on him: "Just found out that Obama had my wires tapped in Trump Tower just before the victory."

Trump's statements regularly touched off a firestorm. His opponents found cause to denounce his every utterance even as the same words rallied his supporters. But this was different. He'd accused the president of the United States of spying on a political campaign, his. It was unthinkable. Yet sources had shown Nunes that Barack Obama administration officials had asked for the identities of Trump transition team members to be unredacted from intelligence reports.

Typically, the identities—names, titles, and so on—of US citizens are redacted, i.e., "masked," to protect their privacy rights. Unmasking is not illegal, and there are legitimate reasons to ask for the identity of an American to be unmasked. But Nunes had seen evidence of an extensive campaign of unmaskings, for no apparent purpose except to spy on the Trump team.

Nunes, wearing a blue pin-striped suit, approached a group of several dozen reporters, photographers, and TV cameramen assembled at the bottom of a staircase in the Capitol Hill Visitor Center. He stood at a narrow lectern with a dozen microphones to accommodate all the media. The event was carried live on several networks. He unfolded a prepared statement and began.

> *While I said there was not a physical wiretap of Trump Tower, I was concerned that other surveillance activities were used against President Trump and his associates. First, I recently confirmed on numerous occasions, the US intelligence community incidentally collected information about US citizens in the Trump transition. Details about US persons associated with the incoming administration, details with little or no apparent foreign intelligence value were widely disseminated in intelligence community reporting. I have confirmed that additional names of Trump transition team members were unmasked. Fourth and finally, I want to be clear, none of the surveillance was related to Russia or the investigation of Russian activities, or of the Trump team.*

The Obama administration had unmasked the identities of Trump associates. The wide dissemination of information identifying them had increased the likelihood that it would be leaked to the media.

Nunes had touched on the essence of what would eventually be understood as the political operation to destroy Trump. It began in the winter of 2015–2016. It consisted of two components, intertwined.

One involved senior Obama officials from the US law enforcement and intelligence communities as well as the diplomatic corps. They had used electronic surveillance and confidential human sources to spy on and entrap the Trump team. They had leaked classified information to the press to portray Trump and his circle as compromised by hidden ties to the Russian government. That was a political espionage campaign, often conducted clandestinely.

The other component was the media campaign. The press had published leaks of classified intelligence as well as political dirt provided by Clinton operatives to build an echo chamber smearing Trump as a Russian agent.

The operation had had two separate legs: it was designed, first, to undermine his campaign; after Trump won, the operation continued, but now its goal was to bring down the president.

Nunes continued:

> *The House Intelligence Committee will thoroughly investigate surveillance and its subsequent dissemination to determine . . . who was aware of it? Why was it not disclosed to Congress? Who requested the additional unmasking? Whether anyone directed the intelligence community to focus on Trump associates. And whether any laws and regulations and procedures were violated.*

When Nunes left Capitol Hill for the White House that afternoon, everything changed. He'd just begun to scratch the surface of a scandal that would split the country. The media attacks on him started immediately.

"Why are Republicans trusting Devin Nunes to be their oracle of truth?" asked MSNBC analyst Elise Jordan. "A former dairy farmer who House Intel staffers refer to as 'Secret Agent Man,' because he has no idea what's going on."

Roll Call's David Hawkings dismissed him as a rube: "The match between his backstory and his prominence seems wholly incongruous, and helps underscore the perception that Nunes is cavalierly playing at a very high-stakes game while in way over his head."

The "resistance" eventually targeted his family as well, with political operatives paid millions of dollars to destroy him. Nunes was no longer just a public figure, the representative from California's Twenty-second Congressional District. He'd become, as Theodore Roosevelt put it, "a man who is actually in the arena, whose face is marred by dust and sweat and blood."

———————————

Crawdaddy's is a large restaurant with a big horseshoe-shaped bar and live music at the end of Main Street in Visalia, California. Two years after Nunes's journey began, I'm there with him and a group of his friends—Ray Appleton, a radio talk show host, and the Kapetan brothers—listening to the house band.

The lead singer, in a dark bob haircut, go-go boots, and a miniskirt, is belting out covers. The band's led by another of the congressman's buddies, the restaurant's owner, Keith Korsgaden, on guitar. They're good, say Nunes's friends, all musicians.

During a pause in the music, a man with a graying beard in a black turtleneck walks up to the stage, has a quick word with the band, then turns to the audience. "This next one," he says into the mike, pointing at Nunes, "is for you." Nunes looks up from his plate and freezes. Was this another protestor, part of the camp that regularly denounces him at protests staged outside his local offices?

Keith rips into the first few licks of "Jumpin' Jack Flash," and the singer tips his driving cap toward Nunes. "I was born," he sings, "in a crossfire hurricane."

A surprised smile passes across Nunes's face, and he nods back. The crowd erupts in cheers.

"Crossfire Hurricane" is the name that the FBI gave to the investigation it opened on the Trump campaign. The probe was named not after the Stones' 1968 classic but rather the 1986 Penny Marshall film *Jumpin' Jack Flash*.

In the late-Cold-War-era comedy, a quirky bank officer played by Whoopi Goldberg comes to the aid of Jonathan Pryce, who plays a British spy being chased by the KGB.

The FBI's code name alludes to the former British spy whose allegedly Russian-sourced reports documented the Trump team's supposed ties to the Kremlin, ex–MI6 agent Christopher Steele.

Hired by Clinton campaign operatives to smear Trump, Steele is credited with authoring a thirty-five-page collection of memos, the "Steele Dossier," that the FBI used to obtain a Foreign Intelligence Surveillance Act (FISA) warrant to spy on Trump and his associates. Informants were also sent to spy on and entrap the Trump team.

The dirty tricks operation turned into an attempted coup after Trump's election. Since he was elected without the consensus of the ruling party representing the coastal elite, Barack Obama's intelligence chiefs, including CIA director John Brennan, FBI director James Comey, and FBI deputy director Andrew McCabe, as well as Director of National Intelligence James Clapper, believed that his election was illegitimate. It was permissible, they believed, to remove him from office.

They'd justify it by continuing the FBI's investigation and expanding on the Clinton campaign's dirty tricks operation contending that Trump was controlled by a foreign power, Russia.

Brennan initiated the coup with an official report produced by his handpicked team of analysts. Their January 2017 intelligence community assessment claimed that Russian president Vladimir Putin himself had interfered with the election to help Trump win.

Comey's March 2017 congressional testimony set up the

president for a series of traps intended to bring obstruction charges leading to Trump's ouster. After Comey's dismissal in May 2017, Mueller was named special counsel and inherited control of the FBI's investigation and therefore the coup. His job was to fulfill Comey's mission and continue the investigation until he could trap the president in an obstruction of justice charge.

The crowd at Crawdaddy's understood that for two years, Nunes had been the only thing standing in the way of the coup called "Crossfire Hurricane."

———————————

It's early spring in Tulare, California, Nunes's hometown. The snowcapped peaks of the Sierra Nevada will soon melt and fill the Central Valley with the water that makes it the world's most fertile agricultural region. "It's the breadbasket of the solar system," Nunes says, smiling.

We're driving by what used to be the Tagus Ranch, the 7,000-acre fruit farm that was the destination for thousands of migrants who fled the midwestern dust bowl for California in the 1930s. Much of John Steinbeck's *The Grapes of Wrath* was set around Tulare. Nunes's ancestors preceded the Oklahomans by decades, but even today some of his family members speak with that same drawl.

The Nunes family is originally from the Azores, an autonomous region of Portugal consisting of a chain of islands 850 miles west of the Iberian Peninsula. "It's a beautiful place but also a tough place to live," says Nunes. "You never starve, but you never have a lot either."

In the late nineteenth century, his ancestors left their small farms in the Azores for small farms in the San Joaquin Valley and helped settle the land. "The Azoreans are tough people," says Nunes. "They have to be—living in the middle of the Atlantic, they're isolated and know they have to count on themselves."

The Nunes family was poor but always made it through, even through the depression. "My ninety-nine-year-old grandmother will tell you they had everything they needed," says Nunes. "They had a small farm, and they were growing what they needed, and they survived."

Nunes was born in Tulare on October 1, 1973, and grew up on the family farm. He attended Tulare Union High School, earned an associate degree at College of the Sequoias, then his bachelor's and master's degrees in agriculture at Cal Poly, San Louis Obispo, about a two-hour drive southwest from Tulare.

The congressman has the self-deprecating humor of a Jimmy Stewart character. Tall at six feet, one inch, a family man, and slow to anger, Nunes is relentless in pursuit. "I raised cattle as a teenager," he says. "My father broke away from the family farm and started his own business—he was a sharecropper. My mother kept the books. He encouraged us to get out on my own, so my brother, Anthony, and I started a harvesting business. I bought my own farm and tended row crops while I was still working on the family's farm."

He later sold the farm and used the profits to invest in Alpha Omega, a maker of world-class wines in Napa Valley.

In 2001, President George W. Bush appointed him California state director of the United States Department of Agriculture's Rural Development section. He was first elected to the House of Representatives in 2002, promising to take on environmentalists who wanted to divert water into the ocean and choke the soil.

Chance rules farm life. Contingency drives the luckless off the land and shapes the stalwart. Farmers are hard not by nature but to weather the nature that determines their fate. If it rains, your crops grow; if it rains too much, they rot; if it doesn't rain, you starve. It is a career of black and white; things are, or they are not.

Nunes says that sensibility shaped his understanding and actions during the last two years. The collusion narrative was nonsense, cover for something else that was going on. He read the terrain quickly.

What he had to learn along the way was how to manage a team in the midst of a crisis like no one had seen before—a coup against a US president.

Nunes assembled a number of distinct and complementary talents: former intelligence officials who knew how to find and identify evidence of corruption; lawyers deeply knowledgeable about esoteric congressional procedures; experts on the history of intelligence; a former DOJ national security prosecutor, Kash Patel, who knew the nature of the enemy—his former colleagues; his communications director, Jack Langer, who went on offense against the hostile press corps; and the late Damon Nelson, the HPSCI staff director, who kept the team together during its hardest times. They called their wide-ranging investigation of the myriad abuses and crimes committed by senior US officials "Objective Medusa."

For nearly two years, Nunes's team pulled at the threads of the operation and found widespread corruption at the top levels of the federal government. They had to press forward carefully to hold the ground they'd won. The rogue law enforcement and intelligence officials, Clinton operatives, Obama aides, and the press were waiting for them to make a mistake.

"Every time we took a shot," says Nunes, "we had to hit them between the eyes."

The Objective Medusa team rarely missed.

They discovered in October 2017 that the Steele Dossier had been funded by the Clinton campaign. A February 2018 report known as the "Nunes Memo" laid out how the dossier had been used as evidence to obtain the FISA.

The Objective Medusa team discovered the role played by DOJ official Bruce Ohr and his wife, Nellie, in pushing the anti-Trump operation.

Objective Medusa uncovered the role State Department officials played in the anti-Trump operation.

Nunes's team won release of the text messages between FBI agent Peter Strzok and his mistress, FBI lawyer Lisa Page, that gave evidence of the extent and nature of the anti-Trump operation. They found that Strzok's "insurance policy" text referred to something specific the FBI had done to obtain the spy warrant.

Objective Medusa investigators pushed to find out how many spies the intelligence community had sent after the Trump campaign.

They set up a congressional task force to widen the investigation into the corrupt FBI investigators who had tried to frame Trump.

Finally, they asked the president to declassify federal law enforcement documents giving further evidence of Deep State corruption.

In giving their full accounting of the abuses and crimes committed during the FBI's investigation of Trump, Nunes and his team returned the House Permanent Select Committee on Intelligence (HPSCI) to its origins: investigating the abuses and possible crimes committed by American spies.

"The committee started in 1977," says Nunes's communications director, Jack Langer. "The House of Representatives passed a resolution to set up a committee monitoring the intelligence community in the wake of widespread abuses. The CIA, FBI, NSA, and others were spying on Americans."

In 1975, two congressional investigatory panels were tasked to look into allegations of intelligence community (IC) abuses: the Church Committee, led by Senator Frank Church of Idaho, and the Pike Committee, chaired by Representative Otis Pike of New York. The two panels established permanent committees in both houses that would be responsible for constitutional oversight of the US intelligence community: the Senate Select Committee on Intelligence and HPSCI.

"It was a pretty quiet committee before the 2016 elections," says Langer. Much of HPSCI's work involves authorizing spending for the intelligence community and providing it with necessary support and assistance. "The public wasn't really following what we do, and if the press had questions for us, we usually couldn't comment, since most of our work is classified."

Nunes and his Democratic counterpart on the committee, Adam Schiff, worked well together the last two years of the Obama administration. As late as 2016, the two said good things about each other on the House floor. That changed when Trump was elected and Schiff lost his bearings.

Nunes's March 2017 trip to tell the White House he'd seen evidence of spying on the Trump team was the opening move in a protracted struggle to bring the truth to light.

I've asked Nunes several times if he ever thought of walking away and just leaving the whole thing alone for someone else to deal with. "No," he says. "Never. Not once. I knew the more times they came after me, the more they hit me, I knew that I was right over the target."

Lots of people know they're right, but not everyone is willing to pay the price for it.

"What happens if you don't do the right thing?" says Nunes. "I wasn't raised that way. How do you look yourself in the mirror? How do you explain to yourself five, ten years down the road that you could have done something but you didn't?"

This book is an effort to present the known, as well as previously

unreported, details in the anti-Trump operation. The basic outline of
the story, however, is shockingly simple. Hillary Clinton's campaign
used political operatives and dirty cops to frame her opponent.
When she lost, Obama officials employed the resources of the federal
government to try to topple President Trump.

What readers may find surprising in this account is the extent
of the role of the press. The media weren't simply partisan or lazy
or complicit—they have been an integral component of both legs
of the operation from the beginning until the present. All in all,
it is a tragic story about criminality, corruption, and a conspiracy
of lies at the highest levels of important US institutions that were
designed to keep the public safe, such as the FBI, and free, such
as the press. But there is another story running parallel to that.
account, and that is a story about a small handful of Americans,
public servants, who stood up, assumed responsibility, and did the
right thing at a crucial time.

"If it weren't for eight people," Patel tells me over a beer one
snowy evening in Washington, "no one would know what happened."

The Objective Medusa team was outgunned by a confederation
with unlimited financial resources and far superior numbers: the
national security bureaucracy, political operatives, and the majority
of the press. Still, they brought the truth to light. This story credits
them for their actions and courage and, I hope, may give some
readers cause for optimism in what looks like a dark moment in
our history and even inspire others.

To tell that story, for nearly two years I spoke with Nunes,
Patel, Langer, and other Objective Medusa investigators who could
not speak on the record. What they accomplished together speaks
for all of them: they uncovered the biggest political scandal in
American history.

Chapter 2

ENEMIES OF THE STATE

DEVIN NUNES and Kash Patel dispute the FBI's claims that the Trump investigation began on July 31, 2016. "We actually think it began in late 2015, early 2016," says Nunes.

It's winter 2019, and I'm sitting in a sushi restaurant in downtown Washington with the congressman and Kashyap "Kash" Patel, the former DOJ prosecutor who led much of the House Intelligence Committee's investigation of the FBI's handling of the Trump-Russia probe.

An athletically built thirty-nine-year-old with a dark, close-cropped beard, Patel was born to Indian parents who had moved from Africa, Uganda, and Tanzania, to Jackson Heights, Queens, a New York City melting pot of Indian, Asian, Latin American, and African immigrants. After graduating from the University of Richmond, he went to law school in New York. He moved to Miami and became a public defender before taking a job in Washington.

"I was a terrorism prosecutor at Main Justice," says Patel, referring to DOJ headquarters. "It was a great place, a dream job, going after bad guys with great colleagues. Running those counterterrorism operations gave me a profound respect and love for the department and the FBI."

During his time at DOJ, Patel also served as a civilian in the military at Joint Special Operations Command (JSOC). "I worked alongside our Tier 1 special forces community conducting global targeting operations," he says. "It was one of the greatest honors of my career."

At Main Justice, he worked with many of the same people he would come to investigate as part of Nunes's team. After spending nearly two years investigating the origins of the Russia collusion investigation, Patel agrees that the anti-Trump operation began in winter 2015–2016.

"January 2016," says Patel, "is when Glenn Simpson, Christopher Steele, and Bruce Ohr start speaking together about a bunch of things they're up to." Their business concerns were related to Russia and Trump.

Simpson, a former *Wall Street Journal* reporter and founder of the opposition research firm Fusion GPS, Steele, a former British intelligence officer, and Ohr, a senior Justice Department official, are central figures in the anti-Trump operation. They'd known each other for years, sometimes working together. Simpson met Steele in 2009, shortly after they separately started private research firms. Steele and Ohr met in 2007. Simpson and Ohr first met around 2010 at networking events. In the early winter of 2016, their career paths intersected again as they engaged in an email correspondence regarding a number of Russia-related business concerns.

After ending his government career on the Russia desk in London, Steele picked up a number of Russia-related jobs in the British capital, home of a large Russian diaspora. He was hired, for instance, to lobby on behalf of Oleg Deripaska, a Russian government–linked aluminum magnate. Deripaska's US visa had been withdrawn years before due to his alleged ties to organized crime. In January 2016, Steele notified Ohr that the situation seemed close to resolution and asked him to monitor developments. Ohr told him he'd "keep an eye on it."

That Steele, the author of the reports alleging Trump's ties to the Kremlin, was himself lobbying a DOJ official on behalf of a Putin-allied oligarch was peculiar enough. The early 2016 manifestation of the anti-Trump plot's central network of Steele, Ohr, and Simpson shows that the operation was seeded long before the FBI says it initiated the Trump-Russia collusion investigation.

Indeed, Simpson had hired Ohr's wife, Nellie, in October 2015 to compile research on Trump, his family, his aides, and their business ties to Russian and other former Eastern Bloc individuals and institutions.

That was only part of the Ohrs' role in the operation. Along with Steele, the husband-and-wife team was a conduit for information passed between Fusion GPS and the small FBI team that managed the Crossfire Hurricane investigation. The Crossfire Hurricane group consisted of a handful of FBI officials at Washington, DC, headquarters, most notably deputy director Andrew McCabe, deputy assistant director for counterintelligence Peter Strzok, and Lisa Page, McCabe's special counsel.

The claim made by Justice Department and FBI officials that the investigation into four Trump team officials—Carter Page, George Papadopoulos, Paul Manafort, Jr., and Michael Flynn—was opened by the end of July 2016 was purposefully misleading. US law enforcement authorities constructed a false chronology of the investigation in order to obscure their wrongdoing and rationalize withholding documents from Congress.

"The FBI wanted to erect barriers to protect themselves," says Patel. "So they say the investigation began on July 31. That's wrong. It's just the FBI saying that date is a big deal, so we'll give you all the documents we have after that date and we don't have anything before that date because there was no investigation. But it's an arbitrary date, and it doesn't mean that nothing happened before then."

Nunes and Patel explain that an investigation doesn't just appear out of thin air; it needs a long runway. "There are levels of authorizations that you need in order to get a counterintelligence investigation off the ground," says Patel. "We said there's stuff before July 31, and FBI said 'No, no, there's nothing.' And then we found a couple of things. Like Ohr and Simpson and Steele talking and texting in January 2016."

There's more evidence suggesting that the Crossfire Hurricane team started looking into Trump officials by early 2016. In addition to the Steele-Simpson-Ohr correspondence, there's Michael Flynn.

Lieutenant General Michael Flynn was regarded as the top military intelligence officer of his generation. He revolutionized the nature of intelligence collection in battlefield settings by circumventing the intelligence bureaucracy. His work in Iraq helped defeat Al Qaeda during the 2007 surge.

Flynn's seminal 2010 article "Fixing Intel: A Blueprint for Making Intelligence Relevant in Afghanistan" put the US intelligence community on notice. The essential problem, he argued, was the Beltway bureaucracy, through which information might circulate for days or weeks before it came back to the field.

"Moving up through levels of hierarchy," he wrote, "is normally a journey into greater degrees of cluelessness."

Flynn was speaking for the collector in the field, often a soldier, who needed actionable intelligence on the spot. Success in battle, and keeping Americans safe, required minimizing the role of the bureaucracy. He wanted to apply the lessons he had learned in combat settings across the intelligence community. Thus his proposed revolution threatened the budgets, jobs, and prestige of thousands of spies who constituted the intelligence bureaucracy.

They noticed. By the time the three-star general was named head of the Defense Intelligence Agency (DIA) in 2012, the bureaucracy saw him as an enemy. He'd also alienated the Obama White House.

Flynn repeatedly challenged Obama's policies. In particular, he was skeptical of the administration's key foreign policy initiative, the nuclear deal with Iran. The Islamic Republic had been directly responsible for killing thousands of Americans in Iraq and indirectly responsible for many more. The documents captured during the raid on Osama bin Laden's compound in Pakistan showed evidence of Iran's relationship with Al Qaeda. Flynn pushed for release of the bin Laden documents, and the White House was furious. Publishing them would complicate Obama's ability to convince Congress of the wisdom in striking a nuclear deal with a terror state devoted to murdering Americans.

"Flynn was in a knife fight with the White House," says Derek Harvey, a retired army intelligence officer who works with Nunes and knows the former DIA head.

Flynn announced his resignation from DIA in April 2014 and started a consulting firm that worked with foreign clients. He did media appearances and advised several GOP candidates for the 2016 nomination: Ben Carson, Ted Cruz, Carly Fiorina, and Scott Walker, as well as Trump. He told reporters he'd moved into public life because he thought the country was at risk. He told friends he saw the Clintons and their corruption as a threat to the republic. He was willing to talk to anyone if it would help keep Hillary Clinton out of the White House.

But it was Trump who fit Flynn best. The candidate who promised to drain "the Swamp" was the only real vehicle for Flynn's campaign against the intelligence bureaucracy. Unless that bureaucracy was shorn of power, it would continue to risk the lives of more Americans, especially those in uniform.

Trump in turn trusted the former spy chief. He had detailed knowledge of the Beltway establishment because he'd fought it— just as important, the Swamp saw Flynn, as it did Trump, as an enemy. But both underestimated the establishment's will to power and the many weapons in its array.

For the intelligence bureaucracy, the situation became increasingly urgent as 2015 was coming to a close and Flynn was drawing closer to a GOP front-runner who promised to upend the system.

In December, Flynn's Beltway adversaries saw an opportunity— an event and a photograph capturing a moment of it. The operatives targeting Flynn must have seen its potential value immediately. It was a picture of the former DIA chief sitting next to Vladimir Putin. The Russian president is in suit and tie and Flynn is in a tuxedo, evidence that he's not working but celebrating with Putin. They're seated at the table of honor at a Moscow banquet commemorating the tenth anniversary of the Russian government–owned news network, Russia Today, now RT.

Flynn's speakers' bureau had arranged the trip and paid him to deliver a speech at the banquet. He had been given a defensive briefing by intelligence officials before he left and debriefed his former colleagues on his return. Flynn said that he had used the occasion to advise the Russians to bring their ally Iran into line, to stop wreaking havoc across the Middle East. But those details were erased in most subsequent press reports. To paint Flynn, and by extension Trump, as Russian assets, the former spy chief's Beltway adversaries used techniques famously employed by Moscow's spy services.

Josef Stalin's spies understood that photographs are useful instruments in pushing propaganda. A picture tells a story. Frame it correctly, and the caption writes itself. To change the story, Soviet propagandists changed the picture. Stalin, for instance, had his rivals erased from photographs. Former colleagues and friends became enemies of the state, vanished down the memory hole. Similarly, details of Flynn's visit to Moscow for the RT banquet were "disappeared." The true account was replaced with a false narrative. In this telling, Flynn wasn't just sitting close to Putin, as the photograph showed, he was actually *close* to Putin—much more than anyone knew.

The operatives targeting Flynn needed to assemble a backstory to explain how the former US general had come to sit near the Russian president. They drew on data points scattered throughout Flynn's past.

In February 2014, Sir Richard Dearlove, a former director of the United Kingdom's foreign spy agency, MI6, hosted a dinner for Flynn in his campus apartment at Pembroke College. The dinner was to celebrate a joint initiative between the DIA and the Cambridge Security Initiative (CSI). CSI was a private intelligence firm directed by Dearlove, Christopher Andrew, the official historian of Great Britain's domestic intelligence service, MI5, and Stefan Halper, a US political operative with family ties to the Central Intelligence Agency. Their idea was to draw on their past reputations and market the in-house talents of Cambridge specialists, including Svetlana Lokhova, a Moscow-born British historian of Soviet intelligence. She is precise in relating the details of Flynn's 2014 visit.

"Flynn gave a public talk, and then there was a dinner by private invitation only to honor him," she says. "It was big event to celebrate Flynn. The organizers wanted to show off for the DIA boss and prove how knowledgeable the group was."

But CSI's analysts had no experience in intelligence work. They were academics, graduate students. "I was invited to the dinner because CSI had been contracted to do a project that involved the Middle East and Russia and I was one of two Russian speakers involved in CSI," says Lokhova.

There were twenty or so guests, mostly academics. Dearlove was seated across from the guest of honor. Andrew, a University of Cambridge professor, sat next to Flynn. The third CSI director, Halper, was absent. At the end of the dinner, Andrew asked Lokhova to show their American guest an example of what she'd found during her research studying the Soviet archives.

"I opened my iPad," says Lokhova, "and showed Flynn a sample of Stalin's handwriting on the back of a postcard."

Flynn wanted a copy of it to show to a delegation of Russian military intelligence officers due to visit DIA the next month. The trip was canceled because of Russia's invasion of Ukraine.

Andrew asked Lokhova to stay in touch with Flynn. He hoped that Flynn might visit Cambridge again. He didn't, but the 2014 dinner would become an important chapter in the story designed to destroy him.

———————————

The University of Cambridge is one of the world's oldest and most prestigious universities, the centerpiece of a medieval English city less than an hour from London by train. From the station, it's a fifteen-minute walk to Market Square, dodging students rushing to class on their bikes.

It was winter 2019 when I visited Cambridge, cool and gray, and the grassy courtyards of the residential colleges were wet with frost.

The university enjoys a uniquely storied reputation as a breeding ground for spies. The Elizabethan playwright Christopher Marlowe, a rival of William Shakespeare, was recruited here as a student to serve Her Majesty's government.

Nearly four hundred years later, five of the university's students, most notoriously Kim Philby, first enlisted at Cambridge in a cause, communism, intended to destroy their society and committed themselves to careers in espionage on behalf of the Soviet Union.

And it was here in the mid-1980s that one of Dearlove's future employees, undergraduate Christopher Steele, was tapped to play a role fighting the Cold War.

Lokhova escaped post–Cold War Russia by moving to England in 1998. "There were breadlines and the violence was so bad that boys in my school brought guns to class," she says of mid-1990s Moscow. I can hear traces of her Russian accent. She speaks hurriedly, as her two-year-old wants her mother's full attention.

"When I arrived here," she says, "I did everything possible to integrate myself into British society and distance myself from that. I celebrated when I became a British citizen."

In 2012, after a career in London's financial sector in the mid-2000s, she returned to academia, where she'd already started to make a name for herself. Her book, *The Spy Who Changed History: The Untold Story of How the Soviet Union Won the Race for America's Top Secrets*, is based on documents drawn from the Soviet archives dating back to the 1930s.

She thrived at Cambridge, cherishing the painstaking research. "Documents have a story in them," she says. "If you spend time with them, they'll start to speak to you." So do timelines, she says. Her research of the culture and methods of Soviet spy agencies prepared her for how to understand the story that US intelligence officials, political operatives, and the media used to smear her in order to get at Flynn.

They concocted a false account of the 2014 dinner, claiming she was a Russian spy and had compromised the DIA director. She became notorious as images of her strawberry blond hair and blue eyes were splashed across the media on both sides of the Atlantic. But that fraudulent narrative of the 2014 dinner wasn't planted in the press until several years later, in the winter of 2016–2017. It was only when Trump was ascendant that the fictional account became useful, an account that dirtied Flynn and by extension Trump. Lokhova, a Russian and a woman, was a convenient instrument. No one blinked when her former Cambridge colleagues threw her to the wolves. Nonetheless, she still speaks sympathetically of the Cambridge group. "They're people who had done something in the past. They wanted to be treated with respect and feel they should be consulted because of their service to the world. But they're men in their midseventies who tend to get drowsy while listening to lectures."

The American, said Lokhova, was unlike Dearlove and Andrew. "Most of these Cambridge people are very gentle," she explains. "Halper stood out because he was incredibly rude. Also, he regularly made a point of making anti-Russian comments."

Halper was another central figure in the anti-Trump operation. It was he who told the US and British press that Flynn had been compromised by Russian intelligence and that the agent of Flynn's undoing had been Lokhova.

Stefan Halper graduated from Stanford in 1967 and earned a PhD from Oxford in 1971. He worked for three Republican administrations—Richard Nixon's, Gerald Ford's, and Ronald Reagan's—and was once married to the daughter of the CIA's director of intelligence Ray Cline. Halper's family ties to the agency won him a leadership position in a dirty tricks operation targeting a presidential campaign.

Halper ran a campaign war room for Reagan's 1980 presidential run. He was hired by David Gergen, a prominent former Republican official and current CNN political analyst, to manage a network of retired CIA officers. Halper's job was to collect foreign policy information from inside the Jimmy Carter administration.

Carter, a famously unpopular president, enjoyed two brief surges in the run-up to the 1980 elections. The first time was when Iranian revolutionaries seized American hostages in November 1979 and took over the US Embassy in Tehran. The public sided with Carter again in April 1980, when he ordered an ultimately unsuccessful mission to rescue the hostages.

Reagan's CIA director, William Casey, and Reagan's campaign director said that the Republican candidate's team had been concerned that Carter might take some sort of dramatic action to free the hostages on the eve of the election and overtake Reagan at the polls. The Reagan camp referred to it as an "October surprise." Halper's job was reportedly to spot plans for an "October surprise" in time to develop a campaign strategy to counter it.

Halper is a well-known figure in the Washington, DC, policy community and the author of several relatively popular books on foreign affairs. He earned another doctorate from Cambridge in 2004. He stayed on to teach at Cambridge, where he directed dissertations in the Department of Politics and International Studies and convened conferences and panels with important figures from the intelligence world. For instance, he brought a former head of Russia's foreign intelligence service, Vyacheslav Trubnikov, to Cambridge twice, in 2012 and 2015.

On campus, Halper was known to be generous with his money. Part of his wealth came from the US taxpayer. In addition to CSI's contract with the DIA, he drew income from the Office of Net Assessment (ONA), an internal Pentagon think tank, to write research reports on strategic threats facing the United States. Between 2012 and 2018, ONA paid him more than $1 million—$600,000 alone for two contracts in 2015 and 2016 for academic research related to Russia. He claimed that one of the sources for his reports on Russia had been the former spy chief Trubnikov.

Halper's work, says a Defense Department official who requested anonymity, "didn't meet the standards of the Office of Net Assessment or merit the money he was paid. Halper's work typically consisted of a collection of essays he'd paid other researchers to write. These were hardly the top names in the field, and the work was substandard."

According to the *Washington Times*, Halper's research claims were falsified. More than a dozen of the expert sources Halper claimed to have consulted for his projects said they had had nothing to do with his work.

It appears Halper misrepresented the nature of his professional relationship with a number of well-known academics and intelligence officials, including former CIA director General Michael Hayden. *Washington Times* reporter Rowan Scarborough asked Hayden if he had contributed to Halper's work as the contractor claimed. Hayden responded, "No memory of project or person."

Pentagon whistle-blower Adam Lovinger contended that ONA was being used to funnel money to favored Beltway insiders such as Halper. In addition, according to records submitted to Congress, Lovinger reported to ONA director Andrew D. May that Halper, a contractor, was being used to "conduct foreign relations," a violation of federal regulations. Instead of investigating Halper, Lovinger's supervisors investigated him.

It appears that Halper was paid not for his research but rather for pet projects that were best kept off the books. The FBI's Crossfire Hurricane team used Halper as an informant to spy on Trump campaign advisers, including Flynn.

The Cambridge scholars who'd met Flynn in 2014 kept track of him after he announced his resignation from the DIA. They noticed when, more than a year later, his name started to appear in the press as an adviser to the Republican front-runner, Donald Trump.

"It seemed odd," says Lokhova. "He'd crossed sides, from Obama official to Trump supporter."

That got Halper's attention as well. Flynn was whispering things in Trump's ear that threatened the ecosystem that sustained Halper and his Beltway associates. It didn't matter that Trump's chances of winning the White House were slim. The logic of power dictates that the powerful use the instruments at their disposal in order to maintain power.

Richard Nixon had the Democratic National Committee wiretapped because he could. The fact that he was destined to crush his Democratic opponent, George McGovern, in the 1972 election was irrelevant. It was because he had the power to spy on his rivals that he did.

Halper was such an instrument. His job was to push favorites across the winning line, just as he'd helped ensure Reagan's victory over Carter more than thirty-five years before.

Nearly two years after the February 2014 dinner that he didn't attend, Halper saw how a report of it might be useful: it could serve as the backstory for the photograph of Flynn at Putin's table. A few short weeks after the RT celebration, Halper directed Christopher Andrew to host him for a dinner and invite Lokhova. "Chris emailed me in January 2016 and insisted I come to dinner with Halper the next month," says Lokhova. "I'd never spoken with him. It was very strange I'd be invited to a dinner with him. But Chris was insistent."

She didn't understand why until later. Halper was running an operation to dirty Trump and several associates as Russian assets. "I was being set up," she says. A Cambridge colleague and friend of Halper later confirmed to her that Halper had been spying on her to get to Flynn.

Halper wanted to probe her to get information on Flynn that he could leak to the press and deliver to his associates in the intelligence bureaucracy. He was looking for material with which to write the false backstory of the Flynn-Putin photograph.

How did the former DIA chief wind up at Putin's table in December 2015 to celebrate a Kremlin-owned TV station? He'd been compromised by the Russians back in February 2014, Halper would eventually tell journalists. In his account, which finally surfaced in December 2016, the postcard with Stalin's signature had been an erotic come-on from Lokhova, the prelude to a seduction. They had left the dinner together. She was a Russian agent.

The premise of that story, says Lokhova, is ridiculous.

"Richard Dearlove, the former head of MI6, hosted the dinner, in his apartment," she says. "It has obviously been cleared with the intelligence services. They're not going to let someone they haven't checked out dine at the home of the former head of the foreign intelligence service while he's hosting the active chief of American military intelligence."

Nonetheless, Halper's account became part of the narrative that Flynn had been compromised by the Russians.

"On this telling," says Lokhova, "at the end of the evening I supposedly walk off alone with Flynn for some rendezvous, and no one says a thing—not his security detail, not the former head of MI6. Instead, everyone just finishes their port and cheese without saying a thing."

Lokhova declined the February 2016 invitation to meet with Halper at Andrew's home, but the anti-Flynn operation launched nonetheless. A February 26, 2016, Reuters article by Mark Hosenball and Steve Holland was the first public evidence of it.

Trump adviser Michael Flynn, according to the article, "raised eyebrows among some U.S. foreign policy veterans when he was pictured sitting at the head table with Putin at a banquet in Moscow late last year celebrating Russia Today, an international broadcasting network funded by the Russian government."

Political operatives turned Flynn into an enemy of the state by erasing facts from the real account of his Moscow trip and the RT banquet. And the photograph of him seated with Putin became the first piece of falsified evidence in the dirty tricks campaign alleging that the Trump team had been compromised by the Kremlin.

Chapter 3

FRAMING TRUMP: THE RUSSIA JOB

IN EARLY SPRING 2016, the press began to fill with stories expressing alarm about Trump's often favorable opinions regarding Vladimir Putin. That was odd. The media had never concerned itself with the sitting president's Russia policy, no matter how many US interests and allies were damaged because of it.

To the contrary, the press had fully backed Obama's efforts to improve ties with the Kremlin, the vaunted Russia "reset" policy managed by former secretary of state Hillary Clinton.

Obama and Clinton's "reset" amounted to turning a blind eye to Putin's aggressions—Russia's invasion of Ukraine, annexation of Crimea, cyberattacks against the United States' Baltic allies, military intervention in Syria, where it had established air bases, and a naval base on the Mediterranean.

All that time, the press had failed to note the dangers of Obama's Russia policy, even as Putin participated in a genocidal campaign in support of his Syrian client Bashar al-Assad. Obama appeased Russia by withdrawing missile defense from the United States' central European allies Poland and the Czech Republic. The US president even ignored Russian cyberattacks on the Pentagon in 2015 and State Department in 2014.

Nunes, watching from his perch on the House Permanent Select Committee on Intelligence, believed that the Obama White House was letting Putin get away with murder.

We're sitting at a long table in Nunes's office in the Longworth House Office Building on Capitol Hill. The jerseys of two Portuguese soccer legends, Luís Figo and Rui Costa, hang on the wall behind him, and a large TV is at the other end of the room. Pictures of his family, his wife, Elizabeth, and his three daughters, Evelyn, Julia, and Margaret, fill the bookcases. It's a seven- to eight-hour trip to get home for the weekends, and often he's traveling far abroad for committee work.

In the summer of 2014, he'd just returned from a trip to Ukraine, where the Russians had downed a passenger jet. He wrote an op-ed for the *Washington Times* warning about Russian aggression—drawing particular attention to the Kremlin's international disinformation campaign—and advocating active steps to counter Putin's actions. "We cannot afford to be a mere bystander as his destabilizing actions begin to threaten the economies of the Baltics and other NATO allies, possibly including our own."

When Nunes became HPSCI chairman in 2015, he set out to address the problem. "The committee got the intelligence community more money for Russia," he says. "Millions. But they didn't use it."

They didn't want the money because Russia wasn't an Obama priority. "There are plenty of people in the intelligence community who know lots about Russia," he explains. "But the IC takes direction from the administration. And the Obama White House wasn't interested in focusing on Russia because it needed Moscow on board for the Iran deal."

The administration believed that Russian support for sanctions designed to bring the Iranians to the negotiating table was vital to striking the deal. Thus Obama showed early on his willingness to accommodate the Russians on other matters.

During a July 2009 trip to Moscow, Obama gave a speech at the New Economic School, where he spoke of a sixty-day review for a proposed US missile defense shield protecting Poland and the Czech Republic. The Russians strongly opposed the shield, a George W. Bush–era initiative, believing that it targeted their nuclear arsenal.

In September, Obama scrapped the program, much to the dismay of Warsaw and Prague, as well as the foreign policy establishment.

When Obama was caught on an open microphone in spring 2012 telling outgoing Russian president Dmitri Medvedev that after his election he would "have more flexibility" in dealing with issues such as missile defense, it lent further evidence to the case that he was appeasing Moscow.

That's how Trump saw it. He was critical of Obama's Russia policy even before he announced his candidacy. Trump said that Mitt Romney had been right to say that Moscow represented a geostrategic threat to US interests. Trump was in favor of sanctioning Russia for invading Ukraine.

"There are a lot of things we could be doing economically to Russia," Trump told a TV interviewer in 2014. "Russia is not strong economically, and we could do a lot of different things to really do numbers on them if we wanted to."

But Trump also wanted good relations with Moscow. There was nothing incongruous about holding the two ideas at the same time. It had been the mainstream bipartisan position since the end of the Cold War: harsh criticism and hope for friendly relations. Starting with George H. W. Bush, every US president, Democratic and Republican, sought to get off on a good footing with Russia. And since George W. Bush's first term that had meant trying to get along with Putin.

But Trump's pedigree was unorthodox—he wasn't a politician—so his style was, too. From Trump's perspective, with him as president, Putin would be dealing with a US leader who had a source of wealth and prestige independent of his office, a business leader who had holdings around the world. In Trump's view, Putin would be dealing with someone even more famous than he was.

To hear Trump tell it, he already had the Russian strongman's respect. Putin, he boasted, had sent him a present during the 2013 Miss Universe contest in Moscow. In contrast, said Trump, Putin "has zero respect for Obama or the US." He argued that the foreign policy elite, Democratic and Republican, had repeatedly shown its incompetence over the last two decades in the form of endless wars and bad deals.

The Bush administration had been responsible for the war in Iraq and the never-ending battle to win in Afghanistan. The Obama White House had concluded the nuclear agreement with Iran—a catastrophe, Trump said on the campaign trail, the worst deal ever made. As for Putin, said Trump, he's "eaten Obama's lunch, therefore our lunch, for a long period of time."

———

Trump, like most of the foreign policy community, misread Obama in one important respect: Obama's dealings with Russia were not entirely a result of his weakness. In fact, Obama believed he was dealing from a position of strength. He used Russia as an instrument to secure the foreign policy goal he most cared about: the nuclear deal with Tehran.

The testing ground was the Syrian war, where Iran and Russia had teamed up in support of their client Bashar al-Assad. The United States' allies in the region implored Obama to arm Syrian rebel factions to defeat Assad and weaken Iran—which was precisely what Obama sought to avoid.

He knew that the nuclear deal would be off the table if he targeted the Syrian regime. Accordingly, he saw Moscow as a partner rather than an adversary.

In late summer 2013, Putin showed he was willing to team up with Obama, so long as it advanced Russian interests. Months before, Assad had deployed chemical weapons, crossing a red line set down by Obama. If Obama enforced his red line with military strikes on Assad, he risked pushing the Iranians from the negotiating table. But if he failed to act, he'd pay a steep political price for backing down.

The Russians proposed a solution: there was no need for Obama to hit Syrian regime facilities to make his point; Moscow would persuade Assad to turn over his chemical weapons arsenal. For Obama officials, it was a win-win. Putin would save his client Assad, and Obama would keep hope of the Iran deal alive. Obama aides called it a diplomatic masterstroke. In exchange for Putin's favor, Obama turned a blind eye when the Russians escalated their troop presence in Syria in September 2015.

"The Obama administration said they were caught by surprise," says Nunes.

That was not possible. US intelligence had seen it unfolding in real time. Moscow had been sending troops and weapons through the Bosporus, an international waterway controlled by a NATO member, Turkey.

"Of course the White House knew what was happening," Nunes says.

For months after the Russian escalation, Nunes had been trying to get out word regarding the administration's dangerous dance with Moscow. "I wanted to get one of the big papers to cover it," says Nunes.

But the press had little interest in a story critical of the White House's Russia policy. It was embarrassing to an Obama-allied media that in coordinating with Putin, the Nobel Peace Prize–winning president was complicit in the campaign of sectarian slaughter in Syria, the largest humanitarian catastrophe of the twenty-first century.

Trump would win no favors from the press.

Trump had been the front-runner since December 2015 and, after big primary wins on March 1 and March 15, was the presumptive candidate. Nevertheless, there was already talk of a brokered convention in July, in which the establishment would fight Trump for the nomination. It seemed unlikely, but the Republican political and ideological leadership that Trump had rejected had in turn rejected him.

Early in March, a foreign policy website, War on the Rocks, published an "Open Letter on Donald Trump from GOP National Security Leaders." Signed by 122 former Republican diplomats, intelligence officials, senior policy makers, analysts, and other foreign policy figures, the letter listed Trump's alleged national security flaws. For example: Trump's "admiration for foreign dictators such as Vladimir Putin is unacceptable for the leader of the world's greatest democracy."

The signatories vowed to oppose him. "As committed and loyal Republicans," the letter concluded, "we are unable to support a Party ticket with Mr. Trump at its head. We commit ourselves to working energetically to prevent the election of someone so utterly unfitted to the office."

The men and women who signed the letter were mostly serious people with a good understanding of their areas of interest, from Europe to the Middle East, from nuclear proliferation to counterterrorism. Group letters, however, are not serious. Republicans signed many during the Obama years in protest of policies they were powerless to affect.

But this early manifestation of "Never Trump" Republicanism carried real consequences. The Republican establishment's abandonment of the candidate left the campaign with a thin foreign policy bench.

The foreign policy letter and negative media attention caused the Trump campaign serious problems. In a March 9, 2016 *Washington Post* column ("Why can't Donald Trump close the deal with any foreign policy advisers?"), Daniel Drezner made a timeline of Trump's promises to announce a foreign policy team dating back to September 2015. For six months, Drezner wrote, the GOP candidate had been promising the "finest team anyone has put together."

That was the substance of the first question the *Washington Post*'s publisher, Fred Ryan, asked Trump when he sat down with him for a March 21 interview with the DC policy establishment's hometown newspaper. He asked the GOP front-runner if he could share some names from the foreign policy team he was planning to announce later in the week.

"I wouldn't mind," said Trump. "Do you have that list," he

asked an aide. "I'll be a little more accurate with it. Okay, you ready?" He sounded nervous. The journalists laughed.

There were only five foreign policy advisers on his list. Trump read them off. "Carter Page," said Trump. George Papadopoulos was another. "Excellent guy," said Trump. None of the journalists had heard of either one. They'd certainly never published in the *Post.* The editorial board, men and women with direct lines to leading US statesmen going back decades, from Henry Kissinger and George P. Shultz to Madeleine Albright and Condoleezza Rice, had no idea who Page and Papadopoulos were.

"Trump reads those names off, and that's what puts them in Fusion GPS' and the Obama administration's crosshairs," says Nunes. "Now they're looking for anything they can get on Trump's two new advisers."

It wasn't until May that Papadopoulos hit the press when he volunteered for an interview with a British newspaper. The Trump adviser said that Prime Minister David Cameron should apologize for insulting Trump and criticizing his proposal to deny US visas to nationals from certain Muslim countries. The interview touched off a firestorm in the small London community of politicians, diplomats, and intelligence officials.

But the first story on Carter Page dropped two days after Trump's talk with the *Post.* Lachlan Markay of the Washington *Free Beacon* explored Page's history. An energy investor who "advised Russian-state-owned energy company Gazprom," wrote Markay, "Page has blasted NATO states' 'biased philosophies and draconian tactics,' their 'targeted discrimination and interventionist policies,' and their 'misguided and provocative actions.'" According to the article, "Trump's selection of Page may indicate the reality-star-cum-politician's opposition to U.S. policies that counter Russian interests in key global theaters." But choosing an unknown and

unpaid campaign adviser from a small pool of candidates eager
to embrace Trump signaled no such thing. The campaign to tar
Trump as suspiciously Kremlin friendly was under way.

In a March 31 *Free Beacon* article, Markay zeroed in on another
Trump campaign aide. This time he reported on the connections
between newly named Trump campaign convention manager Paul
Manafort and a Ukrainian businessman with ties to Russian political
and criminal figures. Manafort, the story asserted, was part of a web
of Russia-linked Trump associates, like Page "a staunch defender of
Putin's regime and highly critical of U.S. efforts to counter Russian
influence in Ukraine and the rest of Europe." At the center of it
was the candidate himself. "Trump's praise for Russian president
Vladimir Putin," wrote Markay, " . . . has drawn criticism from
Republican rivals and experts on U.S. policy toward Russia."

The *Free Beacon* had the Washington, DC-based firm Fusion
GPS under contract to compile opposition research on Donald
Trump. The publication's major donor, hedge fund manager Paul
Singer, had used the outfit previously. Singer, who supported other
Republican candidates for the nomination, tasked Fusion GPS to
look into Trump.

In May 2016, after it became clear that Trump had locked up
the GOP nomination, the *Free Beacon* cut off the Trump-related
research, and in January 2017 it discontinued its relationship with
Fusion GPS. But by the end of March 2016, Fusion GPS had already
found a different sponsor for its Trump research. Rumors circulated
that Clinton supporters were funding Simpson.

According to former CIA official Robert Baer, in the March–
April period there were other Clinton operatives trawling for
rumors of the GOP candidate's ties to the Kremlin.

Cody Shearer, an associate of Hillary Clinton's private spymaster, Sidney Blumenthal, compiled two unpublished reports on Trump's ties to Russia. Shearer wrote that *Wall Street Journal* reporter Alan Cullison had told him that Fusion GPS principals Glenn Simpson and Peter Fritsch had been hired by the Democratic National Committee.

Simpson and Fritsch had "uncovered info," according to Shearer, on Trump's newly named campaign convention manager, Paul Manafort, and his connections to Ukraine. But Simpson was already familiar with the lobbyist's work for Ukrainian politicians. He'd written about Manafort and his relationship with former Ukrainian leader Viktor Yanukovych nearly a decade before, when he had been with the *Wall Street Journal*. Along with Flynn's RT dinner, Manafort's work for Yanukovych became one of the media operation's key talking points. It was meant to provide further evidence that Trump was close to the Russians, via a campaign adviser. Shearer wrote that Fusion GPS had "nothing directly on Trump." That didn't matter. By April, a media campaign tying the New York billionaire to Russian interests was in full swing.

An April 3 article on Politico by former Obama official Evelyn Farkas claimed that Trump posed as much of a threat to the West as Putin did. "Trump," according to Farkas, a Russia specialist, ". . . is seeking to turn the United States into a post-factual society analogous to Putin's Russia."

Another Politico article, "The Kremlin's Candidate," this time by Michael Crowley, also posted in April. It alleged that the Russian government–owned English-language TV station, RT, favored Trump over Clinton. The article cast a suspicious eye at Michael Flynn for attending the December 2015 banquet. "It was extremely odd that he showed up in a tuxedo to the Russian government propaganda arm's party," one former Pentagon official told Crowley. A senior Obama administration official said, "It's not usually to America's benefit when our intelligence officers—current or former—seek refuge in Moscow."

An April 28 story in *New York* magazine by Jonathan Chait, "Why Is Donald Trump a Patsy for Vladimir Putin?" argued that Trump's desire to find common ground with Putin signals "a clear turn in American policy." The explanation, Chait concluded, is that "Trump is Vladimir Putin's stooge." The piece linked to Crowley's article as well as one by Franklin Foer, the former editor of *The New Republic*. Foer and Chait would become among the most active operatives in the Trump-Russia media campaign.

In Foer's April 28 article on Slate, he profiled Manafort with a long section on his business with the Ukrainians, with special attention to Yanukovych. "Why," asked Foer, "would Paul Manafort so consistently do the bidding of oligarchs loyal to Vladimir Putin?" Manafort's hiring, Foer asserted, had been more evidence of Trump's "admiration for Putin's bare-chested leadership."

At the time, Nunes was still trying to get out word of the Obama administration's disastrous Russia policies. "Finally," says Nunes. "I did a CNN interview in which I got in my points regarding Russia."

"The biggest intelligence failure we've had since 9/11," Nunes said in an April interview with CNN's Jake Tapper, "has been the inability to predict the leadership plans and intentions of the Putin regime in Russia."

Under normal circumstances, an unequivocal statement like that from the chairman of the House Intelligence Committee would likely attract widespread attention. But there was little room for Nunes's criticism of the White House's Russia policies in the midst of the anti-Trump media frenzy. So what if Obama had repeatedly prioritized Russian interests over those of our allies? So what if Obama had wanted to coordinate military operations in Syria with the Russians and share intelligence?

According to the press, the real concern was that the GOP candidate said he wanted friendly relations with Putin, and one of his senior advisers, a former army officer, had sat next to Putin at a dinner in Moscow.

None of that was news or analysis. Rather, it was evidence that top media organizations had become the platform for an information operation targeting the Trump campaign. Just as Obama had seen Russia as an instrument to advance his foreign policy objectives, now Democratic operatives were deploying Moscow as a weapon in a presidential race. The media were part of the anti-Trump operation from the beginning.

Chapter 4

THE PROTODOSSIERS

IN APRIL 2016, Hillary for America, Hillary Clinton's presidential campaign operation, and the DNC hired Fusion GPS to build a Trump-Russia echo chamber. Fusion GPS was paid more than $1 million to compile information about Trump's ties to Russia and distribute it to the press. By the end of the spring, every major US media organization was involved in pushing the big story about the Republican candidate: Trump and his associates were tied to Russian and other former Soviet Bloc business interests.

Fusion GPS was the Clinton campaign's shadow war room—and subsequently became its dirty tricks operations center. Founded in 2010 by Glenn Simpson and Peter Fritsch, both former *Wall Street Journal* employees, Fusion GPS had worked on presidential campaigns before. In 2012, it had been hired for Obama's reelection drive to smear Republican presidential candidate Mitt Romney. Fusion GPS had dug up the divorce records of a Romney donor and labeled him a "bitter foe of the gay rights movement." Fusion GPS understood what liberal media audiences wanted to believe about the world. The company became an important part of the media ecosystem because it also knew what journalists needed to get their stories published: sources, background, and above all a compelling narrative.

"Lots of these investigative firms are made up of ex-cops or ex–FBI guys," a former editor tells me over breakfast at a DC hotel in February 2019. "They do solid work, but it's dull, plodding, like reality itself most of the time. Simpson and Fritsch are former journalists. They're unique in that they know what makes for a front-page story."

Fusion GPS typically refers to the opposition research documents it disseminates as "dossiers." Most famously, former British spy Christopher Steele's Trump-Russia reports became known as the "Steele Dossier."

By the time Fusion GPS hired Steele in May 2016, the company had already produced several separate dossiers on Trump and his circle's relations to Russia and former Soviet-bloc states.

At the end of breakfast, my friend hands over a large yellow folder containing four documents along with clips of dozens of news stories from major media outlets that relied on Fusion GPS's open-source research. The number of stories, the repetition of themes, subject matter, names, and even phrases used in press reporting, show that the four documents drove the media campaign targeting Trump and associates that began in early spring 2016. Those four documents were protodossiers. They constituted the skeleton of the dossier that would come to be attributed to the former British spy. The sheer volume of research involved in compiling the four protodossiers, culled from US and foreign media sources, shows that the anti-Trump project was in an advanced stage many months before Steele came on board.

All four protodossiers are footnoted with links to press reports, including Russian-language media. Nellie Ohr, the wife of senior DOJ official Bruce Ohr and onetime professor of Russian history, began working for Fusion GPS in October 2015. (Edward Baumgartner, who also has Russian-language skills, was reportedly rolled into the Trump project after finishing another job for Fusion GPS around June 2016.)

Ohr was hired, as she put it, to look "into the relationship of Donald Trump with Russian organized crime figures." She said that part of her work involved researching the travels and business dealings of Trump's children. That work is reflected in the protodossiers. For instance, one passage claims that in 2004, "Donald Trump Jr. and Ivanka Trump travelled to Moscow with convicted felon Felix Sater of the Bayrock group to explore additional deals." Nellie Ohr is almost certainly an author, likely the primary author, of the protodossiers.

Two of the protodossiers deal specifically with one of Glenn Simpson's recurrent subjects, Beltway lobbyist Paul Manafort. Those dossiers were titled "Paul Manafort—Ukraine and Lichtenstein" and "UPDATE—Paul Manafort." The two Manafort documents were produced after Manafort was named campaign convention manager at the end of March 2016. They deal extensively with his business in Ukraine, focusing on former president Viktor Yanukovych.

Another protodossier is a twelve-page document with five separate reports dealing with topics regarding Trump's connection to the former Eastern Bloc states: "Trump in Azerbaijan"; "Trump's Business Partners in the Trump SoHo" (the partners named are figures from the former Soviet states); "Trump in Russia"; "Trump in Georgia"; "Trump in Serbia." According to sources, the undated document was distributed to the media in April and May 2016.

The most significant of the four protodossiers is a fifteen-page document titled "Donald Trump and Russia" and dated May 20, 2016. This looks like the road map for Steele's research, as it highlights the Trump campaign advisers whose activities he would report to the FBI allegedly starting in early July. By that time, Fusion GPS had been briefing the press on the same Trump associates—in particular Manafort, Page, and Flynn—for several months.

A key difference between the protodossiers and Steele's seventeen memos is that the former discuss Trump's supposed connections to Russian and Eastern Bloc figures alleged to have ties to organized crime and also possibly to Russian state interests. Steele's documents, by contrast, deal almost exclusively with alleged ties connecting Trump and his associates to Russian government officials and figures publicly known to be close to Kremlin leadership.

The header of the May 20 protodossier reads "PRIVILEGED—PREPARED AT THE INSTRUCTION OF COUNSEL." "Counsel" apparently refers to Perkins Coie, the law firm that retained Fusion GPS on behalf of the Clinton campaign and DNC. "Donald Trump's connections to Vladimir Putin's Russia are deeper than generally appreciated and raise significant national security concerns," the document begins. It continues:

> *Trump has partnered on real estate deals with several alleged Russian mafia members. Several of his closest advisers have recently worked for Russian oligarchs loyal to Putin—arguably the world leader most hostile to U.S. and European interests.*

The protodossiers are thick with atmosphere, as sketchy figures from the Eurasian criminal underworld and former Trump associates circulated among New York and Moscow, Toronto, Baku,

Florida, Kazakhstan, and other locations. But for all the novelistic texture, there wasn't much connecting Trump to the Russian figures named in the documents.

Ohr and her colleagues were constantly grasping at straws—and coming up empty. "Trump's relations to Russia and the Russian mob," the document suggests, may date back to his father, Fred, who "began by developing properties in the heavily Russian neighborhoods of Brooklyn."

One former Trump partner, the same document alleges, "was linked to a murder-for-hire plot of his former business partner in the former Soviet Union." He was connected to someone else who was involved in organized crime, who was alleged to have donated to Rudy Giuliani's mayoral campaigns—"which could suggest closer ties to Trump." And from another passage: "Trump and his children have travelled to Russia on multiple occasions over the past thirty years, ostensibly to license his name to local partners. The deals never materialized."

The author of the protodossiers tried to find the missing link, but even the innuendo misfired. Trump marketed luxury apartments to Russians, the May 20 protodossier reported. "The head of Trump marketing was a Russian émigré," it noted ominously, who "recently passed away."

The salacious bits were tepid: "Credible anecdotal evidence suggests Trump was at least as interested in meeting Russian women on these trips as inking deals." What did that mean to a celebrity who'd appeared in the pages of the New York Post for decades with beautiful women on his arm?

There was no fire, not even much smoke. What reporter handed an opposition file like the May 20 protodossier had time to look into twenty-five-year-old media reports "of Russian mobsters living in Trump's public housing buildings in Brighton Beach"?

It wasn't front-page material. Still, the protodossiers provided journalists with some leads. Four pages were devoted to Felix Sater, a Moscow-born businessman, convicted of assault in a bar fight and alleged to have ties to organized crime. Sater had an office in Trump Tower. The May 20 protodossier provided links to reports of his involvement in several projects with Trump, such as the Trump SoHo building. Two paragraphs in the May 20 document were devoted to Aras Agalarov, an Azerbaijani businessman who, along with his son, Emin, had produced the 2013 Miss Universe contest in Moscow for Trump. Several sources, the document claimed, said the Agalarovs "are close to Putin." The same document contended that the Agalarovs had been "integral to the Trump Tower in Baku, Azerbaijan" and "close to an investor" involved in the aborted Trump Tower project in Georgia.

The Azerbaijan and Georgia projects were further detailed in the "Trump in Azerbaijan" and "Trump in Georgia" reports from the undated protodossier. The May 20 document noted Carter Page, saying that he worked at "Merrill Lynch in Moscow," where the firm's clients, the document notes, included Alfa Bank. Also, the dossier notes that Page "regularly writes about enhanced cooperation with Russia in energy policy and is against sanctions."

In addition to the two separate protodossiers on Paul Manafort, the May 20 document includes a paragraph on him.

The May 20 report also points at Michael Flynn, who, as the document concluded in its last line, "showed up at a Moscow dinner honoring the Russia Today channel, seated near Vladimir Putin."

Page, Manafort, Flynn, the RT dinner, Alfa Bank, Sater, and the Agalarovs—those were the names and themes that populated media accounts of Trump's relations to Russia as stories derived from the protodossiers started to fill the press in the spring, summer, and fall. Aside from Sater, they were also the names that would come to feature prominently in Steele's memos.

———————————

Stories hitting Fusion GPS talking points began appearing in early April 2016. An April 5 *New York Times* story by Mike McIntire recounted the Trump SoHo saga, featuring Felix Sater and two Kazakh businessmen, Tevfik Arif and Alexander Maskevich, whose parts were outlined in the May 20 document. The last two had starring roles in the "Trump's Business Partners in the Trump Soho" report from the undated dossier.

Customarily, editors are reluctant to assign stories that repeat news or analysis that's already published, unless there's some fresh angle or new detail. That went out the window with the Trump-Russia series, as the same names, projects, and allegations were recycled repeatedly, and nearly identically, before the election and even after it. The purpose of the stories wasn't to break news but to inundate the voting public with the same message: that Trump and his team had been compromised by Russians.

An April 26 *Washington Post* article by Steven Mufson and Tom Hamburger delved into Manafort's business in Ukraine and relationship to Abdul Rahman al-Assir, a Middle Eastern arms dealer featured in one of the separate Manafort dossiers.

On April 27, *The Guardian* published an almost identical article about Manafort's Ukraine work. Reporter Peter Stone quoted a longtime aide of Senator John McCain. "Advising Yanukovych is like putting lipstick on a pig," said David Kramer.

Franklin Foer's April 28 Slate profile of Manafort rounded out the three-day, three-pronged attack on the Trump adviser, probing his connections with Yanukovych.

A May 17 *Washington Post* article by Rosalind S. Helderman and Tom Hamburger reported on Sater's Trump-related business, hitting on themes from the May 20 protodossier. The *Post*'s Hamburger had known Glenn Simpson for more than a decade. They had shared a byline on stories when they had both worked at the *Wall Street Journal.*

A *Washington Post* article with a May 30 Baku dateline by Kevin Sullivan reported on the Trump project in Azerbaijan, starring Anar Mammadov. His family's exploits, alleged criminal ties, and relationship with Iran were detailed in the "Trump in Azerbaijan" report and briefly mentioned in the May 20 protodossier.

Five days later, June 4, the AP's Jeff Horwitz published virtually the same story on Trump, Azerbaijan, and the Mammadovs. It also included accounts of Trump's ties to Sater.

On June 17, the *Washington Post*'s Hamburger and Helderman went to the well once more. Joined this time by Michael Birnbaum, the *Post* team hit as many of the four protodossiers' talking points as possible: Manafort and the "Russia-aligned Ukrainian president" (Yanukovych), Page's work in Moscow, Flynn (who "stunned the diplomatic community by sitting near Putin at a 2015 Moscow dinner honoring RT"), and the 2013 Miss Universe pageant in Moscow, which Trump coproduced with the Agalarovs. Indeed, a quote from the article repeats the major key of the May 20 document: "Since the 1980s, Trump and his family members have made numerous trips to Moscow in search of business opportunities, and they have relied on Russian investors to buy their properties around the world."

According to the article, a *Post* reporter had recently spoken with the Agalarovs in Moscow. The father and son said they were close to Putin. The Russian president had "awarded the elder

Agalarov the 'Order of Honor of the Russian Federation.'" The
Agalarovs had wanted to go into business with Trump. "I convinced
my father it would be cool to have next to each other the Trump
Tower and Agalarov Tower," Emin told the *Post*. They appreciated
Trump's respect for Putin. "He keeps underlining that he thinks
Putin is a strong leader," the younger Agalarov said.

John McCain aide David Kramer, who would later play a key
role in disseminating the Steele Dossier to the press, also popped up
in the *Post* piece, saying he was "'appalled' by Trump's approach"
to Russia.

There were two seminal Trump-Russia articles in that time frame.
One was Josh Rogin's July 18 *Washington Post* article. Titled "Trump
Campaign Guts GOP's Anti-Russia Stance on Ukraine," the article
was angled to push the narrative that Trump was a Kremlin asset.
Rogin referred to Manafort's work for Yanukovych. Rogin reported
that the Trump campaign had "stripped out the platform's call for
'providing lethal defensive weapons'" to Ukraine. According to
the article, the Trump campaign had weakened the Republican
National Committee's support for Ukraine in its convention
platform.

That was not true. As *Washington Examiner* columnist Byron
York explained, a delegate for candidate Ted Cruz had proposed an
amendment that supported providing "lethal defensive weapons" to
the Ukrainian armed forces. A Trump campaign official had altered
the proposed amendment to use a more diplomatic construction
that promised "appropriate assistance" to the Ukrainian army—
which does not rule out lethal weapons. In other words, the Trump
campaign had slightly softened the Cruz delegate's amendment, but
the adoption of that amendment actually strengthened the RNC

platform's stance on Ukraine. Nevertheless, Rogin's article was recycled through numerous subsequent pieces to push the narrative that Trump was pro-Kremlin.

So was the second key story from that period, another Franklin Foer piece, "Putin's Puppet," published July 4 on Slate. That piece was routinely cited by other journalists joining the messaging campaign. It included figures from the May 20 protodossier rarely mentioned in other reports, such as Richard Burt. The former US ambassador to Germany, Foer noted, sat on the board of Alfa Bank. At the end of October, Foer would write about the bank's alleged ties to the Trump Organization, an article immediately debunked by the FBI and external experts. In the same piece, Foer again zeroed in on Manafort and his work for Yanukovych, the second time in three months. But he went after the new targets as well, discussing Sater at length. Sater, wrote Foer, "worked in Trump Tower; his business card described him as a 'Senior Advisor to Donald Trump.'"

Page was mentioned in the article as well. In the 2000s, he had "advised the state-controlled natural gas giant, Gazprom," wrote Foer, "and helped it attract Western investors." Foer hammered Flynn, too, with Fusion GPS talking points. The retired general "journeyed to Moscow and sat two chairs away from Putin at the 10th anniversary gala celebrating *Russia Today*."

The media operatives quoted one another to fill out their lack of original reporting. Foer cited Michael Crowley's April article in Politico about RT and Flynn's appearance at the December banquet. In turn, Foer's July 4 story was quoted by Jonathan Chait in a July 18 *New York* magazine article. Trump's "relationship with Russia," Chait wrote, "is disturbing and lends itself to frightening interpretations." Chait extravagantly claimed that Putin had overthrown the Ukrainian government "through Paul Manafort, who is now Trump's campaign manager." Chait also repeated Rogin's story on the RNC platform regarding Ukraine. In Chait's view, the platform change "suggests that the candidate's extensive, fulsome praise for the Russian dictator is more than a passing fancy."

———————————

At the tail end of July, another group of writers and national security experts expressed worry that a President Trump would abandon NATO, fracture the international order, let Ukraine fall to Russia, and embrace totalitarian despots the world over.

The articles cited the now-familiar names from the May 20 protodossier—Page, Manafort, and Flynn—and quoted the main takeaways from the Foer and Rogin articles.

In a July 21 *Washington Post* column, Anne Applebaum cited both stories: "The extent of the Trump-Russia business connection has already been laid out, by Franklin Foer at *Slate*," she wrote. She also referenced the article written by her *Post* colleague Rogin: "Earlier this week, Trump's campaign team helped alter the Republican party platform to remove support for Ukraine." She named Page and noted his "long-standing connections to Russian companies." She argued that a "Trump presidency could destabilize Europe." For Applebaum, the only way to explain why Trump would express skepticism about NATO was that he was trying to appease Putin. Her approach was hardly subtle. Beginning her column by invoking the film *The Manchurian Candidate*, she portrayed Trump as an outright Russian asset. "Russia," she alleged, "is clearly participating in the Trump campaign."

In an article published the same day in *The Atlantic*, Jeffrey Goldberg made many of the same observations. Titled "It's Official: Hillary Clinton Is Running Against Vladimir Putin," the article opens: "The Republican nominee for president, Donald J. Trump, has chosen this week to unmask himself as a de facto agent of Russian President Vladimir Putin." As evidence, Goldberg repeated the false claim that "Earlier this week, Trump's operatives watered down the Republican Party's national-security platform position on Ukraine." Goldberg cited a speech that Page had delivered in July during a trip to Moscow and wondered "whether the U.S., under [Trump's] leadership, would keep its [NATO] commitments" or if he "would bring an end to the postwar international order."

In a July 24 *Weekly Standard* article, "Putin's Party?," the magazine's editor, William Kristol, an early and vehement Republican Trump opponent, listed the ostensibly shady connections the Trump team had to Russia through Page, Manafort, and Flynn, who "was paid to give a speech at a Russian propaganda celebration and was seated next to Putin." Kristol also recycled the false story that the Trump campaign had changed the GOP's platform "to weaken language supporting Ukraine."

In an article from the same period, "Trump and Putin: A Love Story," *New Yorker* editor David Remnick cited the "original reporting" of Foer's Slate article. He mentioned Manafort and his work with Yanukovych, "the pro-Russian (and now deposed) leader of Ukraine." The *New Yorker* chief also noted Page's "longstanding ties to . . . Russia's energy industry." Remnick, like Applebaum, Goldberg, and Kristol, was worried that Trump "declared NATO 'obsolete.'"

Oddly, this handful of writers, all of whom hit the same talking points—the RNC platform, NATO, Page's job in Moscow, Manafort's work for Yanukovych, Flynn at the RT banquet, and so on—all had extensive experience covering foreign affairs as well as national politics. Yet not one of them seemed to notice that everything they feared about a Trump presidency had already transpired under Obama. Most glaringly, their concern that Trump would pull support from Ukraine neglected the fact that the Obama White House had refused to supply the Ukrainians with arms.

There were other·issues the national security experts couldn't have missed by accident. Surely it couldn't have escaped Applebaum's notice that Obama had scrapped missile defense for the United States' central European allies, the Czech Republic and Poland. She's a naturalized Polish citizen. Her husband had served as defense minister and foreign minister of Poland. How could she have missed what had happened under Obama's watch?

Goldberg had interviewed Obama five times, most recently in March 2016. Had Goldberg, fretting about the future of NATO, forgotten in only four months that it was under Obama that Moscow's escalation in Syria put Russian forces on NATO's southern border and on the borders of two other US allies, Israel and Jordan?

In 2010, Remnick published a biography of Obama, but had he, too, paid no attention to the policies of the man he had interviewed frequently over nearly a decade? Remnick knew Russia, too, having headed the *Washington Post*'s Moscow Bureau as the Cold War ended. Did he really believe that having a campaign adviser who held a stake in the Russian energy sector suggested that the candidate had questionable loyalties?

Of all those exercises in staged ignorance, Kristol's article was the most willfully vicious. At the *Weekly Standard*, Michael Flynn was regarded as a hero.

I worked at the magazine for seven years, writing mostly on the Middle East—the Syrian war, the Iran nuclear deal, and Obama's partnership with Iran and Russia, all issues that Flynn tackled in and out of the Obama administration. He was a hard-charging intelligence officer who killed terrorists and saved American lives in the Middle East. After Flynn left the DIA, Kristol and Stephen Hayes, a *Weekly Standard* writer who eventually became editor-in-chief, used him as a source for articles about the Osama bin Laden documents, as in this August 2015 piece:

> *"There are letters about Iran's role, influence, and acknowledgment of enabling al Qaeda operatives to pass through Iran as long as al Qaeda did their dirty work against the Americans in Iraq and Afghanistan," Lieutenant General Michael Flynn, former director of the Defense Intelligence Agency, tells* The Weekly Standard. *"What Congress should demand is to see all the UBL [Osama bin Laden] documents related to Iran and all the documents related to intentions of AQ into the future—they are very telling."*

Now, less than a year later, Kristol was suggesting that a retired three-star general, a combat veteran who'd served his country for thirty-three years, had a suspicious relationship with an adversarial power because he had once sat at the same table as Putin.

––––––––––

Fusion GPS had done the job, or part of the job, the Clinton campaign had paid for; with the anti-Trump echo chamber, it had built a solid thing. It was made of the same human matter the Obama administration had used to sell the Iran nuclear deal. As Obama's deputy national security adviser, Ben Rhodes, explained, the echo chamber included officials drawn from the administration, as well as newly minted experts from the think tank and academic communities, and the press. "They were saying things that validated what we had given them to say," Rhodes told *The New York Times Magazine* in May 2016.

Rhodes spoke in the article about exploiting younger journalists, twenty-seven-year-olds who "literally know nothing." But the real core of the echo chamber was the older, experienced journalists, the men and women at the top of their profession whom Rhodes had manipulated for two terms. All they wanted was access to Obama, and as the deans of American journalism, they deserved no less. Rhodes had granted Goldberg five interviews with Obama. Remnick was given enough time with the president to write a biography. They were reliable. It's hardly a coincidence that they were among the first to push the Trump-Russia story.

The other big names were equally useful to Fusion GPS's campaign. Applebaum was an award-winning author who had written extensively about the post-Soviet landscape. If she was calling Trump a Kremlin stooge, it was expert insight. Kristol was the intellectual impresario of the neoconservative movement. As a Republican, he lent the Russia echo chamber the appearance of bipartisan depth.

The paper of record, the *New York Times*, weighed in as well, giving the Fusion GPS–generated campaign its stamp of approval.

Columnist Andrew Rosenthal pondered over Flynn's appearance at the RT dinner. In a July 20 article, the son of the paper's former executive editor A. M. Rosenthal concluded that "the idea that there is some nefarious undertone to Trump's obsession with Putin—is the Russian leader flattering Trump to somehow gain control over him?—somehow does not seem entirely crazy."

On July 22, the *Times*' Paul Krugman filed "Donald Trump, the Siberian Candidate." The Nobel Prize–winning economist thought it was suspicious that the GOP platform on Ukraine "was watered down to blandness on the insistence of Trump representatives."

These weren't twenty-seven-year-olds grinding out copy but opinion leaders. They were authors, top validators, and once you got them to say something, the pack was sure to follow.

And just in time, for the Clinton campaign was preparing for potential problems.

Chapter 5

THE FUSION RUSSIANS

FUSION GPS had joined the Clinton campaign in March to fill the media echo chamber with reports of the Trump team's suspicious ties to the Kremlin. At the same time, there was an analogous operation under way in the shadows. Trump associates were repeatedly approached by figures offering them Kremlin-sourced dirt on Clinton.

Sometimes the dangles were more specific: Trump advisers were told about Clinton's emails and that the Russians had them.

There were six known suspicious approaches made to the Trump team between the time Fusion GPS was hired and the Democratic National Convention, which began on July 25. The operatives who came after Trump associates all had ties to the FBI, other Western intelligence services, or the Clintons. Taken together, it looks like a sting operation targeting the Trump circle.

GEORGE PAPADOPOULOS
George Papadopoulos was one of the five foreign policy advisers named by Trump in his March interview with the *Washington Post*.

That same month, he traveled from London to Rome on a delegation sponsored by his then employer, the London Centre of International Law Practice (LCILP). In Rome, he was introduced to another LCILP employee, Joseph Mifsud, a former Maltese diplomat.

Mifsud taught intelligence and law enforcement officers in London as well as Rome, where he worked at Link Campus University. The university trains intelligence and law enforcement officials from several NATO countries. US intelligence officials from the CIA, NSA, and FBI lectured and researched at Link. Mifsud's professional network comprised high-ranking western European politicians, diplomats, and spies. He was especially well connected in British and Italian circles.

Mifsud told Papadopoulos he had high-level Russian contacts. He connected him by email to a director of a Russian think tank. In London, Mifsud introduced Papadopoulos to a young Russian woman he said was Putin's niece. She wasn't.

In April, Mifsud emailed the Trump adviser from Moscow, where he was participating in an academic conference. On returning, he met Papadopoulos for breakfast in a London hotel April 26. Mifsud reportedly told him that the Russians had dirt on Hillary Clinton "in the form of thousands of emails."

Papadapoulos said he had never told anyone on the Trump campaign about the conversation with Mifsud. Neither Mueller nor anyone else discovered evidence to contradict his claim.

Papadopoulos was in for another strange London encounter two weeks later. Australia's envoy to the United Kingdom asked to meet him in a London wine bar. Papadopoulos said he didn't understand why a senior foreign official like Alexander Downer, formerly Australia's foreign minister, had sought a private meeting with an unpaid campaign adviser.

Downer's circles, like Mifsud's, consisted of high-ranking Western intelligence officials. He'd served on the board of advisors of Hakluyt, a prominent private intelligence firm founded by former MI6 officers. He had ties to the Clintons, too. In 2006, he had arranged a $25 million grant to the Clinton Foundation for its AIDS prevention and education efforts.

Papadopoulos said that Downer kept sticking his phone into his face. He was certain the Australian diplomat was recording their May meeting.

STEPHEN MILLER AND CARTER PAGE

In May and June, Trump advisers Stephen Miller and Carter Page were invited to the University of Cambridge for a July symposium supported by Stefan Halper's academic department. Speakers at the event included Halper's Cambridge colleague former MI6 director Sir Richard Dearlove. Miller declined the invitation. Page accepted the invitation tendered by Halper's associate Steven Schrage. At the symposium, Page was engaged in conversations by Halper and Downer, the Australian diplomat who'd met with Papadopoulos. Halper told Page he knew Paul Manafort; It's unclear what Downer might have discussed with Page.

MICHAEL CAPUTO AND ROGER STONE

Also in May, a man calling himself Henry Greenberg contacted Trump campaign communications adviser Michael Caputo, who arranged for him to meet with another campaign aide, Roger Stone. Greenberg told Stone that he could provide "damaging information" on Clinton in exchange for $2 million. Stone turned him down. Caputo and Stone later learned that Greenberg was a Russian national with a criminal record. In 2015, Greenberg had signed a court affidavit claiming that he had been an FBI informant for seventeen years.

DONALD TRUMP, JR., JARED KUSHNER, AND PAUL MANAFORT

Perhaps the most remarkable episode in the series was initiated by Emin Agalarov, son of Aras Agalarov, the Azerbaijani businessman who played a starring role in Fusion GPS's May 20 protodossier.

The Agalarovs told the *Washington Post* of their friendship and business relationship with Trump. But when they reached out with information that could help his presidential campaign, hurt his rival, and, most important, earn his gratitude, they chose instead to go through intermediaries. The Agalarovs arranged for a British music publicist, Rob Goldstone, to email Donald Trump, Jr. Goldstone wrote the candidate's son that the Agalarovs had "official documents and information that would incriminate Hillary and her dealings with Russia and would be very useful to your father." The phrasing of the email appears designed to frame the Trump team for conspiring with a foreign government: "This is obviously very high level and sensitive information but is part of Russia and its government's support for Mr. Trump."

Trump Jr. promptly responded, "If it's what you say I love it."

It was the only known time a Trump campaign adviser expressed willingness to take damaging information regarding Clinton that was said to be sourced to the Kremlin.

On June 9, Goldstone went to the Trump Tower in midtown Manhattan to meet with Trump Jr., Paul Manafort, and Trump's son-in-law, Jared Kushner. He brought with him a Russian lawyer, Natalia Veselnitskaya. She was sent to convey the information promised to the Trump campaign. The senior campaign officials were disappointed to find out that she had no dirt on Clinton. She wanted instead to talk about sanctions imposed on senior Russian officials under a 2012 US law. She had been hired to help repeal those sanctions. She reported directly to a senior Kremlin official. And Glenn Simpson, who had also been hired to help those efforts, reported to her.

Simpson, says one former journalist familiar with Fusion GPS's operations, is the man with the contacts, while Peter Fritsch is the partner who keeps the trains running on time.

"Simpson is the typical kind of investigative reporter who needs to be reined in from time to time to keep him from wandering into conspiracy theory territory," says the former journalist. "That's Fritsch's role; he's the guy who maintains order there."

Simpson had distinguished himself as an aggressive, if sometimes overzealous, reporter. He had cowritten a 1998 *Wall Street Journal* story alleging that a White House steward had seen Bill Clinton and Monica Lewinsky alone together and found tissues with "lipstick and other stains" following one of their encounters. The story was false, and the *Journal* retracted its account the next week. Clinton White House press secretary Mike McCurry called it "the sleaziest episode in the history of American journalism."

Simpson jumped on the big national security stories of the day: terrorism and the post-9/11 Middle East, as well as organized crime in the post-Soviet Eastern Bloc. He was also interested in Beltway banditry and coauthored a 1996 book with the political scientist Larry Sabato, *Dirty Little Secrets: The Persistence of Corruption in American Politics.*

It was perhaps inevitable that Paul Manafort would get Simpson's attention. The longtime GOP power broker was at the nexus of Washington influence peddling and post-Soviet money. In 2007, Simpson and his wife, Mary Jacoby, also a reporter at the *Journal*, wrote their first of several articles on Manafort and his work for the Ukrainian politician Viktor Yanukovych. It's a piece of straightforward reporting on how the Republican establishment introduced former Eastern Bloc figures like Yanukovych to the ways of Washington. However, Simpson's characterization of Yanukovych as pro-Putin was evidence of his limits as a foreign policy journalist—or that he was pushing against one Ukrainian faction on behalf of others.

A quick glance at a map shows why. Ukraine is a buffer state, weak in relation to its neighbors to the west, Europe, and east, Russia. Russians make up Ukraine's largest ethnic minority, nearly 20 percent. To call a Ukrainian official pro-Putin is meaningless. No Ukrainian head of state can long survive, never mind hold power, with prolonged opposition to Kyiv's mightier, nuclear-armed neighbor in Moscow. The trick for any Ukrainian leader is to find a way to balance Europe and Russia against each other. Manafort advised Yanukovych as president to inch closer to Europe with an association agreement, a trade deal with some political benefits.

In September 2013, Yanukovych was poised to sign and Putin threatened economic measures that were likely to send Ukraine into default. Yanukovych withdrew Ukraine from the agreement, and protestors filled the streets of Kyiv, leading to violence. In February 2014, he went into exile in Russia, from which he described Putin's reannexation of Crimea as a tragedy. EU and US diplomats complained bitterly about Russia's brutal actions in a conflict they'd helped stoke, even as they knew Western leaders would never entangle their interests in a fight on Russia's border.

In the spring and summer of 2016, the US press corps, feeding from Fusion GPS's trough, was happy to accept Simpson's description of Yanukovych as pro-Putin. Since Trump adviser Manafort had worked for the Ukrainian, the fiction further advanced the Trump-Russia narrative.

Experienced Russia hands saw early on that Simpson knew little about Russia or Ukraine and used his conspiracy theory predilections to engage in large-bore theories about what was going on there. "Glenn knew the names of a few Russian oligarchs, and whenever something happened in Russia, he seemed to link those events to one of them," says a national security journalist. "He seemed to know what he was talking about—if you didn't know much about Russia." Oleg Deripaska's is a name that regularly appears in Simpson's Russia reporting. "He was obsessed with Deripaska," says the journalist.

Deripaska is mentioned in a few of the protodossiers. "UPDATE—Paul Manafort," reports that one of his shell companies is pursuing Manafort "for allegedly diverting millions of dollars and not delivering on promised investments." Nevertheless, Simpson's contractor Christopher Steele apparently did not share his concerns about Deripaska. In January 2016, the former British spy lobbied his and Simpson's mutual friend Bruce Ohr on behalf of the oligarch.

Steele and Ohr were among the law enforcement and intelligence professionals who shared Simpson's interest in the chaotic post-Soviet environment. Simpson's interest in uncovering Eurasian organized crime appears to have steered Fusion GPS's work in the opposite direction.

"Fusion GPS started as an opposition research firm," says the national security journalist. "Then their work in Latin America pushed them in another direction, political and dirty." A few years after its founding, the company was working for foreign interests allegedly involved in criminal enterprises.

———————

In 2014, Fusion GPS was hired for a job with Derwick Associates, a firm of five young Venezuelan businessmen with ties to Hugo Chávez's government. Derwick's business practices had attracted unwanted media attention, and they sought help deflecting it.

"Between 2009 and 2011," says independent Venezuelan journalist Alek Boyd, "Derwick bribed their way into twelve no-bid contracts, worth in total about $2.2 billion, of which they stole through overpriced equipment and services about $1 billion."

Derwick has denied this, and a 2013 lawsuit concerning the charges was dismissed.

Boyd explains that the populist Venezuelan government needed help keeping the energy sector afloat and turned to the Russians for help. "As soon as Chávez took over the state oil conglomerate," he says, "he fired some twenty thousand people, so he had to replace their knowledge and experience. He looked to international partnerships, which would take a large percentage but not a majority stake. Russia was a staunch supporter of Chávez."

That created opportunities for Derwick. "Around 2013 Derwick got into a partnership with Gazprombank," says Boyd. "But Derwick had no track record related to oil. All they had was the millions they'd misappropriated and their network of contacts, which they used to provide an expensive loan to Gazprom and insert themselves into a joint oil deal."

When journalists started asking questions of Derwick, the firm threatened legal action. "Most corrupt Venezuelan businessmen get their money and buy a condo in Miami and fly off into the sunset quietly," says Boyd. "But these guys waged an international censorship campaign, and it was the clumsiness of the campaign that got my attention."

Derwick called in Fusion GPS. In 2014, Boyd received a tip that Peter Fritsch had flown to Caracas to meet with Derwick principals. Boyd called another member of the Fusion GPS team he knew, Thomas Catan. "I met Catan when he was covering the 2006 Venezuelan elections for *The Times* of London," he says. He asked Catan about Fritsch's trip to meet the Derwick principals. Catan denied that Fritsch had flown to Caracas. "But I had a copy of a hotel reservation from July 2014 with Fritsch's name on it," says Boyd.

The purpose of Fritsch's visit to Venezuela was to meet with reporters from the *Wall Street Journal* who were working on an investigative article about Derwick. Fritsch and a group of Derwick executives arranged to meet with *Journal* reporter José de Córdoba, Boyd explains. "They said they'd provide de Córdoba with documents to show the contracts were legitimate, but they never did." Boyd says that the purpose of the trip was to bully the *Journal* into silence. Fritsch had once been Córdoba's boss at the *Journal*. Córdoba told a colleague that the "blatant intimidation tactics" had made him feel "uncomfortable." He eventually published a story, but Fritsch apparently derailed a longer investigative piece.

Other journalists covering Derwick were smeared with false allegations, including the Venezuelan journalist and human rights activist Thor Halvorssen. He says Fusion GPS was behind a smear campaign targeting him. He filed a civil Racketeer Influenced and Corrupt Organizations (RICO) Act lawsuit against Simpson, Fritsch, and others in the Eastern District of New York. The lawsuit alleges that Fusion GPS's principals worked for a group of Venezuelan criminals, Derwick, to smear whistle-blowers in a multibillion-dollar fraud in Venezuela. "They circulated a fake dossier about me and placed false accusations in the media that I was a heroin addict, a pedophile, and an embezzler," he says. "Their tactic is to manufacture accusations so appalling that being innocent is not a defense," he continues. "Fusion GPS' strategy is to make you radioactive as a whistle-blower and delete any credibility you may have. What's interesting is that they have a record of engaging in the same pattern of accusations against multiple people. They're mercenaries." These claims are anchored in his RICO suit.

Boyd, too, was smeared on social media, describing him as a drug trafficker, extortionist, car thief, and pedophile. Unknown culprits burglarized his home in London, according to London police reports. Photographs of his young daughters, taken with a telephoto lens, were put into his raincoat pocket. He also received anonymous notes threatening his daughters with sexual abuse.

"Derwick doesn't understand how media works" says Boyd. Fusion GPS was there to lead them and explain it to them. Because of their background, they have an impressive array of contacts they can rely on to discredit someone."

———————

Smear campaigns and press intimidation became signature Fusion GPS tactics.

When the firm was hired in spring 2014 to help Russian officials repeal US legislation sanctioning Putin associates, Fusion GPS targeted the driving force behind the law: the fifty-three-year-old Chicago-born financier William Browder. Browder's company, Hermitage Capital Management, had opened for business in Russia in the mid-1990s and become one of the country's largest investment advisers. In 2005, Browder was expelled from Russia and his offices were raided. Seized documents were later used to misappropriate $230 million in taxes that his company had paid to the Russian government.

Browder hired a Russian tax specialist, Sergei Magnitsky, to investigate. In 2008, Magnitsky was arrested. Russian authorities demanded that he sign a false statement admitting that he had stolen the $230 million. Magnitsky refused. His health steadily deteriorated in prison, and on November 16, 2009, the thirty-seven-year-old Magnitsky was found dead. Independent inquiries showed that he'd been beaten by Russian authorities, leading to his death.

Browder knew that there was nothing to be done in Moscow but that he could hurt Putin and his associates by going after the money they'd parked in Europe and the United States. He found allies on Capitol Hill, and in 2012 the Magnitsky Act, targeting the officials and regime cronies responsible for the Russian's death, was signed into law.

Two years later, the Justice Department opened a case against a Russian holding company, Prevezon, for laundering money stolen in the fraud Magnitsky had uncovered. The company was owned by Denis Katsyv, the son of a former Russian minister who frequently employed Natalia Veselnitskaya. "She's an arm of the Russian government," says Browder. Court documents filed with the Southern District of New York show that she was producing documents for the Russian government in response to requests from the US government. "It shows that she is not just an independent lawyer but is employed by the Russian government," says Browder.

Veselnitskaya was one of Moscow's instruments for undoing the Magnitsky Act. She hired the law firm BakerHostetler to litigate the Prevezon case in the US, and the firm brought on Fusion GPS for "litigation support." Sources explain that their job was to manufacture and market a cover story to the press in order to smear Browder and Magnitsky. "Glenn Simpson was running an advocacy campaign for an agent of the Russian government," says Browder. "He was employed by Veselnitskaya to assist the Russians in discrediting me and the Magnitsky Act."

Veselnitskaya brought on another associate to push the anti-Magnitsky, anti-Browder campaign on Capitol Hill, Rinat Akhmetshin. A relatively well known figure among Washington, DC, journalists working the national security beat, Akhmetshin lobbies on behalf of various Russian-related interests. He's reportedly a former Soviet intelligence officer. "I'd never heard of Akhmetshin until he popped up in this story," says Browder.

Veselnitskaya and Simpson's main line of attack was to deny that Magnitsky had been killed and put forth an alternative narrative. "They said Magnitsky wasn't murdered. Nobody did it. And he wasn't a whistle-blower," says Browder. "Therefore, since the Magnitsky Act was advocated by me under false pretenses, it should be repealed."

Browder tried to interest journalists in a story about the role that Simpson and Fusion GPS had played in the campaign targeting him and Magnitsky. There were no takers. "I discovered that Glenn Simpson was so deeply embedded as a source for different stories, no one wanted to write a story about him," he says. "I was told explicitly by journalists in those organizations that their editors wouldn't touch Simpson, he was so firmly entrenched. I was told by a few journalists who wanted to do a story on Fusion GPS that Simpson called their editor and tried to get them fired."

Simpson had the press on his side. He peddled the fake narrative about Browder and Magnitsky to a number of US journalists and apparently found a taker in NBC News' Ken Dilanian. Browder shared documents with me chronicling Dilanian's reporting on the Magnitsky Act, reporting that Browder says is derived from Fusion GPS's smear campaign. Browder provided Dilanian with voluminous evidence regarding the circumstances of Magnitsky's murder. Yet the reporter continued to contest the facts.

Eventually Browder's lawyers stepped in and responded to Dilanian's employer. The reporter's questions, the lawyers told NBC executives, indicated that he was ignoring the details of the case and the evidence that Browder had produced in response to his questions. "It is inconceivable," wrote Browder's lawyers, "that Mr. Dilanian could publish an article for an esteemed media company such as NBC while ignoring this evidence."

Whatever story Dilanian might have been reporting did not run. But Browder saw the reporter's questions as evidence of a larger maneuver. "April 2016, the smear campaign began in earnest," he says. "The point was to assert that all the facts of the Magnitsky case were not true, so in effect I'd been lying to Congress."

Simpson met with Veselnitskaya the day before and after her June 9, 2016, meeting at Trump Tower. His narrative discrediting Browder and Magnitsky was recycled into her talking points. She brought Akhmetshin with her and repeated much of what Dilanian recited in his correspondence with Browder. She told the Trump aides that Browder was guilty of tax fraud and embezzlement. That was not what Trump team had expected. They'd been hoping for the dirt on Clinton. They stopped the meeting after twenty minutes.

What happened?

Fusion GPS had rolled its smear campaign on behalf of Veselnitskaya into its Clinton-funded smear campaign. After all, the goal of the anti-Trump operation was to tie him to the leadership in Moscow. A meeting with a genuinely Kremlin-linked lawyer would dirty senior campaign officials, including the candidate's son

It was around that time that someone else was rolled into Fusion GPS's Trump job: Christopher Steele, who was already working on at least two other Russia projects.

The former MI6 officer had contacted Bruce Ohr about Deripaska's visa problems. Also, by April, Steele had reportedly completed an investigation for clients, called "Project Charlemagne," that looked into Russian interference in European politics.

It seems that Steele was also already working for the FBI. In February, the ex–British spy had been "admonished"—given specific instructions—by the FBI as a confidential human source.

The various currents of the anti-Trump operation—Russia, Fusion GPS, and the FBI—were merging. Steele was the nexus. The former MI6 man, said Simpson, "doesn't exaggerate, doesn't make things up, doesn't sell baloney." But Fusion GPS had brought on Steele for no other purpose. To market make-believe, Clinton cutouts hired a credentialed Russian expert who was already working for the FBI.

Chapter 6

THE AVATAR

SIMPSON SAID that he had brought on Steele because his company had gathered all the public-record information on Trump and had exhausted open sources. So Fusion GPS hired a specialist who could take the investigation further. Remarkably, in only one month's time, Steele hit the mother lode. Even though his tenure at the Russia desk had ended seven years before and he hadn't been back to Russia since his cover had been blown in the late 1990s, Steele's sources provided him with details that illuminated what Fusion GPS's May 20 report had barely touched.

Note how Steele's June 20 report augmented and expanded the information from a month before.

THE MAY 20 PROTODOSSIER:
Donald Trump's connections to Vladimir Putin's Russia are deeper than generally appreciated and raise significant national security concerns.

THE JUNE 20 MEMO:
Russian regime has been cultivating, supporting, and assisting

TRUMP for at least 5 years. Aim, endorsed by Putin, has been to encourage splits and divisions in western alliance.

MAY 20:

Trump and his children have travelled to Russia on multiple occasions over the past thirty years, ostensibly to license his name to local partners. The details never materialized.

> **JUNE 20:**
>
> So far TRUMP has declined various sweetener real estate business deals offered him in Russia in order to further the Kremlin's cultivation of him.

MAY 20:

Credible anecdotal evidence suggests Trump was at least as interested in meeting Russian women on these trips as inking deals.

> **JUNE 20:**
>
> Former top Russian intelligence officer claims FSB [Federal Security Bureau, Russia›s main security and intelligence service] has compromised TRUMP through his activities in Moscow sufficiently to be able to blackmail him. According to several knowledgeable sources, his conduct in Moscow has included perverted sexual acts which have been arranged/monitored by the FSB.

The pattern is clear: the June 20 memo used the May 20 protodossier as a template. It picked up themes from the earlier document and sensationalized them. Trump, it said, was not merely connected to Russian businessmen in perhaps suggestive ways; he'd in fact been *compromised* by the Kremlin. He wasn't just attracted to Russian women; Russian intelligence had *recorded* him doing perverted things with Russian women.

The May 20 document was only one source for the June 20 memo. Steele's reports incorporated other Clinton-related Trump-Russia research as well.

For instance, the most memorable claim from the June memo appears to have been cribbed from the reporting that, according to former CIA officer Robert Baer, Clinton associates Sidney Blumenthal and Cody Shearer began in March–April 2016. The Shearer-Blumenthal memos relate that an FSB officer claimed there was film of a woman urinating on Trump and that he had been caught on tape in the Moscow Ritz-Carlton in 2013. Clinton operatives must have believed that urination was a compelling theme, for in the June 20 memo, Steele claimed that Trump had hired prostitutes in 2013 to urinate on a bed in the Moscow Ritz-Carlton, where President Obama had once slept.

Like the Shearer report, Steele's memo claimed that Trump's actions had been documented. "The hotel," according to Steele, "was known to be under FSB control with microphones and concealed cameras in all the main rooms."

What had started as an opposition research project that had turned up little of substance had transformed into a smear campaign. But Fusion GPS didn't need Steele for that. It had already shown its ability to dirty targets in its work for the Obama campaign, Derwick Associates, and Veselnitskaya.

So why did Fusion pay Steele a reported $168,000 to put his byline on a dirty tricks operation? The documents themselves provide some clues.

In addition to the tabloid-style revisions of the June 20 report, and the fact there are no footnotes as there are in the protodossiers, there were other differences between the two documents. First, the May 20 protodosser paid extensive attention, three of fifteen pages, to onetime Trump associate Felix Sater. The felon with alleged ties to Russian organized crime was absent from Steele's June 20 report and appeared nowhere in the dossier's subsequent sixteen memos.

Why was Sater, who had reportedly worked as a confidential informant for the FBI and other US government agencies, missing from the Steele Dossier? Had Fusion GPS been advised not to include him?

This raises an even more significant issue. Nellie Ohr said she had been hired to look into Trump's connections to Russian organized crime figures, research reflected in the May 20 protodossier. However, the June 20 report and Steele's subsequent memos described the Trump team's clandestine relationship with a foreign power, Russia. These are two different scenarios.

With the beginning of Steele's reporting, Fusion GPS changed course. From the May 20 protodossier to the June 20 memo, the Clinton-funded operatives moved from opposition research to a document laying the groundwork for a counterintelligence investigation. The radical shift provides evidence that the dossier was written under direction, with an eye to obtaining a warrant to spy on the Trump campaign.

Finally, Steele's report made two claims not found in the May 20 document. First, it alleged that "the Kremlin had been feeding TRUMP and his team valuable intelligence on his rivals, including Democratic presidential candidate Hillary CLINTON for several years." Much of it had come "from bugged conversations CLINTON had made on her various trips to Russia and focused on things she had said which contradicted her current position on various issues. Others were most probably from phone intercepts." However, according to Steele, the Russians had nothing incriminating on Clinton. The file "comprised mainly eavesdropped conversations of various sorts rather than details/evidence of embarrassing behavior."

Presumably, the client that had paid Fusion GPS to distribute Trump-Russia information to the press was relieved to find that the Russians had nothing *embarrassing* on the candidate. Clinton campaign officials couldn't have been more delighted had they dictated the finding themselves.

The next section of the Steele report, however, claimed that the Russians weren't passing information to Trump or to anyone else. Under the "explicit instructions of PUTIN himself," Steele claimed, the Clinton information "had not as yet been leaked abroad, including to Trump or his campaign team. At present it was unclear what PUTIN's intentions were in this regard."

So was Russia passing off intelligence on Clinton to Trump or not? Had they given the Trump team Clinton-related dirt previously but were holding off on newer material? The answer is unclear. However, it seems that whoever was directing Steele's reporting was preparing for the possibility that Clinton's communications were going to be leaked.

It appears that the memo was part of a cover story that would not only defend Clinton but also damage her rival; it was the Russians who gave Clinton's stolen communications to Trump. And he was in the Kremlin's pocket.

––––––––––

On June 12, a little more than a week before the date of Steele's first memo, WikiLeaks founder Julian Assange had told a British TV interviewer that WikiLeaks had "upcoming leaks in relation to Hillary Clinton." Assange said, "We have emails."

It wasn't clear what he was referring to. WikiLeaks had already posted the thirty thousand emails that Clinton hadn't deleted from her server and had been obtained lawfully pursuant to a Freedom of Information Act request. Was Assange talking about the more than thirty thousand emails she said she'd deleted and couldn't be located?

Clinton claimed they had been emails about her daughter, Chelsea's, wedding, "condolence notes to friends as well as yoga routines, family vacations, the other things you typically find in inboxes." In other words, she had deleted them because they were no one's business but her own. But what if she'd tampered with official government records? What if she'd destroyed evidence?

Her emails and the private, unsecure server on which she'd conducted official government business during her term as secretary of state constituted one of the campaign's major worries. In July 2015, the FBI had opened an investigation into her possible mishandling of classified intelligence. Peter Strzok led the FBI investigation, called "Midyear Exam." In February 2016, Andrew McCabe took on oversight when he was named deputy FBI director.

There were concerns inside the FBI that McCabe had a conflict of interest. In March 2015, longtime Clinton associate Terry McAuliffe had encouraged McCabe's wife to run for a Virginia state senate seat and then arranged for nearly $700,000 in campaign contributions. FBI higher-ups reasoned that since McCabe had taken over the Clinton probe after his wife's unsuccessful run had ended in November 2015, there was no conflict of interest. That was a poorly reasoned decision; just because his wife's campaign was over didn't mean McCabe was no longer indebted.

In any case, the Clinton campaign was not concerned primarily with the possibility of the candidate being charged with mishandling classified information. Had charges been brought, virtually every cabinet member with whom she'd communicated would have been implicated, including the president.

Obama had not only exchanged emails with her on her private, unsecure account but had done so while she was on the territory of a foreign adversary: Russia. Clinton had sent an email to Obama during her late-June 2012 trip to Saint Petersburg. In an interview with the FBI, Clinton "stated she must have sent it from the plane." The FBI concluded that "it is reasonably likely that hostile actors gained access to Secretary Clinton's private email."

It was also possible that Russian intelligence, as well as other intelligence services, had more Clinton emails. The US secretary of state's communications are among those most highly prized by intelligence services, friendly and hostile, the world over. Clinton had made hers especially vulnerable by using an unsecure server.

Maybe a spy agency wouldn't release them. They would offer valuable insight into, or blackmail material on, the woman everyone assumed was going to be the next US president. But someone else might drop them: maybe an opposition research shop or just a private citizen eager to hand Trump an "October surprise." Maybe a journalist had them. Maybe Assange did.

Thus, even after FBI director James Comey officially cleared Clinton on July 5 of mishandling classified information—even as he indicated that at least some of the thirty thousand emails she'd deleted had been work related—her problems were far from over. If the deleted emails were published—and there must have been some that would prove hard to explain away—there was no changing the message. But the reception of the news could be shaped by changing the focus: Ignore the content of Clinton-related emails, and pay attention to who dropped them and why.

The Steele Dossier was corroboration of the espionage operation that had been targeting Trump associates since March. Why did mysterious figures approach Trump officials—Papadopoulos, Page, Miller, Caputo, Stone, Trump Jr., Kushner, Manafort—and usually with offers of dirt on Hillary Clinton that originated in Russia? The answer was in Steele's report: the Kremlin wanted to help Trump, the candidate it had been cultivating, according to Steele, for at least five years.

Or imagine watching TV and seeing those figures move in and out of the Trump circle. Without naming Joseph Mifsud, Alexander Downer, Henry Greenberg, Natalia Veselnitskaya, Rinat Akhmetshin, and Stefan Halper, the dossier spelled out their purpose in bold letters at the bottom third of the screen. Steele's June 20 report was the chyron synched to the visuals: *Trump is taking dirt on Clinton from the Russians.*

It looks as though the Clinton campaign was defending against a potential "October surprise."

The same day Comey exonerated Clinton, FBI agent Michael Gaeta visited Steele in London. Gaeta was assigned to the Rome embassy in the FBI's legal attaché office. He had previously worked with Steele investigating corruption in world soccer's governing board, Fédération Internationale de Football Association (FIFA). Gaeta reportedly turned white when he read Steele's memos on Trump. Presumably he was alarmed by Steele's findings. But there were questions the FBI agent might have asked the Brit about his June 20 report.

Why had the Russians been cultivating Trump for five years? How had they known that the host of the top-rated TV show *Celebrity Apprentice* would someday run for president?

Why would a serious intelligence service like Russia's hand over control of an intelligence file on the next president of the United States to Putin's spokesman, Dmitry Peskov? Did Moscow customarily entrust sensitive intelligence operations to press attachés?

And above all, why would Putin go out of his way to provoke the woman everyone assumed would be the next president by helping her opponent?

None of it made sense. Perhaps that's why Steele and his confederates went through Gaeta. They may have seen him as a mark. Otherwise, why wouldn't Steele simply take his reports to FBI counterintelligence? Instead he went to an FBI agent whose focus was organized crime. What did he know about the inner workings of the Kremlin?

The same, of course, could be said of Steele. According to his friend Bruce Ohr, Steele was an expert in Russian organized crime.

Gaeta and Steele had worked together in the past on what had essentially been an organized crime case. Press reports claimed that Steele was celebrated in US law enforcement circles for having helped the Justice Department win dozens of indictments of FIFA officials in 2015.

That was part of Steele's legend. It credentialed his Trump-Russia reports. The FBI officially assessed Steele to be "reliable as previous reporting from [Steele] has been corroborated and used in criminal proceedings." However, it appears that Steele's contribution to the FIFA case was overstated.

In 2009, Steele left MI6, founded a private intelligence firm, Orbis Business Intelligence, and was reportedly hired by a consortium sponsoring England's efforts to win the 2018 World Cup. The England bid's backers wanted to know what their rivals were up to, and Steele was reportedly directed to focus on Russia.

He contacted Andrew Jennings, a then-sixty-six-year-old investigative journalist who'd covered sports corruption for decades. In 2006, Jennings had written a book on FIFA: *FOUL! The Secret World of FIFA: Bribes, Vote Rigging and Ticket Scandals.*

In late 2009, Steele asked to meet the reporter in his hometown in northwest England. "He came up to Penrith for lunch," Jennings tells me by Skype. "He's a very intelligent guy." He says that he talked with Steele about FIFA head Sepp Blatter and some of the more notoriously corrupt local football associations, with particular attention to the Americas and the Caribbean. "I'd been on the story since 2001," says Jennings. "I gave Steele the basic background on FIFA, and he got it pretty quickly. It's an organized crime racket."

It appears that while Steele was working for the sponsors of the England 2018 bid, he contacted the FBI to discuss his research. Shortly after the new year, says Jennings, Steele invited Jennings to London to meet with US law enforcement officials. One was a young FBI agent named Jared Randall. The other two were Michael Gaeta and head of the Department of Justice's Organized Crime and Racketeering Section, Bruce Ohr. The Americans were attentive, and Jennings was enthusiastic. "The FBI guys were very serious," he says. "I'd been working on this for years, and there were no national police in the world who were interested in pursuing corruption in FIFA, and then the FBI turns up at my door. I'm thinking this could be very good."

I ask Jennings if he shared documents with Steele and the US officials. "Not that I remember," says the journalist. He briefed them, as he had Steele.

The last time Jennings spoke with Steele was in 2011. "I tended to trust him," says the journalist. "He didn't seem like the sort of guy to make stuff up, because it wouldn't take long before someone caught on if it wasn't true. And that would discredit all that he's done."

Jennings wrote two more books on FIFA, one published just before the Justice Department handed down more than a dozen indictments in December 2015: *The Dirty Game: Uncovering the*

Scandal at FIFA. DOJ brought no charges against Russian officials or institutions.

There is no public evidence that Steele's research into Russia's 2018 bid panned out. He contributed intelligence he'd collected on Russia to a database regarding rival bids. However, the information on Russia from the database was never officially made public. The intelligence, one source told the press at the time, was "incendiary" but was not thought to be "legally credible."

Finally in 2014, nearly four years after Russia was awarded the World Cup, the work for which Steele had reportedly been hired began to surface. The former British spy leaked his findings to the press. In a report two journalists filed with the British Parliament, Steele is referred to as the "MI6 source." He drew a portrait of a wide-scale Russian government campaign, including top Putin allies, to corrupt the bidding process and win the international tournament. But he had no evidence to prove it.

"What you need to remember about this is the way this was done in Russia is that nothing was written down," Steele told the journalists. "Don't expect me or anyone else to produce a document with Putin's signature saying please X bribe Y with this amount in this way. He's not going to do that. Putin is an ex–intelligence officer. Everything he does has to be deniable."

It would not require the professional habits of an intelligence officer to avoid signing documents providing evidence of a criminal conspiracy. Steele's bluster hid his failure. Indeed, his 2014 account of Russia's World Cup bid foreshadowed his reporting on the Trump team's ties to Russia.

According to Steele, the central figure in the World Cup scheme was Igor Sechin, the CEO of the Russian energy giant Rosneft. Sechin, Steele claimed, was Putin's proxy, offering officials from

Qatar energy deals in exchange for supporting Russia's 2018 bid. Also according to Steele, the key data point was Sechin's visit to Qatar in April 2010 to discuss joint projects to develop gas deposits in the Russian Arctic. "We always suspected and I think there were indications that there were other items on the agenda of which the World Cup was one," he said.

One of Steele's informants—"extremely well placed," boasted the former spy—later confirmed the MI6 veteran's hunch: "We got something from a source saying that this was significantly related to the World Cup." He continued, "Our conclusion was that if there was collusion [between Qatar and Russia] it was done through the energy sector. Gas deals. Igor Sechin went just before the vote."

Steele must have been fixated with Sechin. Just two years after he named him as Putin's bagman for Russia's World Cup bid, Steele identified him as the mastermind of the Kremlin's effort to tilt the US presidential election to Trump.

In a July 19 report for Fusion GPS, Steele claimed that Carter Page had met with Sechin in Moscow. According to Steele's memo, Sechin "raised with PAGE the issues of future bilateral energy cooperation and prospects for an associated move to lift Ukraine-related western sanctions on Russia." He was repeating the precise pattern he had set out in his FIFA investigation: collusion, through the energy sector, with Igor Sechin in control. The ex-spy simply swapped out Qatar for the Trump campaign.

––––––––––

Page, according to Steele's memo, had also met with a Russian official who mentioned the compromising material "the Kremlin possessed on TRUMP's Democratic presidential rival, Hillary CLINTON, and its possible release to the Republican's campaign team."

When the WikiLeaks emails dropped on July 22, three days before the Democratic National Convention began, it wasn't Clinton's thirty thousand deleted emails but emails between DNC insiders about sticking it to Clinton's rival Bernie Sanders.

The Clinton campaign was prepared to identify who had done it. And even explain why.

The cybersecurity firm hired by the campaign, CrowdStrike, claimed it had been a Russian hack.

Clinton campaign manager Robby Mook pushed it one step further—the Russians, he told CNN's Jake Tapper on July 24, had done it to help Trump. "I don't think it's coincidental these emails were released on the eve of our convention here," he said.

The *Washington Post*'s Anne Applebaum reinforced the campaign's messaging. She complained there was too much attention paid to the emails and not enough to who dropped them and why.

"Most of those covering this story," Applebaum wrote in her July 25 column, "are not interested in the nature of the hackers, and they are not asking why the Russians apparently chose to pass the emails on to WikiLeaks at this particular moment, on the eve of the Democratic National Convention. They are focusing instead on the content of what were meant to be private emails."

The echo chamber was primed.

During the convention, the Clinton campaign's communications director, Jennifer Palmieri, and foreign policy adviser, Jake Sullivan, had briefed the broadcast media on what other Clinton operatives had been telling the print press for several months: that the Trump team had suspicious connections to the Kremlin. So when Trump jokingly called for Russia to publish Clinton's thirty thousand deleted emails, the echo chamber roared. In the media environment the Clinton campaign had created, the

GOP candidate unknowingly lent credibility to the disinformation campaign designed to destroy him.

On July 29, CNN's Anderson Cooper asked his guests about the leaked DNC emails, "Do we know how this is going to play out and not just for the DNC but even for the Trump campaign if it, in fact, is shown that Russia is behind this? Not that there would be any Trump collusion with Russia, obviously, but the fact, would there be blowback for the Trump campaign?"

New York Times correspondent Maggie Haberman said that the "Clinton campaign is basically saying that there's collusion between Trump and Russia."

The Clinton campaign was using Steele's language and briefing on it: *collusion* between Trump and Russia.

On July 30, Steele was in Washington and saw the Ohrs, his old acquaintances Bruce and fellow Fusion GPS contractor Nellie. Over breakfast, he told them about the work for which the Clinton campaign had commissioned him. He told them about Carter Page's meeting with Igor Sechin. He talked about Oleg Deripaska's lawyer, who was collecting information on money Manafort might have stolen from the oligarch. He also told them about one of his sources, a high-level former Russian intelligence official.

Steele's most significant finding was nearly identical to claims made by Clinton campaign manager Robby Mook. According to Steele's July 26 memo, the WikiLeaks dump had been evidence of a "well-developed conspiracy between [Trump officials] and Russian leadership." It had been managed, Steele claimed, by Paul Manafort with "Carter PAGE, and others, as intermediaries."

The day after Steele met with the Ohrs, the FBI opened a counterintelligence investigation on the Trump campaign. Australian diplomat Alexander Downer had tipped off a State Department official based in London regarding another Trump intermediary. George Papadopoulos had been told by Joseph Mifsud, a Rome-based academic alleged to have ties to Moscow, that the Russians had thousands of Clinton's emails.

The investigation was opened on a Sunday, which was peculiar enough. Even odder was the fact that the probe—called "Crossfire Hurricane"—was not run out of a field office as it normally would be. Instead, top officials exerted direct control by running the operation out of FBI headquarters in Washington.

Chapter 7

THE INSURANCE POLICY

PETER STRZOK WAS LONELY. It was August 2, and the deputy assistant director of the FBI's counterintelligence division had just arrived in London. His mistress, Lisa Page, was back in Washington. Strzok had wanted her to come with him, but she couldn't. They both had their jobs to do now that the Bureau had officially opened a counterintelligence investigation into the Trump campaign.

Strzok was the lead agent. Page was special counsel to Deputy Director Andrew McCabe. She had come up with the name for the investigation: Crossfire Hurricane.

The same top FBI officials who had been running the Clinton investigation—McCabe, Strzok, and Page—were now officially investigating the other presidential campaign. They opened the investigation on the Papadopoulos information, but the parameters of the probe included Page, Flynn, and Manafort as well. From the FBI's point of view, they were all satellites circulating in Trump's orbit; the Bureau was investigating the candidate.

Not all of the FBI's investigations, for instance, typical criminal investigations, are classified at high levels. Counterintelligence investigations are classified at least at the Secret level, cordoning off the investigation from colleagues. The FBI has oversight mechanisms for counterintelligence investigations, but the Bureau's highest-ranking officials—number one, Comey, and number two, McCabe—were participants in the operation.

Crossfire Hurricane was run out of headquarters, which meant that the agents involved were more adept at bureaucratic infighting. They were political by necessity. Further, running it out of the FBI's main office—from the counterespionage section of the counterintelligence division, to be exact—ensured that it would be as closely held as possible. The conspirators, up to the highest level, could update one another in person with less risk of leaving a record of their communications.

The fact that Strzok and Page texted on their FBI phones is an index of their arrogance. They were in communication all the time. They regularly complained about bureaucratic rivals. He liked to text her about the important things he was doing, the things they were working on together. "And damn this feels momentous," he had texted her just before he left for England. "Because this matters." Strzok was in London to interview sources. He met with the Australian diplomat Downer and likely with Halper, too.

Lisa Page told Strzok that he was "meant to protect the country."

He texted back: "I can protect our country at many levels."

He liked having her approval. He was needy. They were both married to other people.

She tended to believe what the media said about Trump. Many of the stories in the press were the same stories that Steele was feeding to the FBI.

Glenn Simpson was introducing Steele to reporters in the late summer and early fall. It was as if Simpson was afraid to let Steele go out on his own. He escorted the former spy to the offices of the *Washington Post* and the *New York Times* and met with a *New Yorker* reporter at a Washington restaurant.

No one was publishing any of Steele's claims yet, but the press was looking into them, especially the story about the tape of the urinating prostitutes. In the meantime, journalists were publishing Trump stories synced to the protodossiers.

On August 14, Gary Silverman published an article in the *Financial Times* about Felix Sater and Tevfik Arif, both in the May 20 protodossier.

Kenneth Vogel's August 18 piece on Politico reported on Manafort's work for Yanukovych and his "closeness" to a Ukrainian political operative, Konstantin Kilimnik. It appears that whoever identified the "Russian Army–trained linguist" for Vogel didn't tell him that Kilimnik was also a source for the State Department.

A September 23 *Newsweek* article by Kurt Eichenwald described Trump's foreign business ties to people such as Anar Mammadov, the key figure in the "Trump in Azerbaijan" protodossier.

On October 19, the *Financial Times* again reported on Trump's connections with Sater and Arif.

A November 6 story on The Daily Beast by Michael Weiss, Catherine A. Fitzpatrick, and James Miller detailed Trump's connections with the Agalarovs, Sater, and Arif.

Editors at prominent publications continued to break standard journalistic protocol, assigning and publishing stories about Trump and his Russian connections that others had already printed.

That didn't matter to Lisa Page. Articles about Trump and Russia interested her. She sent Strzok the link to a *New York Times* article about Manafort. She sent her boyfriend the link to another *Times* article about Trump and Russia, "The Real Plot Against

America." Trump scared Lisa Page. "Trump is a loathsome human," she texted Strzok.

"Omg he's an idiot," he replied.

"He's awful," she wrote.

"God Hillary should win 100,000,000–0," he texted.

Strzok's bias against Trump was a problem. He was the lead agent, and it compromised the investigation. But he was also just a man telling a woman what he thought she wanted to hear.

"Congrats on a woman nominated for President in a major party!" he'd texted during the Democratic National Convention. "About damn time!"

Strzok wanted to believe that Hillary was deserving. He led a phony investigation of the Democratic candidate's handling of classified material to clear the way for her inevitable electoral victory. And now he was point man on an operation to dirty a presidential campaign. Had that ever happened at the FBI before, even in the Hoover era? It was third-world stuff, like in Egypt or Argentina. But it was happening in the United States of America.

Page told him he was protecting the country because that was what they meant to each other: they reflected back to themselves confirmation of their self-images. They were narcissists, just like the candidate they were protecting.

Clinton had little to offer voters except the promise that they would share in her redemption. Her husband had humiliated her publicly. It seemed the only thing that could make her whole was the presidency. She resented having to earn it; she felt she deserved it. Her supporters understood that. Strzok wanted to show Page that he did, too.

Page and Strzok shared Clinton's worldview. Trump supporters were loathsome, deplorables. The two FBI officials were sad that their boss, McCabe's, wife, Jill, had lost her race for the Virginia state senate. She had run on the Democratic ticket: "Disappointing, but look at the district map," Strzok texted, "it's still largely ignorant hillbillys."

The intermingling of their self-love bred contempt for others. "Just went to a southern Virginia Walmart," Strzok texted her. "I could SMELL the Trump support."

"Yup," she replied. She was lunching with another FBI lawyer who had a role in Crossfire Hurricane, Sally Moyer. "We both hate everyone and everything," she texted.

That was the sensibility of the public servants who decided to spy on Americans exercising their constitutional rights by participating in a political campaign. That was the character of the intelligence bureaucrats who took it into their hands to interfere in an election because they didn't like their neighbors and the candidate they had chosen to govern the republic. They had a plan to stop Trump.

"I want to believe the path you threw out for consideration in Andy's office—that there's no way he gets elected," Strzok texted her, "but I'm afraid we can't take that risk. It's like an insurance policy in the unlikely event you die before you're 40."

———————

When Strzok returned from London, he briefed Comey, who then reported to Obama's chief of staff, Denis McDonough. "POTUS," Page texted Strzok, "wants to know everything we're doing."

Other Obama administration principals had also been enlisted, including CIA director John Brennan. At the end of August, Brennan was briefing congressional leaders in classified settings. Brennan testified that he "provided the same briefing to each of the Gang of Eight members." He may have tailored his briefings to his audience.

The briefing he gave Nunes was lacking on details. "I'll tell you what he didn't brief me on," says Nunes. "Whatever he told Harry Reid, he didn't tell me."

He didn't brief Nunes on the dossier. On August 25, Brennan briefed the Senate minority leader.

Subsequently, on August 27, Reid wrote in an open letter to Comey, "I have recently become concerned that the threat of the Russian government tampering in our presidential election is more extensive than widely known." In the letter, he referenced "a Trump advisor which was Carter Page.

Reid's letter was another channel to get the dossier information to the FBI. It seems it was also an instrument Brennan used to motivate the Bureau. He took credit for getting the probe off the ground.

He later testified before Congress: "I was aware of intelligence and information about contacts between Russian officials and U.S. persons that raised concerns in my mind about whether or not those individuals were cooperating with the Russians, either in a witting or unwitting fashion, and it served as the basis for the FBI investigation to determine whether such collusion—cooperation occurred."

The more sources feeding the FBI with Steele's reports, the more authentic they appeared to be. Reid was also a vehicle to get Trump-Russia rumors into the press. Just as Fusion GPS was giving Trump-Russia stories to the media, Obama's intelligence chiefs were feeding congressional leaders the same material, counting on the likelihood that they, too, would give it to reporters.

On September 8, Comey, Secretary of Homeland Security Jeh Johnson, and Obama's homeland security advisor, Lisa Monaco, summoned congressional leaders for an unusual briefing. Obama had sent them, reportedly to urge a "show of solidarity and bipartisan unity" against Russian interference in the election.

"They pulled us into the House Intelligence Committee room

for an all-hands briefing," Nunes recalls. "They called it a Gang of Twelve meeting, which was out of the ordinary."

The Gang of Eight is an informal name for the congressional leaders from both parties and the chairs and ranking members from the House and Senate Intelligence Committees, who are briefed on classified intelligence matters by the executive branch.

"Gang of Twelve," says Nunes, "included the chair and ranking member from Homeland Security committees in the House and Senate. There had never been a Gang of Twelve meeting before. They were trying to create a stir."

The subject of the meeting was Russia and what the intelligence agencies said they were picking up about Russian efforts to shape the upcoming presidential election. However, they provided no details.

"They had no evidence of anything," says Nunes. "I was wondering, Why aren't you giving us information about what they're up to? Is there anything abnormal about what the Russians are doing? If not, if they're just doing what they always do, which is interfere with elections, why aren't you, the executive branch, taking care of it? Why are you coming to us with it?"

Comey and the others wanted to light a fuse. "They were trying to create the impression that there had been a major occurrence and the Russians were behind it," Nunes says. "They were trying to coerce Congress to come out with a joint statement of some kind: the Russians were up to something. And they orchestrated a bigger group—'Gang of Twelve'—to increase the likelihood of leaks."

Obama's intelligence chiefs succeeded in getting more leaks, but the Republicans refused to produce a joint letter. They weren't taking the bait.

"Comey and the others wanted to create a panic," Nunes says, "but I knew that something wasn't on the up-and-up. [Senate majority leader Mitch] McConnell knew it was a setup. And [House speaker Paul] Ryan knew it was a setup. I remember the Speaker talking to McConnell's people, asking what the hell are they doing?"

With Comey, Johnson, Monaco, and Brennan laundering the Trump-Russia story through Congress, Obama's intelligence community had merged with Clinton operatives.

On July 26, *Wall Street Journal* reporter Damian Paletta texted Carter Page: "We are told you met with Igor Sechin during your recent Moscow trip and discussed energy deals and the possibility of the US government lifting sanctions on him and others." Paletta also asked if he had met with a senior Kremlin official who said Russia had compromising material on the candidates.

Page denied the allegations. He texted the reporter that the point about sanctions lifting was a "ridiculous idea."

Soon Page heard from more reporters with similar questions. Fusion GPS was talking to the press about the findings Steele was taking to the FBI. One of the reporters looking into the story about Sechin and Page was Michael Isikoff of Yahoo! News. He'd been briefed by Steele, under Simpson's supervision.

On September 23, the story about Carter Page that Fusion GPS had been trying to place since late July finally launched. Isikoff's story quoted Steele as "a well-placed Western intelligence source." The ex–MI6 spy said he had given US officials intelligence reports claiming that during Page's three-day trip to Moscow, he had met with Sechin, who had discussed the possibility of lifting sanctions.

The Isikoff story illustrated how Clinton operatives and the Crossfire Hurricane team pushed the operation. The stories that Fusion GPS fed the press were the same reports that Steele was pushing into the FBI. The Crossfire Hurricane team used the stories to corroborate the memos. Together, the stories and memos allowed the little FBI group to legitimize spying on the Trump campaign—and enhance their surveillance powers of the GOP candidate.

As it had in July, the Clinton campaign's messaging reinforced the information operation that it was funding. Shortly after the Isikoff story broke, the campaign released a statement regarding "the bombshell report"—without mentioning that the story's source, Steele, was being paid by the campaign. "It's chilling," according to the statement, "to learn that U.S. intelligence officials are conducting a probe into suspected meetings between Trump's foreign policy adviser Carter Page and members of Putin's inner circle while in Moscow."

After months of fending off reporters' questions about the false stories, Page was shaken to see them in print, and decided to leave the campaign. "There's so little time between now and the election," he told a reporter. "This is in the best interests of the candidate. It's so ridiculous I want to have it behind us."

On September 25, Page addressed an open letter to Comey, offering to speak to the FBI in order to clear his name and "put these outrageous allegations to rest while allowing each of us to shift our attention to relevant matters."

Thinking about it today, Nunes shakes his head in disbelief. "Page wrote Comey a letter offering himself for an interview," says Nunes, "and the director of the FBI turns around and says, 'To hell with him, forget the interview, let's go spy on him.'"

The Crossfire Hurricane group took its anti-Trump operation to a new level after the FBI was forced to reopen the Clinton email case.

In September, the FBI's New York field office and New York Police Department discovered Clinton emails on a laptop belonging to Anthony Weiner—the subject of a sex crimes investigation for his contact with an underage girl—and his wife, Clinton aide Huma Abedin. McCabe found out about the emails on September 28 and briefed Strzok. He and McCabe stalled for a month before reopening the Clinton case. It was during that monthlong lapse that the Crossfire Hurricane team obtained the warrant to spy on Carter Page.

"After they reopen the Clinton case," says Nunes, "the little cabal—Strzok, Page, McCabe—are desperate. They've convinced themselves they're going to find something on the Trump campaign."

It didn't matter that Carter Page had left the campaign the month before; a FISA warrant allowed the FBI to monitor his past communications as well as his ongoing ones. "It was his past communications they wanted," Nunes says, "going back as far as they still existed and weren't deleted."

Monitoring Page's communications would serve as an entry point into the entire campaign. Whatever the Crossfire Hurricane group came up with would serve the purpose. The target was Trump. "But there was no way they were going to the FISA court and say they needed a warrant to spy on Trump," says Nunes. "So they made it sound like it was just about this one bad actor. They loaded up everything they had on Page, hoping to strike oil."

———————

The FISA program is the US government's most intrusive form of intelligence collection. In the wake of the intelligence community's vast abuses uncovered during the 1970s, the 1978 Foreign Intelligence Surveillance Act (FISA) set out the proper procedures for the electronic and physical surveillance and collection of foreign intelligence information between foreign powers and agents of foreign powers.

Title I FISAs allow federal law enforcement agencies to go into the National Security Agency's massive database, culled from service providers, and retrieve the target's phone calls and emails. Title III FISAs deal with physical searches.

To obtain a warrant, the requesting agency presents evidence before a judge in the Federal Intelligence Surveillance Court (FISC). The target of the warrant has no legal representation at the FISC, which relies on the probity of federal officers.

Though it is an exaggeration to call it a rubber-stamp court, the FISC rarely refuses to grant the warrant. The Crossfire Hurricane team had reportedly attempted at least once during the summer to get a FISA on the Trump campaign but had been denied.

The FISA application stated that Page was a foreign agent and had been recruited by Russian intelligence in 2013. That was inaccurate. Page had been approached by Russian agents working undercover at the UN Consulate in New York. He had assisted the FBI in apprehending them.

The centerpiece of the application was the Steele Dossier. Also in the application was the Isikoff article, which was sourced to Steele's reporting. The application also cited other press reports, including Josh Rogin's *Washington Post* article claiming that the Trump campaign had watered down the RNC platform's position on support for Ukraine.

Also included in the application was an article that appears to be Michael Crowley's August 3 story in Politico ("Trump changed views on Ukraine after hiring Manafort") that built on Rogin's j124 RNC story. According to Crowley, Trump's position on Ukraine had shifted because of "his recent association with several people sympathetic to Russian influence in Ukraine." Crowley cited Manafort and Page, "who has extensive business ties in Russia."

But the Crossfire Hurricane group still wasn't sure that would get them the warrant. "They knew that once they pulled that trigger and got the FISA, it lives forever," says Nunes. "For months their operation was all compartmentalized as a counterintelligence investigation, classified and siloed off from the rest of the FBI and everyone else so only their little group knew about it. So if they're going for it, they better make sure they get the FISA. They needed an insurance policy."

According to Nunes, the "insurance policy" that Strzok and Page texted about, the issue they'd discussed in McCabe's office, was not simply the operation against Trump that they planned to roll into a coup in the event he was elected.

"It has a deeper meaning, it's more specific than that," he says. "It's what else they did to get the FISA, to ensure they got the warrant on Page. It's as bad or worse than using the dossier. It's another thing they hid as part of a counterintelligence investigation."

What did they do? Nunes spreads his arms in the air. "Something we hope to have declassified. Something the American public should know about."

On October 21, the FBI obtained the warrant. "They were sure they were going to find something," says Nunes, "the golden ticket."

Nunes says the FBI knew Carter Page was not a Russian spy. "They were just using him," says Nunes. "They were sure they were going to find that he had talked to a Russian or had an email from a Russian, an email from Rosneft, or something, anything. Then they'd leak it to the press. They assumed something had to be there, because they thought Page had all these Russian contacts. They only needed one thing. And they couldn't even get that."

The anti-Trump operation was designed in part to defend against a possible "October surprise" involving Clinton's communications. Now its other purpose was evident—it was an offensive weapon, too, tailored to obtain the spy warrant. They were breaking in to the Trump campaign. The dossier would find the Crossfire Hurricane group an "October surprise" to deploy against Trump and put an end to the GOP candidate once and for all.

But they found nothing. And then they panicked.

Another letter from Harry Reid to Comey, dated October 30, inadvertently put the Crossfire Hurricane team under the spotlight. Reid complained that the FBI had reopened the investigation into Clinton while sitting on "explosive information about close ties and coordination between Donald Trump, his top advisers, and the Russian government."

But the Crossfire Hurricane team's fishing expedition had come up empty, and they had no leverage in case they were caught.

An October 31 article in *Mother Jones* set off alarm bells. David Corn's breathless report regarding Trump's ties to Russia quoted Steele—"a former Western intelligence officer"—extensively. He said that the FBI's response to his revelations had been "shock and horror." The FBI, he said, had "requested more information from him" and told him that "there was or is a pretty substantial inquiry." Steele had showed Corn the reports he'd been sharing with the FBI, excerpts of which were published in the article: "Russian regime has been cultivating, supporting, and assisting TRUMP for at least five years. Aim, endorsed by PUTIN, has been to encourage splits and divisions in western alliance." Corn also passed Steele's reports to the FBI—another channel meant to legitimize a conspiracy theory.

His story was successful in advancing the Trump-Russia narrative, but it also sent the Crossfire Hurricane team looking for cover.

The Bureau terminated its relationship with Steele, because, it said, he'd violated the terms of his relationship as a confidential source by talking to the press. But the Crossfire Hurricane team must have already known that Steele was briefing the media. In September, he met with multiple media outlets: CNN, *The New Yorker*, the *New York Times*, and the *Washington Post*, as well as Yahoo! News. He was obviously the source for Isikoff's article.

"The reason they fired Steele," Nunes says, "is because they'd obtained nothing useful through their FISA. Steele was evidence they'd done something bad. They fired him because they were covering up their tracks."

A *New York Times* article published on October 31 looked like more housecleaning to HPSCI investigators. The FBI illegally leaked to the press the existence of a classified counterintelligence investigation on the Trump campaign. But after they'd gotten the FISA and found nothing on Page, the Crossfire Hurricane group wanted to leave evidence, through the *Times* report, that they'd shut it all down.

———————

As Clinton's numbers started to drop, however slightly, the Crossfire Hurricane group became increasingly anxious. Days before the election, Page texted Strzok, "The American presidential election, and thus, the state of the world, actually hangs in the balance."

But it wasn't just mankind on the precipice. What if Clinton didn't win and someone started poking around to see what the Crossfire Hurricane team had been cooking up against Trump? A sting operation, dating back to late 2015, designed to undermine a presidential candidate—who now lived at 1600 Pennsylvania Avenue.

On election day, Page wrote, "OMG THIS IS F*CKING TERRIFYING."

"Omg," Strzok replied, "I am so depressed."

Nunes thought Trump was going to win. "I didn't think so until a week before the election," he now says. He hadn't endorsed anyone in the primaries but had waited to see who'd win the nomination and then support the Republican candidate.

"Then about a week before the election," he said, "I started seeing reports about Puerto Ricans in Florida being mad at Trump because of his promise to build a wall on the Mexican border."

Nunes called up Florida congressman Mario Diaz-Balart for a reality check. "I said, Mario, this doesn't make sense," he recalls. "They're Americans, what do they care about a wall? And he agreed. It told me they were putting fake news into the press because they were worried. I said to him, 'Now I think he'll win Florida.' And Mario said, 'Yes, I think he'll win.'"

As the press kept pushing that story line, Nunes remembers, "I knew Clinton lost Florida for sure. Then I knew that North Carolina was gone. So then the question was, Can he unlock any of the other pathways to victory—like Pennsylvania, Wisconsin, Michigan?"

That's the path Trump took to the White House. Hillary was gone. Now the Crossfire Hurricane team was on their own and searching for their next move.

Page texted Strzok. She told him she'd bought and read *All the President's Men*. "Figure I needed to brush up on Watergate," she wrote.

For the Crossfire Hurricane team, the real-life political thriller was a how-to book. The *Washington Post* reporters who had broken the Watergate story, Bob Woodward and Carl Bernstein, had had a well-placed source in the law enforcement bureaucracy. They had referred to Mark Felt, the FBI's second-highest-ranking official, as "Deep Throat." He had spilled the secrets that had brought down Nixon. Strzok and Page worked for the Bureau's number two, Andrew McCabe. More than forty years later, the Crossfire Hurricane team was poised to reenact the Watergate legend. They were going to take down a president.

Chapter 8

OBAMA'S DOSSIER

AFTER DONALD TRUMP was elected forty-fifth president of the United States, the operation designed to undermine his campaign transformed. It became an instrument to bring down the commander in chief. The coup started almost immediately after the polls closed.

Hillary Clinton's communications team decided within twenty-four hours of her concession speech to message that the election was illegitimate, that Russia had interfered to help Trump.

Obama was working against Trump until the hour he left office. His national security advisor, Susan Rice, commemorated it with an email to herself on January 20, moments before Trump's inauguration. She wrote to memorialize a meeting in the White House two weeks before.

On January 5, following a briefing by IC leadership on Russian hacking during the 2016 Presidential election, President Obama had a brief follow-on conversation with FBI Director Jim Comey and Deputy Attorney General Sally

Yates in the Oval Office. Vice President Biden and I were also present.

President Obama began the conversation by stressing his continued commitment to ensuring that every aspect of this issue is handled by the Intelligence and law enforcement communities "by the book." The President stressed that he is not asking about, initiating or instructing anything from a law enforcement perspective. He reiterated that our law enforcement team needs to proceed as it normally would by the book.

From a national security perspective, however, President Obama said he wants to be sure that, as we engage with the incoming team, we are mindful to ascertain if there is any reason that we cannot share information fully as it relates to Russia. . . .

The President asked Comey to inform him if anything changes in the next few weeks that should affect how we share classified information with the incoming team. Comey said he would.

The repetition of "by the book" gave away the game—for there was nothing normal about any of it.

Rice wrote an email to herself. It commemorated a conversation from two weeks before. The conversation was about the FBI's investigation of the man who was about to move into the White House—an investigation from which Obama was careful to distance himself. During the conversation, the outgoing president instructed his top aides to collect information ("ascertain") regarding the incoming administration's relationship with Russia.

"To any rational person," says Nunes, "it looks like they were scheming to produce a get-out-of-jail-free card—for the president and anyone else in the White House. They were playing Monopoly while the others were playing with fire. Now the Obama White House was in the clear—sure, they had no idea what Comey and Brennan and McCabe and Strzok and the rest were up to."

Meanwhile, Obama added his voice to the Trump-Russia echo chamber as news stories alleging Trump's illicit relationship with the Kremlin multiplied in the transition period. He said he hoped "that the president-elect also is willing to stand up to Russia."

The outgoing president was in Germany with Chancellor Angela Merkel to discuss everything from NATO to Vladimir Putin. Obama said that he'd "delivered a clear and forceful message" to the Russian president about "meddling with elections . . . and we will respond appropriately if and when we see this happening."

After refusing to act while the Russian election meddling was actually occurring, Obama responded in December. He ordered the closing of Russian diplomatic facilities and the expulsion of thirty-five Russian diplomats. The response was tepid. The Russians had hacked the State Department in 2014 and the Joint Chiefs of Staff in 2015. And now Obama was responding only on his way out.

Even Obama partisans thought it was weak. "The punishment did not fit the crime," said Michael McFaul, Obama's former ambassador to Russia. "The Kremlin should have paid a much higher price for that attack."

But the administration wasn't retaliating against Russia for interfering in a US election; the action was directed at Trump. Obama was leaving the president-elect with a minor foreign policy crisis in order to box him in. Any criticism of Obama's response, never mind an attempt to reverse it, would only further fuel press reports that Trump was collaborating with the Russians.

In the administration's last days, it disseminated intelligence throughout the government, including the White House, Capitol

Hill, and the intelligence community (IC). Intelligence was classified at the lowest possible levels to ensure a wide readership. The White House was paving the way for a campaign of leaks to disorient the incoming Trump team.

The effort, including the intended result of leaks, was publicly acknowledged in March 2017 by Evelyn Farkas, a former deputy assistant secretary of defense in the Obama administration.

Obama's biggest move against Trump was to order CIA director John Brennan to conduct a full review of all intelligence relating to Russia and the 2016 elections. He requested it on December 6 and wanted it ready by the time he left office on January 20. But the sitting president already knew what the intelligence community assessment (ICA) was going to say, because Brennan had told him months before.

Brennan's handpicked team of CIA, FBI, and NSA analysts had started analyzing Russian election interference in late July. In August, Brennan had briefed Harry Reid on the dossier and may have briefed Obama on it, too. Earlier in August, Brennan took reports.

When Brennan reassembled his select team in December, it was to have them reproduce their August findings: Putin, according to Brennan, was boosting the GOP candidate. And that's why only three days after Obama ordered the assessment in December, the *Washington Post* could already reveal what the intelligence community had found.

"The CIA," reported the December 9 edition of the *Post*, "has concluded in a secret assessment that Russia intervened in the 2016 election to help Donald Trump win the presidency, rather than just to undermine confidence in the U.S. electoral system."

The story was the first of many apparently sourced to leaks of classified information that were given to the *Post* team of Adam Entous, Ellen Nakashima, and Greg Miller. The reporters' sources weren't whistle-blowers shedding light on government corruption—rather, they were senior US officials abusing government resources to prosecute a campaign against the newly elected commander in chief. The article was the earliest public evidence that the coup was under way. The floodgates were open, as the IC pushed more stories through the press to delegitimize the president-elect.

The same day, a *New York Times* article by David E. Sanger and Scott Shane echoed the *Post*'s piece. According to senior administration officials, "American intelligence agencies have concluded with 'high confidence' that Russia acted covertly in the latter stages of the presidential campaign to harm Hillary Clinton's chances and promote Donald J. Trump."

A December 14 NBC News story by William M. Arkin, Ken Dilanian, and Cynthia McFadden reported that "Russian President Vladimir Putin became personally involved in the covert Russian campaign to interfere in the U.S. presidential election, senior U.S. intelligence officials told NBC News."

The ICA that Obama ordered gave political operatives, the press, and his intelligence chiefs a second shot at Trump. They'd used the Steele Dossier to feed the echo chamber and obtain surveillance powers to spy on the Trump campaign. The dossier, however, had come up short. Trump had won.

But now, on his way out of the White House, Obama instructed Brennan to stamp the CIA's imprimatur on the anti-Trump operation. As Fusion GPS's smear campaign had been the source of the preelection press campaign, the ICA was the basis of the postelection media frenzy. It was tailored to disrupt the peaceful transition of power and throw the United States into chaos.

Because Trump hadn't been elected by the US public, according to the ICA, but had been tapped by Putin, he was illegitimate.

Therefore, the extraconstitutional and illegal tactics employed by anti-Trump officials were legitimate.

The ultimate goal was to remove Trump from office.

"If it weren't for President Obama," said James Clapper, "we might not have done the intelligence community assessment . . . that set off a whole sequence of events which are still unfolding today."

Nunes agrees. "The ICA," he says, "was Obama's dossier."

Nunes is sitting in his office in the Longworth House Office Building along with his communications director, Jack Langer, a forty-six-year-old former book editor and historian with a PhD from Duke University.

"The social media attacks on Devin began shortly after the election," Langer remembers. "They're all hinting at some vast conspiracy involving Russia that the chairman of the Intelligence Committee is part of. And we have no idea what they're talking about."

Nunes points out that his warnings about Russia fell on deaf ears for years. "And all of a sudden I'm a Russian agent," says the congressman.

Now Langer and Nunes see that the attacks were first launched because the congressman had been named to Trump's transition team. "I put forward [Mike] Pompeo for CIA director," says Nunes. "He came from our committee."

The attacks on Nunes picked up after the December 9 *Washington Post* article. The assessment provided there was not what the HPSCI chairman had been told. The assessment had been altered, and Nunes asked for an explanation. "We got briefed about the election around Thanksgiving," he says. "And it's just the usual stuff, nothing abnormal. They told us what everyone already knew:

'Hey, the Russians are bad actors, and they're always playing games, and here's what they did.'"

By providing that briefing, the IC had made a mistake. When it later changed the assessment, the November briefing was evidence that Obama's spy chiefs were up to no good. "I bet they'd like to have that back," says Nunes. "They briefed us before they could get their new story straight."

Nunes acknowledges that he was caught off guard by many things back then. "We still thought these guys were on the up and up," he says. "But if we knew, we'd have nailed them by mid-December, when they changed their assessment. 'Wait, you guys are saying this now, but you said something else just a few weeks ago. What's going on?'"

After the *Post* story, Nunes wanted an explanation. "We expressed deep concern, both publicly and privately," says Langer. "We demanded our own briefing to try to determine whether that *Post* story was true or false. They refused to brief us. They said, 'We're not going to be doing that until we finish the ICA.'"

Nunes says the fact that the IC conducted an assessment like that was itself unusual. "I don't know how many times they'd done that in the past, if ever," he says. "But if the IC is operating properly, when someone says what can you tell me on X or Y or Z, they have it ready to pull up quickly. The tradecraft is reliable, and the intelligence products are reliable." That was not the case with the ICA. There were problems with how the assessment had been put together.

"If you really were going to do something like an assessment from the intelligence community, then you'd get input from all our seventeen agencies," says Nunes. "They did the opposite. It was only FBI, CIA, NSA, and DNI. They siloed it, just like they had with Crossfire Hurricane. They kept everyone else away from it so they didn't have to read them in."

Nunes released several statements in the middle of December. The HPSCI majority, read a December 14 statement, wanted senior Obama intelligence officials "to clarify press reports that the CIA has a new assessment that it has not shared with us. The Committee is deeply concerned that intransigence in sharing intelligence with Congress can enable the manipulation of intelligence for political purposes."

After the statements warned of political foul play in the IC's assessments, the social media attacks on Nunes became more regular. "They were constant," says Langer.

Anti-Trump operatives recognized that Nunes was going to be a problem. The HPSCI chair had previously called out the IC for politicizing intelligence. "They said that we had defeated Al Qaeda in Iraq and Syria," says Nunes, "and I knew that wasn't true. Then they withheld the Osama bin Laden documents to conceal that Al Qaeda worked with Iran, because the administration was protecting the Iran deal. So when I saw them changing this assessment of the 2016 election in midstream, I knew it was the same old trick: they were politicizing intelligence."

The speed with which Brennan's handpicked analysts produced the ICA and then got a version of it declassified for public consumption was another sign that something wasn't right. "All throughout Obama's two terms, his IC chiefs aren't paying attention to Russian actions," says Nunes. "We give them more money for Russia, which they don't use. But now they know so much about Putin that they manage to produce a comprehensive assessment of Russian intentions and actions regarding election interference in a month—at Christmastime, when everything slows down. And then they produce a declassified version in a manner of weeks. None of this is believable."

Three different versions of the ICA were produced: an

unclassified version, a top secret one, and another highly compartmentalized version. According to a January 11, 2017, *Washington Post* story by Greg Miller, Ellen Nakashima, and Karen DeYoung, an annex summarizing the dossier was attached to the versions that were not declassified.

The FBI had been working from Steele's reports for more than half a year. Including the dossier along with the ICA would provide Comey with ammunition to take on the president-elect. Both he and Brennan were manipulating intelligence for political purposes.

"A lot of the ICA is reasonable," says Nunes. "But those parts become irrelevant due to the problematic parts, which undermine the entire document. It was designed to have a political effect; that was the ICA's sole purpose."

The assessment's methodological flaws are not difficult to spot. Manufacturing the politicized findings that Obama sought meant not only abandoning protocol but also subverting basic logic. Two of the ICA's central findings are that:

- Putin and the Russian government developed a clear preference for President-elect Trump.
- Putin and the Russian government aspired to help President-elect Trump's election chances when possible by discrediting Secretary Clinton and publicly contrasting her unfavorably to him.

To know preferences and intentions would require sources targeting Putin's inner circles—either human sources or electronic surveillance. As Nunes notes, however, US intelligence on Putin's decision-making process was inadequate.

But even if there had been extensive collection on precisely that issue, it would be difficult to know what was true. For instance, the closest you can get to Putin's inner circle is Putin himself. But even capturing him on an intercept saying he wanted to elect Trump might prove inconclusive. It is difficult to judge intentions because it is not possible to see into the minds of other people. How would you know that Putin was speaking truthfully? How would you know that the Russian president didn't know his communications were under US surveillance and wasn't trying to deceive his audience?

Quality control of information is one of the tasks of counterintelligence—to discern how you know what you know and whether that information is trustworthy. There was no quality control for the Trump-Russia intelligence. For instance, Crossfire Hurricane lead agent Peter Strzok was the FBI's deputy assistant director of counterintelligence. Instead of weeding out flawed intelligence on Russia, the Crossfire Hurricane team was feeding Steele's reports into intelligence products. Yet the ICA claimed to have "high confidence" in its assessment that "Putin and the Russian Government developed a clear preference for President-elect Trump." What was the basis of that judgment?

According to the ICA:

> Putin most likely wanted to discredit Secretary Clinton because he has publicly blamed her since 2011 for inciting mass protests against his regime in late 2011 and early 2012, and because he holds a grudge for comments he almost certainly saw as disparaging him.

"Most likely" and "almost certainly" are rhetorical hedges that show the assessment could not have been made in "high confidence." Putin may have held a grudge against Clinton, but there is no way of knowing it.

The supporting evidence deteriorates more the farther the ICA purports to reach into Putin's mind.

Beginning in June, Putin's public comments about the US presidential race avoided directly praising President-elect Trump, probably because Kremlin officials thought that any praise from Putin personally would backfire in the United States.

This is absurd. Part of the evidence that Putin supported Trump is that he avoided praising Trump. It is difficult enough to determine intentions by what someone says. Yet the ICA claims to have discerned Putin's intentions by what he did not say.

There is no introductory philosophy class in logic where reasoning like that would pass muster. Yet Brennan's handpicked group used it as the basis of its assessment that Putin had helped Trump.

Moscow also saw the election of President-elect Trump as a way to achieve an international counterterrorism coalition against the Islamic State in Iraq and the Levant.

This may be an accurate description of how Putin saw Trump. But Trump's predecessor also wanted to coordinate anti-ISIS operations with Moscow. On this view, Trump would have represented a continuation of Obama's ISIS policy. Why would this make Trump's victory suspicious to Obama's intelligence chiefs?

The ICA also pointed to documentary evidence of Putin's intentions: English-language media owned by the Russian government, the news site Sputnik, and the RT network, were critical of Clinton.

> *State-owned Russian media made increasingly favorable comments about President-elect Trump as the 2016 US general and primary election campaigns progressed while consistently offering negative coverage of Secretary Clinton.*

Curiously, just days before the election, the informant the US government sent after the Trump campaign praised the Democratic candidate in an interview with Sputnik. "Clinton would be best for US-UK relations and for relations with the European Union," Stefan Halper told the Kremlin-directed media outlet. "Clinton is well-known, deeply experienced, and predictable. US-UK relations will remain steady regardless of the winner although Clinton will be less disruptive over time."

The ICA includes a seven-page appendix devoted to RT, the central node, according to the document, of the Kremlin's effort to "influence politics, fuel discontent in [*sic*] US."

Adam Schiff appeared on RT in July 2013. He argued for "making the FISA court much more transparent, so the American people can understand what's being done in their name in the name of national security, so that we can have a more informed debate over the balance between privacy and security."

RT's editor in chief, Margarita Simonyan, is a master propagandist, according to the ICA. The document fails to mention that Simonyan heads another Moscow-owned media initiative, *Russia Beyond the Headlines*, a news supplement inserted into dozens of the West's leading newspapers, including the *New York Times*. *Russia Beyond the Headlines* has been delivered to millions of American homes over the last decade. By contrast, RT's US market share is so small that it doesn't qualify for the Nielsen ratings. Virtually no one in the United States watches it.

Taking the logic of Brennan's handpicked team seriously would mean that the publishers of the *New York Times* played a major role in a coordinated Russian effort to elect Donald Trump.

Nunes realized even then the purpose of Obama's dossier. "Devin figured out in December what was going on," says Langer. "It was an operation to bring down Trump."

There was no evidence that any Trump associate had done anything improper regarding the Russians, and Nunes was losing patience. "We had serious things the committee wanted to do," he says. "With Trump elected, we could do some big stuff, like with China."

Still, it was important for HPSCI to maintain control of the Russia investigation. Otherwise, Democrats and Never Trump Republicans were likely to get their wish to convene a bipartisan commission to investigate Russian interference—with the purpose of turning it on Trump.

"Before they started floating the idea of a special counsel, the big idea was a special commission like the 9/11 Commission," says Langer. It was outgoing secretary of state John Kerry who first came forward with the proposal.

The point was to change the power dynamic. "In a normal committee," says Langer, "the majority has the power, and that happened to be us. They wanted to strip our power and make it fifty-fifty."

"Bipartisan" was a euphemism for "anti-Trump." "It would have been a complete joke," says Nunes. "A combination of partisan hacks from the left and people who hated Trump on the right."

Democrats led by Schiff and Senate minority leader Chuck Schumer were joined by the late John McCain, the most active of the Never Trump Republicans. After the election, the Arizona senator had instructed his aide David Kramer to deliver a copy of the Steele Dossier to Comey.

"God only knows who they'd have populated that committee with," says Nunes. "Anyone they could control. It would have been a freak show."

Speaker of the House Paul Ryan defended HPSCI's independence. On the Senate side, Intelligence Committee chairman Richard Burr had only one move. To deflect demands for an independent commission, he effectively ceded control of the Senate investigation to his vice chair, Democrat Mark Warner.

Still, Nunes believed that all the talk of Trump and Russia was a waste of time. "They kept promising us evidence of collusion, week after week, and they came up with nothing."

Nunes's disdain for the ICA forced the Crossfire Hurricane team's hand. "Right around the time that they came out with the ICA, they kept saying that we were waiting on something to show us, something important that was coming in," he says. "They said it was some significant figure who they couldn't quite track down yet."

But the FBI knew exactly where its missing link was, the piece of evidence that they thought would convince hardened skeptics like Nunes that collusion was real. They didn't have to chase him down, because he was sitting at home in Chicago. He submitted to a voluntary interview January 27 and without a lawyer because he had no idea what the FBI had in store for him.

The Crossfire Hurricane team was figuring how they were going to set up the Trump adviser they'd used to open up the investigation in July 2016: George Papadopoulos.

Chapter 9

THE PRESS BREAKS

ON JANUARY 10, 2017, one of the United States' most vital political institutions—the media—imploded. The founding fathers believed that a free press was central to the preservation and advancement of a free people. "Our liberty cannot be guarded but by the freedom of the press," wrote Thomas Jefferson, "nor that be limited without danger of losing it."

Journalists and media organizations around the world are vulnerable—susceptible to the blandishments of self-regarding regimes that would lure them into a career of flattery and, worse, defenseless against the despotisms that would silence them forever.

Very rarely has a free press sacrificed its independence and prestige by putting its rights and privileges into the service of intelligence operations designed to target one faction on behalf of another. But that was what the US media did in the winter of 2017. They became political operatives. The bylines they used were part of the journalistic apparatus that camouflaged the dirty work they were undertaking.

The effect of their campaign was to break men and women, including other Americans, to separate them from their families and friends, to strip them of their liberty, their homes, their savings, simply for exercising their constitutional right to participate in a political campaign.

But from the press's perspective, they'd backed the wrong candidate and he had won, so those on the other side were disposable.

On January 6, CIA director John Brennan, Director of National Intelligence James Clapper, FBI director James Comey, and National Security Agency director Michael Rogers briefed the president-elect on the intelligence community assessment that Obama had ordered in the wake of Trump's election. Comey stayed after to tell Trump alone about the Steele Dossier; he'd made sure that allegations from it were included in an appendix to the ICA.

Comey knew that CNN had the story about the dossier and was only looking for a news hook to justify publishing it. He briefed Trump partly to give CNN the news hook.

The Crossfire Hurricane group was watching closely. McCabe tipped off colleagues that Trump had been briefed on the dossier. "CNN is close to going forward with the sensitive story," wrote the deputy FBI director. "The trigger for [CNN] is they know the material was discussed in the brief and presented in an attachment."

The January 10, 2017, story, "Intel Chiefs Presented Trump with Claims of Russian Efforts to Compromise Him," was coauthored by Evan Perez, Jim Sciutto, Jake Tapper, and Carl Bernstein. The report referred to the dossier's most serious charge, "allegations that there was a continuing exchange of information during the campaign between Trump surrogates and intermediaries for the Russian government."

CNN's story and Comey's briefing touched on different issues. Comey had told the president-elect only about the dossier's claims that the Russians had video of him and prostitutes in a Moscow hotel. Why hadn't Comey told Trump about the much more consequential claims? Because the FBI director was trying to elicit information from Trump.

Prior to meeting with the president elect, Comey had met with McCabe and others including Crossfire Hurricane "supervisors" and discussed whether Trump might "provide information of value to the pending Russia interference investigation." Just a day after Obama had directed Comey and others to gather Russia-related information on the Trump team, the FBI director was spying on the president-elect.

The January 6th briefing was a pivotal episode, for it also showcased the partnership between the press and the national security apparatus.

Comey wasn't the only Obama spy chief who pushed his advantage. There was also the director of national intelligence. After initially denying having discussed the dossier with anyone in the media, Clapper admitted under oath that while he was director of national intelligence he had discussed it with his future CNN colleague Jake Tapper.

Leaks of that magnitude regarding top members of the intelligence community briefing the president and president-elect are rare. And illegal. Leaks of classified information would soon become a regular occurrence.

Hours after the CNN story broke, BuzzFeed published what appears to be the full text of the Steele Dossier. Tapper emailed BuzzFeed editor Ben Smith to complain. "I think your move makes the story less serious and credible," he wrote. "I think you damaged its impact."

Another media outfit had taken the air out of the CNN investigative team's big breaking news story. Because of Buzzfeed, American news audiences could judge the credibility of the dossier—with its lurid tales of golden showers and outlandish allegations of Trump-Russia conspiracies—for themselves rather than take it on CNN's authority.

Publication of the document undermined the story's credibility. CNN had not published an account of prostitutes precisely because it wanted to avoid appearing like a tabloid, because it wanted its *serious* and *credible* report to have an *impact*.

With news consumers now given a wider context in which to judge the CNN report, Tapper was angry. "Collegiality wise," Tapper wrote, "it was you stepping on my dick."

Tapper thought BuzzFeed was unprofessional. "Your guys unlike us don't even seem to know who the former agent i[s]," he wrote.

Tapper was boasting. The CNN team was on the inside. It wasn't until the next day, January 11, it was reported that Steele had authored the memos. CNN had been briefed by Steele himself.

Steele's boss, Glenn Simpson, had worked with CNN's Evan Perez at the *Wall Street Journal*. After he had left the *Journal*, Perez still socialized with the former journalists who founded Fusion GPS.

CNN did not disclose that Perez was friends with the political operatives who had produced and distributed the Clinton-funded dossier that Clapper discussed with the CNN anchorman and that Comey had briefed to the president-elect as a news hook for CNN to break the story. It was a tightly wrapped package, like a bomb designed to blow up on Trump.

"No one has verified this stuff," Tapper wrote to Smith regarding the dossier.

That was true. Months before the election, media organizations had sent reporters as far as Moscow to try to verify the dossier. No one had been able to, which was why CNN needed Comey's briefing to report on it.

The CNN anchor was caught in a contradiction. It was unverified, but CNN ran with it anyway. CNN published a story about intelligence officials briefing a president on national security issues based on information it knew might not be true.

I worked with Tapper nearly twenty years ago at a magazine called *Talk*. He was a very good journalist. And yet he missed the real story here—four US intelligence chiefs had briefed unverified information to the president and president-elect.

No one in the press reported that story because they couldn't— they were themselves part of it. But the CNN story found a way around the traditional measures designed to keep disinformation out of the press: it didn't report on the allegations of the dossier directly but rather on the fact that it was briefed to the president-elect.

The dossier was now out in the open. And under the guise of "news," the press would unleash half a million fictions engendered by a conspiracy theory. After CNN's January 10 story, there was no going back to traditional, fact-based journalism. Reporters had transformed into outright political operatives.

Nunes says he remembers seeing the Steele Dossier in BuzzFeed for the first time. "I showed it to the staff, and everyone was laughing," he says. "It was a joke, *The Onion* magazine version of intelligence products. Peeing on a bed? None of it made any sense."

It was poorly written, incoherent in places, and rife with misspellings. Steele had graduated from one of England's great universities. He was a college journalist and debater. At MI6, he'd written reports for a living. How had he learned to write so poorly?

"We read intelligence products all the time," says Nunes. "The staff, the lawyers, everyone is saying 'No one is going to take this seriously.'"

Nunes also heard from US allies with the most experience of Russian intelligence operations. "Our eastern and central European partners couldn't believe so many people seemed to have fallen for the dossier," he says. "They said, 'This has nothing to do with the Russians, it's not a Russian work product. The Russians would have made sure there were three or four things in there that were dead true.'"

Nunes had traveled extensively in the former Eastern Bloc states. Romanian president Klaus Iohannis had awarded him the Order of the Star of Romania, the highest award given to foreigners, for building a strong alliance between Washington and Bucharest.

"The central and eastern Europeans lived behind the Iron Curtain for half a century," he says. "They're laughing at our intelligence agencies for believing the dossier. The truth is, our IC wasn't buying it; they concocted it in cooperation with the Clinton campaign."

Before Comey briefed Obama and Trump on the dossier, he met with congressional leaders. They asked the FBI director who had paid for the dossier. He said that it had been started by Republicans. That soon became a Comey talking point.

It was still months before news would break that the conservative *Washington Free Beacon* had taken Fusion GPS's Trump opposition research until May 2016 but had had no role in funding Steele's work. When Comey made his claim in January 2017, there was no evidence that Republicans had had anything to do with the dossier. Either Comey was mistaken or was lying, or Fusion GPS had fed him yet another falsehood that served them both.

Comey also failed to disclose to congressional leaders that Steele's reports had in fact been paid for by the Clinton campaign. Unlike his claim regarding Republicans, there was evidence of DNC involvement—which the Crossfire Hurricane team did its best to hide in the application for the spy warrant on Carter Page.

"Comey seemed to know things that aren't so," says Nunes, "and not know things that are so."

The publication of the dossier echoed themes from press stories that had appeared in the months leading up to the election. That was for two reasons: one, Fusion GPS had inserted already published news, such as the misreported *Washington Post* story about the RNC platform, into the dossier to make Steele's reporting seem genuine; and two, because Fusion GPS had given Steele's memos to the press, including the July report on Carter Page and Igor Sechin, to build the Trump-Russia echo chamber.

For instance:

MEMO 80, Dated June 20:

> *The Russian government had sexually compromising material on Trump. The material Moscow had on Clinton wasn't embarrassing and was controlled by Kremlin spokesman Dmitry Peskov.*

That appeared to confirm a Kurt Eichenwald story in *Newsweek* on November 4 that had made those same claims days before the election.

MEMO 94, July 19:

Carter Page met with Rosneft CEO Igor Sechin during his July trip to Moscow and discussed sanctions relief in exchange for bilateral energy cooperation.

That had been reported in Isikoff's September 23 story.

MEMO 95, undated, written after the Democratic National Convention and before July 30, the date of the subsequent memo:

The Kremlin had hacked the DNC.

That had been widely reported in the press, first in a June 14 *Washington Post* article by Ellen Nakashima. The finding had been made by CrowdStrike, a cybersecurity firm employed by the Clinton campaign. CrowdStrike had been hired on the recommendation of former DOJ official Michael Sussman, a lawyer at Perkins Coie— the firm that had hired Fusion GPS for the Clinton campaign.

The Trump team had agreed to sideline the Russian intervention in Ukraine as a campaign issue.

That lined up with the July 18 *Washington Post* story by Josh Rogin claiming, that the RNC had weakened its platform on Ukraine at the behest of Trump officials.

Moscow was using Russian émigrés in New York, Washington, DC, and Miami to run operations.

That claim had appeared in Eichenwald's November 4 *Newsweek* article, reporting that Moscow's "operations have also been conducted in the United States, primarily out of New York City, Washington, D.C., and Miami. Those involved include a large number of Russian émigrés."

MEMO 100, August 5:

> *Reports of conflict between Putin advisers Sergei Ivanov and Dmitry Peskov. Ivanov was angry that Peskov had gone too far in pushing the pro-Trump operation and advised "only sensible course of action now for the Russian leadership was to 'sit tight and deny everything.'"*

Conveniently, the two supposedly rivalrous Putin deputies, Peskov and Ivanov, had been seated at the same table as the Russian president and Flynn at the December 2015 RT dinner. Though most photos of the event were cropped to include only Flynn and Putin, a widened angle shows the two Putin aides.

MEMO 101, August 10:

> *The Kremlin was engaging with several high-profile US players, Carter Page, Jill Stein, and Michael Flynn, and had funded their recent visits to Moscow.*

That referred to the December 2015 RT banquet, at which Stein and Flynn had sat at the same table with Putin. Flynn had explained that he had been paid by his speakers' bureau. It's not publicly known whether Russian officials paid for Page's July 2016 trip to Moscow.

MEMO 105, August 22:

Former Trump campaign convention manager Paul
Manafort had been discussed in a secret meeting between
his former client Ukrainian president Viktor Yanukovych
and Putin.

The press had widely asserted that Manafort's client
Yanukovych was pro-Putin.

Further, claimed the memo, Yanukovych had "authorized kick-
back payments to MANAFORT, as alleged in Western media."

A *New York Times* article by Andrew E. Kramer, Mike McIntire,
and Barry Meier had reported on the payments. The article had
been published on August 20, two days before the date of the memo.
A source for the *Times* article, Ukrainian political operative Serhiy
Leshchenko, was also a Fusion GPS source.

MEMO 112, September 14:

The Russian owners of a financial institution, Alfa Bank,
were close to Putin.

That echoed an October 31 Slate story by Franklin Foer
claiming that Alfa Bank's computer servers were in contact with
those of the Trump organization. Putting the Foer story together
with the dossier memo connected Trump to Putin via Alfa Bank.

Perkins Coie lawyer Michael Sussman was a source for Foer's
article and also passed the information to the FBI.

Immediately upon publication of the Foer article, the Clinton
campaign issued a press release about the story, which Clinton

operatives themselves had planted. Candidate Clinton retweeted the statement on her timeline the day the story was published: "Computer scientists have apparently uncovered a covert server linking the Trump Organization to a Russian-based bank."

MEMO 113, September 14:

> *"Azeri business figure Araz AGALAROV . . . had been closely involved with TRUMP in Russia."*

That seemed to confirm the *Washington Post*'s June 17 story by Tom Hamburger, Rosalind S. Helderman, and Michael Birnbaum in which the Agalarovs had boasted about how close they were to the Republican candidate.

The Agalarovs, featured extensively in the protodossiers, were also reported to have offered Donald Trump, Jr., dirt on Hillary Clinton, leading to the June 2016 Trump Tower meeting.

MEMO 136, October 20:

> *The Prague offices of a Russian "parastatal organization," Rossotrudnichestvo may have been used to host a meeting between Kremlin officials and Trump lawyer Michael Cohen.*

That, too, had been in Eichenwald's November 4 *Newsweek* article, in which he had claimed that "a Trump associate met with a pro-Putin member of Russian parliament at a building in Eastern Europe maintained by Rossotrudnichestvo."

Some memos, however, were out of sync with news reports. For instance, Memo 86 contends that the "FSB leads on cyber within Russian apparatus."

A week before the dossier was published, an Obama administration press release announcing sanctions for election interference had claimed that the GRU, Russian military intelligence, was in charge of cyberactivities, saying that the FSB "assisted." Either a former top MI6 Russianist got it wrong, or the Obama White House was pointing in the wrong direction.

Other memos simply sounded false. Memo 95 claimed that the reason for using WikiLeaks to dump the DNC emails had been "plausible deniability."

WikiLeaks had long been accused of having ties to foreign intelligence services, including Russia's. Julian Assange hosted a talk show in 2012. After WikiLeaks had published the emails, the press had assumed immediately, and with evidence provided only by the Clinton campaign's computer specialists, that the organization was acting on behalf of Russian intelligence.

Memo 111 claims that Putin aide Sergei Ivanov was fired in August because he had "advised PUTIN that the anti-CLINTON operation/s would be both effective and plausibly deniable with little blowback" and was proven wrong. However, according to previous dossier memos, he'd argued against the operation.

In Memo 100, for instance, Ivanov "laments Russian intervention in US presidential election and black PR against CLINTON and the DNC." According to that report, it was his rival Peskov who was the "main protagonist" in the "Kremlin campaign to aid TRUMP and damage CLINTON."

It appears that Steele's sources switched stories in order to explain Ivanov's unexpected dismissal.

Still other dossier claims were definitely false. Memo 105, for example, described a secret August 15 meeting between Yanukovych and Putin near Volgograd, a Russian port city. Putin had indeed visited Volgograd on August 15, for one day. Yanukovych, however, didn't get there until August 18, three days after Putin left. It would have been hard to miss Yanukovych's arrival, since he pulled into the river port on a triple-decker yacht.

Steele's sources got it wrong. Perhaps a Fusion GPS employee had simply pulled the wrong date off the internet.

The publication of the dossier provided a road map of the media campaign. The fact that Comey had briefed Trump on it showed that the press and the intelligence community had joined forces.

Strzok texted Page on January 10 to tell her he was watching CNN as the story about the briefing led the news. "We're discussing whether, now that this is out, we use it as a pretext to go interview some people."

It was standard operating procedure for the Crossfire Hurricane cell. "They use a story they've planted to go out and interview people," says Nunes. "All through their investigation, they planted a story with journalists, then picked it up as a predicate to investigate more. They did it to get the FISA and did it again in January. I don't think that's how most Americans want law enforcement to work, for the FBI to plant bogus stories on people then investigate them."

———————————

How did the US press corps become a partner in a coup?

CNN's January 10 story was seminal. But already by the summer of 2016, when the press had first partnered with the Clinton campaign and intelligence officials, the United States' most prestigious media brands—the *New York Times*, the *Washington Post*, CNN, NBC, and others—were in transformation.

No one had ever doubted that the press leaned left. The last Republican the *New York Times* had endorsed for president had been Dwight D. Eisenhower in 1956. But this was different. It was no longer simply media bias. The press had become a slicker version of third-world media, a state-owned political communications apparatus armed to advance the ruling party's agenda and to threaten and terrorize the opposition.

In a lecture at University of California, Berkeley, the week after he left the *Wall Street Journal*, Glenn Simpson explained the problem succinctly. "It used to be the newspaper model that people who were shopping for used cars would inadvertently subsidize investigative journalism," he said. "People looking at bottom lines don't even consider investigative journalism a loss leader any more. They just consider it a loss."

The old financial model of newspapers depended on advertising: retail, like department or jewelry stores, and classified. The three big categories in classified advertising were employment, real estate, and automotive—the used cars that Simpson was referring to.

The *Village Voice*, America's first, and now defunct, alternative weekly, was sustained largely by its real estate classifieds. New York City apartment hunters lined up at the Times Square newsstand late Tuesday night to make sure they had an early copy of Wednesday's paper.

I was at the *Voice* in the 1990s when the meteor hit, vaporizing the old financial model on contact. With the advent of the internet, all those listings now appeared on line, for free. Craigslist alone, with classified listings for urban areas around the country, demolished the economic pillar of virtually every media market in America. The press panicked. The *Voice*'s publisher decided that the paper was going free. How could he keep charging $1 for what consumers could get for nothing?

Thus it was the media itself that first devalued the media. By making news, reporting, and opinion free, the press told consumers as well as producers—journalists—that its product, journalism, was worth zero.

By crippling newspapers, the internet had damaged the entire ecosystem. Newspapers were at the core of the US media, the content not only filling their own publications but also feeding other media, particularly television.

TV is an expensive medium. Producers can't afford to waste valuable airtime on stories that scare or bore advertisers. The print press allowed producers to watch a story unfold over a few days or weeks to see whether it was worth dispatching a news crew and chewing up valuable broadcast minutes.

Local newspapers fed the magazine industry, too, stories as well as talent. The most ambitious writers in smaller papers across the country—investigative journalists, feature writers, humorists— all hoped for the day they'd get tapped to write for the big glossy magazines, regional publications, such as *Texas Monthly*, or the giants, such as *Esquire* or *The New Yorker*.

When the press's ad-based revenue model collapsed, why didn't media executives do the logical thing and *raise* the price to consumers? Yes, they would have lost some readers and have had to cut staff and departments, but they'd have established a fundamental defense of the product, the industry, and the institution itself—that news is worth paying for.

It took the *New York Times* more than a decade to settle on billing consumers—after giving away content, charging for it, giving it away again, then billing for "premium content," and so on. By then it was too late. The financial collapse of the press was followed by its professional and ethical collapse. Entire papers went under, and even at those that survived, the most prestigious enterprises, the costliest, went first.

"All these newspapers used to have foreign bureaus," Ben Rhodes, Obama's deputy national security advisor for strategic communications, told *The New York Times Magazine* in 2016. "Now they don't. They call us to explain to them what's happening in Moscow and Cairo. Most of the outlets are reporting on world events from Washington."

That was true of the Trump-Russia beat, too. All of it came out of Washington or New York and was sourced to anonymous US officials. No one covering a national security story allegedly about a foreign government controlling the commander in chief thought to report from what was, by the logic of the Trump-Russia narrative, the real center of power: Moscow.

Investigative teams were hit as hard as foreign bureaus. Those units had always been considered financial drains, swallowing up salaries that supported investigations lasting weeks or months that might not pan out in the end.

But just as Obama's communications team had rotated in for the foreign bureaus, the investigative teams were replaced by opposition research firms—such as Fusion GPS. "We're hoping to continue to do investigative work," Simpson told the Berkeley audience in 2009. He explained that he'd "formed a private company to pioneer yet another new model to fund investigations. We hope that people who have an interest in ferreting out corruption will come to us and fund us, they don't even have to have pure motives. They might want to investigate a competitor."

The press outsourced investigative work, reporting, because it couldn't afford it. So who would pay? Corporate clients, law firms, and lots of political groups.

It is always election season in the United States, national or state or municipal, and there's always a paying client who wants the dope on his or her opponent—and wants it distributed to the press.

But publishing that material puts the media into the middle of political operations. Whether media organizations and journalists take sides in those operations or not is irrelevant; the content they produce is a political instrument paid for by groups pushing their political interest. Eliminate that content—content that the press can no longer afford to produce—and an enormous chunk of media disappears, taking thousands of jobs with it.

Thus there was no chance that journalists would ever report honestly about Fusion GPS's role in driving the anti-Trump operation. Sure, journalists were scared of crossing Glenn Simpson and Peter Fritsch, but the problem was much more fundamental: opposition research is the cornerstone of the media's new financial model.

Scores of journalists and press organizations had seen or been briefed on the Trump-Russia protodossiers months before Steele's name was stamped on the weaponized version, but none of them had ever come forth to say what they knew. They couldn't afford not to join the plot against Trump. The culture of journalism had changed along with the economic model.

As Washington became the country's media mecca, the city's sociology replaced that of the former press capital. It's difficult to imagine the hundreds of wizened New York reporters and editors who since the 1970s had run thousands of stories about Donald Trump—the loudmouthed real estate mogul, the tabloid celebrity, the sharp with the model on his arm, the TV star—falling for the line that he was a Russian spy.

Any reporter could have figured it out in the time it took to ride the subway out to Brighton Beach, home of one of the world's largest

Russian diasporas, and ask a handful of bouncers and bartenders. After the first half dozen laughed, after the first three vodkas, a savvy journalist would have gotten the picture.

The sociology of Washington, on the other hand, is not only more political but also more gullible, more cynical. It's a city of half a million student council presidents, ready to adopt any opinion that advances their careers.

The press had become a testing ground for operatives, earnest, underpaid, and dense. Without its absolute commitment to the anti-Trump plot, the coup would never have stood a chance.

Chapter 10

BLOOD IN THE WATER

OBAMA HAD WARNED TRUMP about hiring Michael Flynn. It was two days after Trump's victory. The president-elect was bewildered. Of all the things Obama could have been discussing with his successor, he devoted valuable time to running down Flynn. That should have told Trump that something was up.

The outgoing president's primary concern was to protect the Iran nuclear deal. Flynn had been critical of it even while inside the Obama administration. Now, as counselor to a commander in chief who'd called the agreement catastrophic, Flynn had a shot at dismantling the forty-fourth president's signature foreign policy initiative.

According to officials, some of Obama's concerns about Flynn were Russia-related. There was his attendance at the 2015 RT banquet in Moscow, as well as "other contacts with Russia."

Flynn had first gone to Russia in June 2013 as Obama's DIA chief to visit military intelligence headquarters and meet with senior officers. Flynn believed it was possible to cooperate with the Russians on counterterrorism. Obama wanted to coordinate operations in Syria and share intelligence with the Russians.

The only other reports related to Flynn and Russia were the false allegations Stefan Halper had made about Flynn's 2014 visit to the University of Cambridge and his supposed dalliance with Moscow-born British historian Svetlana Lokhova.

Was Obama aware that Halper was running a dirty tricks operation to frame Flynn? We don't know, though it's clear that Obama wanted to be kept in the loop on the Crossfire Hurricane investigation. The president, Lisa Page had texted Peter Strzok, wanted to know everything about what they were doing.

Strzok said he was worried that if Trump was elected, some of the people they were investigating "might be named to senior national security positions." Strzok was referring not to Carter Page or George Papadopoulos or even Paul Manafort but to the former head of the DIA, Michael Flynn.

Obama had allies throughout the intelligence community, hundreds of them. And they had their own reasons to go after Flynn. "Flynn was talking about remaking the NSC staff and getting rid of the Obama holdovers to put Trump's people in there," says Nunes. "He was going to cut the NSC staff down to a third of its size under Obama."

Even more significantly, Flynn was going to address the problems with the intelligence community as a whole. "He wanted to remake the entire IC," says Nunes. He had Trump's ear. They were going to drain the Swamp.

"Flynn was going to have everyone in the senior intelligence service turn in their resignations," says Nunes. "That's hundreds of people, all across the IC spectrum. That didn't mean they were all going to go, but they had to justify what they were doing."

Most wouldn't have made the cut. "There were lots of bad apples," says Nunes. "Flynn served with many of them. They'd been appointed by Obama, and he knew what they were like. Lots of them didn't do anything. They were put in those places by bad characters. Look at the Crossfire Hurricane group. How do you think they managed to have all those people in exactly the right place with no one watching them?"

Flynn was an existential threat to hundreds of Americans whose job was to spy on foreigners, undermine the ability of their governments to function properly, and then lie about it with a straight face. They had turned that skill set against their own government. They regarded, with some justification, the man who was to be Trump's Swamp drainer as their enemy.

———————

The 2017 intelligence community assessment flagged RT as a major cog in the Kremlin's disruption operations, though practically no one in the United States watches it. But the fact that it was featured in Obama's dossier was intended to underscore the seriousness of Flynn's appearance at the network's Moscow banquet the previous year. Obama's intelligence apparatus knew the real story: that Flynn's speakers bureau had arranged the trip, which had been cleared with his former agency.

Nonetheless, reporters had been told that Svetlana Lokhova was behind the RT dinner. "The UK and US press were briefed on my supposedly compromising Flynn at the February 2014 Cambridge dinner," says Lokhova. "And my alleged involvement arranging Flynn's attendance at the December 2015 RT banquet."

It appears that Halper took his story public well after her brief contact with Flynn. Had Halper sent the story back to Washington immediately after the February 2014 meeting, it's unlikely that Lokhova would've been put in front of the next DIA chief as well. A May 1, 2015, email from Cambridge Security Initiative invited her to meet with General Vincent Stewart when he visited Cambridge for the joint DIA-CSI project that Flynn had arranged.

It was a full year after the RT dinner that Halper spread his story to the press. Lokhova says that an American journalist told her that the briefings about her and Flynn had started in December 2016. "He said no one could publish the stories then because they only had one source at the time," she says.

It was Halper's Cambridge colleague Christopher Andrew, Lokhova's professor, who gave a boost to the stalled media campaign against her and Flynn. Andrew wrote a February 29, 2017 article for the London *Sunday Times* hinting at the possibility that Flynn had been ensnared by a Russian agent. "After that article," says Lokhova, "all the journalists could report it. Andrew's piece stood up the rumors Halper started."

Now the media operation was in full swing, and by late winter, Lokhova was fielding calls from British reporters, including Nick Hopkins from *The Guardian* and American journalists, as well as Rob Barry from the *Wall Street Journal*.

A March 18 *Wall Street Journal* story by Barry, along with Carol E. Lee, Shane Harris, and Christopher S. Stewart, claimed that Flynn didn't report "his interaction with Ms. Lokhova to security officials in the Defense Department." According to the article, the contact between Flynn and Lokhova "came to the notice of U.S. intelligence." The source of the story was "a former senior U.S. official with knowledge of the matter." In the manner of typical Trump-Russia journalism recycling past, uncorroborated articles, the article quoted extensively from Andrew's piece about the Cambridge dinner. "Andrew," the *Journal* reported, "described a woman of dual British-Russian citizenship who showed Mr. Flynn a number of historic Russian documents, including an 'erotic postcard' that Joseph Stalin sent to a young woman in 1912.'"

The Cambridge professor had set up his student on behalf of Halper, who had been tasked to destroy Flynn. According to Andrew, the *Journal* story continued, "Flynn asked the woman to travel with him as a translator to Moscow on his next official visit but that the trip never materialized."

Andrew, an auxiliary of Halper's operation, had insinuated that his former student was a Russian spy who'd honey-trapped Flynn. Lokhova pauses briefly. Her daughter is playing at her feet. In painting her as a Russian spy, Andrew suggested she'd betrayed England, the country where she'd made her life whole.

"He betrayed me," says Lokhova. "My old professor. I'd studied with him since I was eighteen years old, half my life. I'd just given birth, and now the press is laying siege to me and my new family. It was horrible. I guess anyone can betray anyone."

But at the time, Lokhova still didn't understand what Andrew was doing. Her former professor had also convinced her to speak with *Washington Post* journalist David Ignatius. "He told me that he trusted Ignatius and I should speak to him," she says. "He said Ignatius had the 'inside track' on Flynn."

Ignatius is an intelligence community insider, his column a traditional platform for both information and disinformation leaked by US as well as foreign intelligence services. He was in London in early March and offered to come up to Cambridge to meet her.

"Ignatius wanted to talk about Flynn and the 2014 dinner," says Lokhova. "But I told him not to bother, the story was nonsense. Ignatius said he was surprised because he'd always found Stefan Halper to be a very reliable source."

There were two operations targeting Flynn in which Ignatius

was offered a part. He eventually passed on the one smearing Lokhova and accepted the other.

————————————

On January 12, 2017, Ignatius published a story entitled "Why Did Obama Dawdle on Russia's Hacking?" The White House hadn't taken more serious action prior to the election, Ignatius explained, because it "probably feared that further action might trigger a process of escalation that could bring even worse election turmoil." That made no sense. Just a week prior to the Ignatius article, Obama's spy chiefs had produced an official document claiming that Russia had interfered in an election to help elect its preferred candidate, Trump. If that had been true, then from the perspective of the losing party, Obama's party, nothing could have caused "worse election turmoil."

Ignatius's column was really a platform to attack Flynn. He cited Obama's dossier and Fusion GPS's talking points about the RT dinner:

> *Retired Lt. Gen. Michael T. Flynn, Trump's choice for national security adviser, cultivates close Russian contacts. He has appeared on Russia Today and received a speaking fee from the cable network, which was described in last week's unclassified intelligence briefing on Russian hacking as "the Kremlin's principal international propaganda outlet."*

Then Ignatius threw a bomb:

> *According to a senior U.S. government official, Flynn phoned Russian Ambassador Sergey Kislyak several times on Dec. 29, the day the Obama administration announced the*

expulsion of 35 Russian officials as well as other measures in retaliation for the hacking. What did Flynn say, and did it undercut the U.S. sanctions?

Intercepts of foreign officials are classified. The Ignatius story was more evidence that senior Obama officials were waging a criminal campaign by leaking classified intelligence as part of a political operation against the Trump team.

That was the real story: US officials were waging a criminal campaign against the president-elect.

"If we'd had a real press on the job," says Nunes, "the story would have been about who leaked the intercept and Flynn's name. Not the fact that he talked to the Russian ambassador; that was his job. A normal media would have pointed out that a crime had been committed and then looked for the criminal who leaked to the press."

But the January 10 CNN story had changed all that. It had ushered in the postdossier era, in which the United States' most prestigious media organizations enlist themselves in political operations.

"On January 10, the dossier comes out in the press and it's a joke," says Nunes. "It flopped. But two days later, Russia was back in the news. Flynn was used as the catalyst. They leaked the fact that he was speaking with the Russian ambassador to blow the Russia investigation sky high. The Russia story was reenergized with the Flynn leak."

Ignatius alleged that Flynn had crossed a line by speaking with Kislyak about Obama policy. "The Logan Act," he wrote, ". . . bars U.S. citizens from correspondence intending to influence a foreign government about 'disputes' with the United States. Was its spirit violated?"

Jack Langer remembers the media uproar over the 1799 law,

which had never been successfully prosecuted. "It was ridiculous," he says. "No one takes the Logan Act seriously, including reporters, and no one gets in trouble over it. It's just something both sides in Washington, for messaging purposes, like to accuse each other of violating. But the press was acting like Flynn had murdered somebody. A reporter asked Devin a question about it and Devin said, 'Oh, you're a Logan Act guy?' Then he smiled."

Still, the media noise further pressured the already harried transition team. The incoming administration's anxiety was evident days later when Vice President–elect Mike Pence appeared on *Face the Nation*. During the January 15 interview, Pence disputed the Ignatius allegations and said that Flynn had not discussed the sanctions with the Russian ambassador.

"I can confirm, having spoken to him about it," said Pence, referring to Flynn, "those conversations that happened to occur around the time that the United States took action to expel diplomats had nothing whatsoever to do with those sanctions." Reportedly, a US official who knew about the intercept said at the time that "either Flynn had misled Pence or that Pence misspoke."

The first scenario became the standard version of events. It appears it was more complicated than that.

As a career intelligence officer, Flynn knew that the communications of the Russian ambassador were regularly monitored. As the incoming national security advisor, it was his job to speak with foreign officials. He would have been derelict in his duties had he not asked for patience from an ambassador whose country had been put into the middle of a dirty tricks campaign engineered by the outgoing administration.

Here's what actually happened: There were reports December 28 that the Obama administration was planning to take punitive measures against the Russians. That evening Kislyak texted Flynn:

"Can you kindly call me back at your convenience." Flynn put him off. He was working with his deputy, K. T. McFarland, and the transition team to formulate a response. The transition team was concerned that the sanctions would affect the incoming White House's foreign policy goals and did not want Russia to escalate.

On the 29th, McFarland sent an email to transition team members about the sanctions and said that Flynn was speaking with Kislyak that evening. It's not clear whether Pence was briefed on the phone call at the time or on sanctions. As head of the transition team and vice president–elect, he probably should have been.

But the transition period was chaotic, hampered by a lack of bureaucratic discipline that reflected the president-elect's lack of political experience. On top of that, the outgoing administration had put into question its successor's legitimacy; Obama's dossier claimed that Trump owed his victory to Putin. Every day the transition team was fending off some new story linking Trump and his associates to the Kremlin.

Perhaps most important, the sanctions issue was itself complex. There were two relevant rounds of sanctions that could easily have been confused.

First, there were the sanctions the Obama White House had imposed after Russia's 2014 invasion of Ukraine and annexation of Crimea. The latest sanctions, however, had been imposed as the Obama administration was walking out the door. They had been intended to box Trump in and add further luster to the collusion narrative.

Flynn denied to the *Washington Post* that he'd discussed sanctions with Kislyak. It's likely he didn't think of the actions that Obama had taken against the Russians in December as real sanctions; Nunes didn't.

"Anyone who knows the Russia sanctions issue knows that the

real sanctions are the ones we imposed with our allies for annexing Crimea," he says. "I never considered what Obama did in December to be sanctions. It was a classic Obama move: make noise and do nothing. Everyone shrugs their shoulders and laughs."

It's not hard to see how in that environment the transition team's communications regarding Flynn's call with Kislyak might have been muddled.

The day after the Ignatius story appeared, a transition team official told the *Post*, "I can tell you that during his call, sanctions were not discussed whatsoever."

The same day, incoming White House press secretary Sean Spicer said that the conversation between Flynn and Kislyak had dealt with "the logistics" of a postinauguration call between Trump and Putin. "That was it," said Spicer, "plain and simple."

Whatever the reason for the miscommunication, whether the burden was on the transition team or on Flynn, the Crossfire Hurricane group saw the gap between Pence's televised statements and what Flynn had told Kislyak as a window of opportunity.

Comey waited until after the inauguration. More than a week after Pence's TV interview, he told McCabe to send agents to interview Flynn. The FBI director admitted that it was something he "probably wouldn't have done or maybe gotten away with in a more organized . . . administration." With other administrations, he said, "if the FBI wanted to send agents into the White House itself to interview a senior official, you would work through the White House Counsel and there'd be discussions and approvals and it would be there. And I thought, it's early enough, let's just send a couple of guys over."

Just as Comey had deceived Trump two weeks before and interviewed him as part of a counterintelligence investigation, he had the Crossfire Hurricane team to do the same to the national security advisor. McCabe called Flynn and told him that "people were curious about his conversations with Kislyak."

Flynn replied, "You know what I said, because you guys were probably listening."

McCabe dispatched Strzok and another FBI agent, Joe Pientka, to interview him at the White House. They asked if he "recalled any conversation with Kislyak in which the expulsions were discussed, where Flynn might have encouraged Kislyak not to escalate the situation, to keep the Russian response reciprocal or not to engage in a 'tit for tat.'"

Flynn hedged. "Not really," he said. "I don't remember. It wasn't 'don't do anything.'"

On January 26, Acting Attorney General Sally Yates went to the White House to warn lawyer Donald McGahn that Flynn might have misled the vice president. She said that since the Russians knew that there were discrepancies between what Flynn had said to Kislyak and what he had apparently told Pence of their conversation, the national security advisor might be vulnerable to blackmail.

Yates was fishing. The FBI knew what Flynn had said—it had the intercept—and Flynn knew the FBI knew what he had said. Since everyone knew what the national security advisor had said, there were no grounds for blackmail.

But Pence was still in the dark. The Crossfire Hurricane team planned to enlighten him. They bided their time.

McCabe was scheduled to brief Pence's staff on February 10. The briefing appears to have been timed to another leak of classified intelligence.

On February 9, the *Washington Post* published the parts of the Flynn-Kislyak intercept that contradicted Pence's account. The story, coauthored by Greg Miller, Adam Entous, and Ellen

Nakashima, was sourced to "nine current and former officials, who were in senior positions at multiple agencies at the time of the calls."

All of those officials said Flynn's references to the election-related sanctions were explicit. Two of those officials went further, saying that Flynn urged Russia not to overreact to the penalties being imposed by President Barack Obama, making clear that the two sides would be in position to review the matter after Trump was sworn in as president.

When McCabe appeared at the White House the next day, he was called into Pence's office. Priebus and McGahn were there, watching news coverage of the leaked intercept. They were upset. They asked to see the information McCabe had on Flynn.

McCabe showed the vice president what he had on Flynn. "This is totally opposite," said Pence. "It's not what he said to me."

Nunes remembers telling senior administration officials that they were out of their minds if they were thinking of firing Flynn. "I told Priebus he'd be next, along with Bannon and McGahn. I told them leave it alone and calm down and revisit it later."

The problem was an inexperienced White House staff pressured by the FBI leaking through the press. "The FBI are making it so that Flynn has to go and the media is backing them," says Nunes. "Remember, Flynn wanted to remake the entire IC."

Nunes warned the administration that it didn't have to satisfy the press's demands for blood. "What did Flynn actually do?" he asks. "Nothing. Every man has his flaws, but Flynn didn't have too many of them. People knew he was a man of action and a brilliant tactician. I told the administration that 'if you give in, they'll know they can come after any of you. There'll be blood in the water, and they're not going to stop.'"

The national security advisor was fired February 13, three days after McCabe's meeting with Pence in the White House. Trump told former New Jersey governor Chris Christie that the "Russia thing is all over now."

How did Trump not understand what was in store? The rules of the jungle—always attack, never give in—had governed his candidacy. Yet as president, he sacrificed a trusted adviser to the same intelligence officials he openly disdained.

"He was getting bad advice from some of his advisers," says Nunes. "He didn't understand that after they got Flynn, they'd have momentum. After Flynn went down, they believed they could get the president, too."

The day after Flynn left the White House, as the press uniformly vilified the general as a liar and a Russian stooge, Nunes issued a statement with a different message:

> *Michael Flynn served in the U.S. military for more than three decades. Washington, D.C. can be a rough town for honorable people, and Flynn—who has always been a soldier, not a politician—deserves America's gratitude and respect for dedicating so much of his life to strengthening our national security. I thank him for his many years of distinguished service.*

The HPSCI chair was one of the few people inside the Beltway who saw what the Flynn affair signaled. Flynn was only the first casualty in a chain of events initiated by the forty-fourth president of the United States. The plot was only just getting off the ground.

Chapter 11

BECOMING DEEP THROAT

RUSSIAGATE, the press claimed, was just like Watergate, but bigger. The commander in chief of the United States wasn't just corrupt; he'd been corrupted by a foreign power to which he owed his presidency.

But it was nothing like Watergate. The scandal that had ended with President Richard Nixon's resignation had begun with a crime.

On Saturday June 17, 1972, a security guard at the newly completed office and residential Watergate building complex caught five men breaking into the offices of the Democratic National Committee.

It's often forgotten that the burglars were charged for violating federal wiretapping laws and that the main purpose of the break-in was to put Nixon's opponents under surveillance. He wanted to know what they were doing and find out what they knew about him. The aides who planned the Watergate break-in were also running the "White House plumbers," a unit tasked to find out who was leaking sensitive material from the White House.

In that regard, then, it was Obama who was most like Nixon, because Trump's predecessor used the resources of the federal government, sensitive surveillance programs and staff, to spy on his opponents. It started many years before the collusion narrative swallowed the media.

As the Russiagate hoax unfolded, it was clear that most of what the Clinton operatives, intelligence and law enforcement officials, and Obama aides had engineered had been rehearsed during the battle over the Iran deal. Most obvious was the echo chamber, created by Ben Rhodes to win the Iran deal and repurposed to push the Trump-Russia story.

And it was during the Iran deal that the Obama administration first ran a smear campaign to tar political opponents as disloyal. If it was easy to convince the press that the Trump campaign was full of Kremlin assets, it was because just two years before, the Obama White House had gotten the media on board for a campaign employing anti-Semitic tropes to paint Iran deal opponents as more loyal to Israel than to the United States.

At the same time, the administration spied on its opponents. The White House monitored the communications of Israeli officials to reverse target the US congressional and Jewish community leaders with whom they were speaking and meeting. Several pro-Israel activists and Jewish community leaders tell me they were aware at the time that they were under surveillance.

"I was warned that my conversations with senior Israeli officials were possibly being monitored," says Noah Pollak, formerly the director of the Emergency Committee for Israel, a nonprofit organization that opposed the nuclear agreement with Iran. He and the other pro-Israel officials recognize that there is good reason to monitor the communications of foreign officials, even those of a friendly state such as Israel. "The Israelis probably do the same to US officials," he says.

But there were no compelling national security reasons to use surveillance programs against Americans engaged in legitimate political activism that, due to the nature of the policy under debate, involved conversations with foreigners. Yet the identities of pro-Israel activists and Jewish community leaders were unmasked in classified intercepts and fed to the Obama White House's war room, where operatives devised strategies to counter their opposition to the Iran deal.

Pollak says he was told of three different instances in which Obama officials responded quickly to conversations between senior Israeli officials and US citizens. "The administration did things that seemed incontrovertibly to be responses to information gathered by listening to those conversations." In one case, he says, "an Israeli official was on the phone with a prominent American rabbi who mentioned that he would be visiting Elie Wiesel in a day or two to encourage him to come out publicly against the deal. The rabbi was shocked to learn, upon meeting Wiesel the next day, that an administration official had just contacted him asking to discuss the Iran deal."

Says Pollak, "At first we thought these were coincidences and we were being paranoid. Surely none of us are that important. Eventually it simply became our working assumption that we were being spied on via the Israeli officials we were in contact with. The administration had defined achieving the nuclear deal as a vital national security interest, and this opened the door to treating those attempting to prevent this achievement—including Americans—as something akin to a threat."

In spying on the representatives of the American people and members of the pro-Israel community, the Obama administration learned how far it could go in manipulating surveillance programs for its own domestic political advantage. In both instances, the ostensible targets—first Israel and then Russia—were simply instruments used to go after the real targets at home.

Obama administration officials also learned which journalists they could trust with sensitive operations. Since leaking classified intelligence is a felony, a crucial concern was the reliability of the intermediaries chosen to publish it. One reporter who earned their trust was Adam Entous.

In December 2015, Entous, then working at the *Wall Street Journal*, reported on the Obama administration's surveillance of Israeli officials. In his telling, it was only by accident that Obama deputies had listened in on Americans.

"The National Security Agency's targeting of Israeli leaders and officials also swept up the contents of some of their private conversations with U.S. lawmakers and American-Jewish groups," wrote Entous. "That raised fears—an 'Oh-s— moment,' one senior U.S. official said—that the executive branch would be accused of spying on Congress."

According to Entous, the blatant abuse of surveillance programs to spy on US citizens was an innocent mistake. The Obama administration was just trying to find out how Israel was planning to oppose the Iran deal. "White House officials," he wrote, "believed the intercepted information could be valuable to counter Mr. Netanyahu's campaign."

But it was only US lawmakers, not the prime minister of Israel, who had the ability to block the deal. Administration officials were going after Americans. They knew that they were doing something bad and worried that they were going to be caught.

As Entous wrote, "Wary of a paper trail stemming from a request, the White House let the NSA decide what to share and what to withhold."

In other words, the chief executive tasked intelligence officials to pass along intercepts of politically important communications involving Americans. Some of the times, those conversations were between Israeli officials speaking about US citizens.

"The NSA has leeway to collect and disseminate intercepted communications involving U.S. lawmakers if," wrote Entous, "foreign ambassadors send messages to their foreign ministries that recount their private meetings or phone calls with members of Congress, current and former officials said."

The Entous story, cowritten by Danny Yadron, had been leaked to defuse a potential scandal and shape it favorably toward the Obama White House.

With Trump's election, Entous became a favored pass-through device for leaks of classified intelligence purposed to damage the incoming administration. He moved to the *Washington Post*, the landing spot for a few *Journal* reporters who wanted to play a more active role in the anti-Trump resistance that the *Post* was leading.

Entous had the lead byline on the December 9 *Washington Post* story mentioned earlier: "Secret CIA Assessment Says Russia Was Trying to Help Trump Win White House." It was through leaks of classified intelligence to the press that Obama's intelligence chiefs announced that they had changed their assessment of Russia's role in the 2016 election. They now believed Putin had worked to help Trump win.

Entous was one of three bylines, along with Greg Miller and Ellen Nakashima, on the February 9, 2017, story leaking the intercept of Flynn's conversation with Kislyak.

Yet the most illuminating of Entous's Russia-related scoops was a December 31, 2016, *Washington Post* article reporting that Russian hackers had penetrated the nation's power grid through the computer system of a Vermont utility company. According to US officials, "A code associated with the Russian hacking operation dubbed Grizzly Steppe by the Obama administration has been detected within the system of a Vermont utility."

After the story posted, the utility company reported to have been hacked, Burlington Electric, released a statement explaining that a laptop unconnected to the company's grid had been affected by malware. There had been no threat to the utility, never mind "the nation's electrical grid," as the anonymous US officials had claimed.

The story was false—which Entous or his cowriter, Juliet Eilperin, would have discovered had they contacted the electricity company before the story was published. They didn't because the story has not been learned from sources on location. Rather, it had *started* with anonymous US officials who had leaked a false story to advance the Russiagate narrative.

If Entous had first earned the trust of Obama officials by shaping the Iran deal surveillance scandal favorably, the Vermont utility story showed that he was willing not to ask basic questions, so long as the narrative was aimed at hurting Trump.

———————

Devin Nunes's communications director, Jack Langer, says that as the collusion narrative developed over time, he saw a sociological pattern emerging. "There was a pecking order of journalists that aligned with the traditional media hierarchy. The *Washington Post* and *New York Times* were the ringleaders or trendsetters. Then you have everybody else who simply follows their lead and is afraid to do anything that strays out of the narrative that's coming down from that clique."

But there was an even smaller group within that elite, a handful of journalists including Adam Entous, Greg Miller, Ellen Nakashima, and Devlin Barrett at the *Washington Post* and Matt Apuzzo, Matthew Rosenberg, Mark Mazzetti, Michael Schmidt, and Adam Goldman at the *New York Times*. They were entrusted with the most sensitive information, often classified, that advanced the anti-Trump operation.

The small group of journalists corresponded to the select Crossfire Hurricane team, insulated from the rest of the FBI and DOJ and responsible for the day-to-day management of the coup: McCabe, Strzok, Page, and Ohr, with Comey as the grand, sometimes distant, leader. Comey took the lead in setting up Trump with the dossier briefing in January.

After Trump's win, the Crossfire Hurricane team supplemented Fusion GPS's work, handing out Trump-Russia stories to media that needed content but no longer had the resources to produce it on their own. And this was a story that drove traffic for an industry hemorrhaging consumers and revenue.

Just as Bob Woodward and Carl Bernstein's Watergate reporting had made the *Washington Post* one of the most famous newspapers in the world, the Russiagate coverage boosted the media's sagging numbers.

Consider Woodward's home, the *Post*. Between 2004 and 2015, the paper's daily circulation shrank by more than half, from 726,000 to 360,000. But in 2017, Russiagate helped double the *Post*'s digital subscription number to one million, landing it in third place behind the *New York Times* and the *Wall Street Journal*.

Everyone wanted a piece of Russiagate. It boosted news organizations as well as individual careers. Reporters who attached themselves to Fusion GPS got promotions, raises, job offers, TV contracts, and book deals. Some reporters even identified themselves as Trump-Russia correspondents. The beat was make-believe, covering a conspiracy theory that Clinton operatives had dropped into the public sphere. It's as if an elite cadre of reporters had been assigned to cover the secret global conspiracy of Jews who rule the world and foment war, as described in the famous Russian intelligence forgery *The Protocols of the Elders of Zion*, and then called themselves "*Protocols* correspondents."

Yet Russiagate was a genuine financial category, a subindustry that drove traffic and thus convinced much of the press that it was producing real news.

Some journalists said they repented having gone too easy on Obama and promised they'd never again flinch from the truth. That was nonsense, for they ignored the massive Obama-era scandal unfolding before them in real time. Obama's FBI had run an espionage operation against a presidential campaign, which his CIA, FBI, and national intelligence directors rolled into a coup.

Naturally, the media congratulated itself on partnering with Clinton operatives and Obama officials to target Trump. Even before Trump's election, the *New York Times'* media reporter, Jim Rutenberg, opined that "normal standards" of journalism might have to be discarded when covering a "potentially dangerous" man such as Trump.

An MSNBC anchor compared journalists to firemen rushing into a burning building to save the truth. The *Washington Post* adopted a new motto, resonant with Orwellian forebodings: "Democracy Dies in Darkness." It was coined by the *Post*'s owner, Jeff Bezos, who said he had heard the paper's own Bob Woodward use the phrase once, when he had been talking about his latest book on Watergate, *The Last of the President's Men*.

Now the entire press corps was Woodward and Bernstein, every journalist a part of something meaningful. They weren't just covering events but had a role in history. The story they were part of—the disinformation campaign they were pushing—was as momentous as Watergate.

The few clear-eyed press critics remaining, such as Howard Kurtz at Fox News, tried to disabuse colleagues of their delusion. He noted that unlike in the case of Watergate, there was no evidence that Trump or his advisers had broken any laws.

From that perspective, the *Washington Post* had come full circle. Having become famous for breaking a big story about the abuse of executive power, four decades later Congress's hometown paper became the flagship of a shadow campaign pushed by executive branch officials such as Brennan, Clapper, Comey, and McCabe.

But there's another way to see the *Post*'s trajectory, a perspective that alters the popular understanding of the Watergate legend. From this point of view, the seeds of the press's collapse were sown at the moment of what is typically characterized to be its greatest triumph.

In the Watergate legend, Woodward and Bernstein's source was a whistle-blower, a man of conscience serving the people he had protected for decades as a federal agent. That was Mark Felt, the second-highest-ranking official at the FBI.

But Deep Throat, Felt's alter ego, was a disgruntled senior bureaucrat who believed he was entitled to succeed J. Edgar Hoover and fumed when Nixon passed him over for the Bureau's top job. Instead of going public with what he knew about a crime, a senior law enforcement official used tactics he'd learned in Hoover's FBI to go after his enemy: the commander in chief.

The real Watergate story, then, is anything but heroic. Rather, it's a tale of ambition and revenge and how those all-too-human emotions play themselves out in the large office buildings scattered along the Potomac, where bureaucratic backstabbing shapes the life of a nation.

The press corps has long seen itself in the starring role of the Watergate legend, an interpretation that two generations of journalists turned into a professional ethos. Accordingly, the job of journalists is to ingratiate themselves with government officials, who use the press to leak information damaging to their rivals. The lesson for aspiring journalists is that if they stay close enough to power, they may someday break a story that will bring down a president—as Woodward and Bernstein did.

That was another reason the media could never expose the truth about the coup. National security reporters could not produce stories without the acquiescence of the intelligence community that fomented the plot. The journalists' jobs, their prestige, the welfare of their families required their loyalty to the men and women who leaked them classified information.

It was appropriate that Carl Bernstein's byline appeared on the January 10 CNN story leaked by intelligence bureaucrats for the purpose of destroying Trump. After more than forty years, he was still paying off the debt he had incurred by becoming Carl Bernstein. He owed them everything.

What's more interesting is to see Watergate through the eyes of the Crossfire Hurricane group. "The way they saw Watergate, the FBI man is the leading man," says Nunes. "The hero isn't Woodward and Bernstein, it's Felt. They all wanted to become the next Deep Throat."

The FBI protagonist sees the press corps for what it is and uses the journalists' vanity, professional ambition, and neediness to do the work that matters to him. He's not interested in Pulitzer Prizes, book deals, or TV contracts. He's running assets. His mission is simply to bring down the president.

Felt managed to take out Nixon almost single-handedly, using two young reporters to push a story that most of the press ignored for months. By comparison, Crossfire Hurricane had not only the number two man at the FBI but also a counterintelligence team, a top DOJ lawyer, and surveillance capabilities that Nixon would have envied.

Their operations were assisted at various times by the FBI and CIA directors and the director of national intelligence, as well as senior Obama White House and State Department officials. Instead of two reporters, Crossfire Hurricane had elite teams at the United States' two most prestigious papers, whose reputations ensured wide buy-in from the rest of the media.

Compared to Felt's operation, the odds were stacked heavily in favor of Crossfire Hurricane. The conspirators had reason to believe they were going to bring down Trump.

———————

A neglected aspect of the Flynn affair is that in portraying a US official as an agent of a foreign power because of his contacts with a foreign ambassador, Obama aides subverted a foundational principle of international diplomacy: An envoy is sent abroad as a line of communications between his home and host countries. This relationship is especially useful in times of crisis between a home and host country.

In falsely accusing Putin of throwing the election to Trump, Obama officials manufactured a potential crisis with Moscow. At the same time, they made the Russian ambassador toxic. For even speaking with Kislyak signaled a willingness to betray the United States.

A March 1, 2017, *Washington Post* piece by Adam Entous, Ellen Nakashima, and Greg Miller broke the news that Attorney General Jeff Sessions had met with Kislyak twice. The article was sourced to intercepts of Kislyak's communications with Moscow in which he had told his superiors he'd met with Sessions.

If the *Post* article is accurate, US officials had exposed the intelligence community's ability to monitor the Kremlin's communications in order to target the country's top law enforcement official.

Sessions had foolishly set his recusal in motion when he had been confirmed attorney general the month before. Upon the publication of the *Post* story, he officially stepped aside.

"Sessions should have known better," says Nunes. "He's an honorable man who sees the good in people, and he didn't realize they were taking advantage of him. He knew that he didn't do anything wrong, so he thought there wasn't going to be a problem. In a perfect world that's what would have happened, but it wasn't what they had in mind."

Nunes's communications director imagines what was going through Sessions's mind. "The media attacks driving the collusion narrative were overwhelming and disorienting for the targets," says Jack Langer. Soon he would experience it himself. "The hysteria can get you to do things you wouldn't normally do," he says. "And you think there's no way out from the pain except to do what they demand from you. For Sessions, it was to recuse."

Trump was outraged that his attorney general had left him exposed to a political operation. Maybe the president had come to regret firing Flynn, for Nunes's warnings had come true. There was no calm for the White House, only more blood in the water. Two days later, the president tweeted: "Just found out that Obama had my wires tapped in Trump Tower just before the victory. Nothing found. This is McCarthyism."

Nunes said at the time that there was no evidence of a wiretap but he was concerned about other possible surveillance activities against the Trump team. And he came to realize that Trump had been right about the rest. "It was McCarthyism," he says. "I said it several times. They used McCarthyism to build a political structure. They used the Russia investigations to rile up their base and as a fund-raising mechanism."

With Sessions's recusal, Democrats started calling for a special counsel. They wanted an investigation with as little oversight as possible. Now that Flynn was gone and Sessions had recused himself, the conspirators, with the Crossfire Hurricane team on point, saw an open field before them. Trump was in their sights. Only Nunes was in the way. They went after him next.

Chapter 12

THE VALLEY OF DEATH

AFTER TRUMP tweeted that his predecessor had spied on him, Nunes said that there was no indication Trump had been wiretapped. There was ample evidence, however, that the national security apparatus was being used against the president and his senior aides.

Trump's January conversations with world leaders had been leaked to the media. His conversation with the president of Mexico had been leaked to *Washington Post* reporters Philip Rucker, Joshua Partlow, and Nick Miroff. The president's call with the Australian prime minister had been leaked to the *Post*'s Greg Miller and Philip Rucker.

An intercept of the national security advisor's communications with the Russian ambassador had been leaked to the *Post*'s team of Miller, Entous, and Nakashima; nine US officials had been directed to confirm it.

An intercept showing that attorney general Jeff Sessions had met with the same diplomat had also been leaked to the *Post*'s Miller, Entous, and Nakashima.

Clearly, there was a political operation under way designed to sabotage the Trump administration.

"Alarm bells should have been going off all over," says Nunes. "The FBI should've been breaking down doors to find out what was going on. 'Hey, we're here to protect you and the country, Mr. President.' Instead," says Nunes, "there was nothing."

But the members of the intelligence community who weren't part of the anti-Trump operation were panicked. The plotters were putting sensitive programs at risk. Whistle-blowers reached out to the HPSCI chair.

"The sources," Nunes says, "told me that Obama officials had been going crazy unmasking people on the Trump transition team."

Nunes will not disclose anything about his sources and cannot say much about the nature of what he uncovered, as it touches on intelligence community sources and methods. But he outlines how he revealed the unmasking of Trump officials and brought it to light. "I slowly put together what happened. But it was difficult. I couldn't just say to the new administration, 'Give me everything that was unmasked,' because I didn't know what I was looking for. I wouldn't have known where to find the records without the sources."

On March 21, Nunes went to the Eisenhower Executive Office Building, adjoining the White House, where the bulk of White House staffers have their offices. "I got my hands on the documents I was looking for and the next morning briefed Speaker Ryan on it," he recalls. "I told him, 'I'm going to go brief the Republican members on the committee and the president. I'm going to be very transparent with the press so that they know what's going on.' So I called a press briefing before I went to the White House to give them what details I could of what I had seen."

As Nunes's staff gathered to discuss the next move, there was concern that the chairman was moving too quickly. "We didn't want him going out there alone on this," says a Nunes aide who asked not to be named. "We wanted another set of eyes on it so he could get some support from the rest of the committee and Republicans."

Damon Nelson, HPSCI's staff director, was particularly wary. He'd known Nunes since high school. "I met him when I was a freshman and he was a sophomore and we had classes right next to each other," says Nunes. "He had long hair and cut class and played pool. Then he seemed to drop from sight. And then, in 2002, I was interviewing for my first legislative director and here's this guy with the same name—Damon Nelson, who graduated from high school, joined the air force, where he met his wife and served in the first Gulf War, and went on to get a bunch of degrees."

It was an amazing transformation, says Nunes. And he came to value Nelson's advice as much as anyone's. But the chairman also knew he had to act quickly. "The window of opportunity to expose what they'd done was closing," he says. "Once they found out I was onto them, they were going to shut down everything. There were still plenty of Obama holdovers in that building, and they were watching me when I came in that day. I had to move quickly."

The staff eventually came to see that their skepticism was misplaced. "He has great political instincts," says the aide. "He's almost always right about that kind of stuff. And besides, after all the debate, we all recognized that he was the one who was elected."

And they knew it was their job to follow him into the valley of death, into which he was surely heading by taking on the intelligence community, political operatives, and the press.

At his March 22 press conference in the Capitol, Nunes stressed that none of the surveillance of Trump team members "was related to Russia or the investigation of Russian activities or of the Trump team." That is, what he'd seen had nothing to do with any investigation of the Trump transition team. "It was never about Russia," he says. "It was simply Obama people unmasking Trump transition people for no legitimate reason."

HPSCI found that huge numbers of unmaskings of Americans had been done by certain Obama officials in 2016, including hundreds by Samantha Power, who wouldn't have seemed to need such constant access to highly sensitive intelligence to conduct her duties as US ambassador to the United Nations. Testifying before HPSCI, former national security advisor Susan Rice acknowledged having unmasked Trump transition officials when they had met in December 2016 at the Trump Tower with the crown prince of the United Arab Emirates. Her testimony was leaked to CNN reporter Manu Raju, revealing the names of the Trump officials she'd unmasked: Michael Flynn, Jared Kushner, and Steve Bannon.

Rice justified the unmasking by saying that she had been frustrated that the Emiratis had not followed protocol for visiting officials and had failed to notify the White House of their stay. But if her aim was to rebuke foreign dignitaries, why unmask the identities of US officials—which were then leaked to the press?

It seems that part of her purpose in unmasking transition officials was to gather intelligence on a future meeting between Trump associates and UAE officials.

A few weeks after the meeting between the Trump officials and the Emirati royal, prominent Trump supporter Erik Prince, the founder of the private security firm Blackwater USA and brother of incoming education secretary Betsy DeVos, met with Emirati officials in the Seychelles. There Prince was introduced to a Russian banker.

Prince denied allegations made in an April 3, 2017, *Washington Post* article that he had been there to establish a back channel with Moscow. Adam Entous had the lead byline with Greg Miller, Kevin

Sieff, and Karen DeYoung on another *Post* article seemingly sourced to a classified intercept.

Prince said he had been shown "specific evidence" by sources from the intelligence community that his name was unmasked and given to the paper. "Unless the *Washington Post* has somehow miraculously recruited the bartender of a hotel in the Seychelles," said Prince, "the only way that's happening is through SIGINT [signals intelligence]."

That was the essence of the political campaign targeting the Trump White House: Obama officials leaked classified intelligence to political operatives with bylines to sabotage Trump.

Because Nunes had uncovered the operation, he had to be crushed. "Finding the unmasking was really deadly to them," he says. "And it should be, and they should all be investigated, and people should be thrown in jail for it. People should be in jail for a long time for what they did to Flynn and others."

And just as they'd pushed Flynn from the White House and forced Sessions to recuse himself, they were going after Nunes. "Right after that March 22 appearance," he says, "they turned their entire apparatus, from super PACs to the press, on me, dumping oppo research and fake news about me everywhere. They did it because they knew they were caught—they were unmasking Trump transition people and leaking it to the press. I broke up their party. They knew they were screwed, so they tried to get rid of me."

Jack Langer's office is down the hall from Nunes's in Longworth. The communications director spent many of his early years in Japan, where his father was a computer executive. After his family returned home to Philadelphia, he went to the University of Colorado Boulder, and once he'd finished college, he moved to

Prague. "I learned Czech and forgot it," he says. "I have a talent for forgetting languages—I forgot the Japanese I used to know, too."

He worked as a reporter and ad salesman for a few English-language publications in the Czech Republic before he came back to the United States to get his PhD at Duke. He wrote his dissertation on imperial Russian history. "I can't believe Team Collusion missed that one," he jokes.

Nunes offered him the communications director's job after he'd edited the congressman's book, *Restoring the Republic: A Clear, Concise, and Colorful Blueprint for America's Future.* "It was a great experience," says Langer, a slender man with a thick, booming voice. "We'd be working on the book late at night and drinking a good bottle of wine from Devin's winery."

Langer remembers when his relationship with the media was good. "Before the Russia stuff, we really had no problems with anybody in the press," he says.

That changed after the March 22 press briefing. An early example of the press's new posture surfaced in a March 24 Daily Beast story by Tim Mak. That kicked off the "Midnight Run" narrative. It was a fictionalized account of how Nunes had learned of the unmasking. According to Mak's sources, Nunes "received a communication on his phone," jumped out of an Uber he was sharing with staffers, switched cars, and went somewhere at night to review the documents.

"The story was sourced to three Intelligence Committee officials and one other official closely tied to the Intelligence Committee," Langer remembers. "So the author is basically acknowledging 'These are Intelligence Committee Democrats who gave me this story.'"

Langer says that four or five different publications called him to confirm details of the "Midnight Run." "Obviously the story was being shopped around," he says. He remembers a call from a

Washington Post reporter. "The writer told me, 'I have this story from three of your own committee's staffers.' I still remember the tone of voice. It was stunned, as if to say, 'I've got this from three people on your own committee. How can you deny it?' When in fact it's three Committee Democrats saying this and the reporter can't imagine that a hostile source may have a reason to invent a story to discredit Devin."

After Nunes unmasked the unmasking, numerous stories were contrived to embarrass the HPSCI chairman. The purpose was to intimidate him and keep him from digging further into the anti-Trump operation.

"I didn't understand what was going on with the press," says Langer. "I was still naive enough that I didn't understand the point of this story or why it was being put out. But then Adam Schiff comes out and labels this 'the Midnight Run,' and then the Democrats and the press start ridiculing Devin and pointing to this as proof he's this weird conspiratorial guy who does wacky things like jump in and out of cars in the middle of the night."

Nunes went on CNN a couple of days later and told Wolf Blitzer the story was false. "He didn't jump in and out of any cars, he didn't go anywhere at night, and he wasn't sneaking around," says Langer. "He stopped and casually chatted with various people he ran into on his way to the Eisenhower building, which has the secure facility where the documents were. But all the denials had absolutely zero effect. To this day, the media reports the 'Midnight Run' story as a fact. It's too perfect of a caricature of Devin for them to let go."

Another story that sticks out in Langer's mind is a *New York Times* piece trying to identify Nunes's sources for the unmasking. "These publications could have sent their journalists out to discover whether or not it was true that Obama people were unmasking

Trump people," he says, "but instead they all tried to hunt down the whistle-blower."

Langer hadn't immediately agreed with the congressman's suggestion to stop talking to the mainstream press. But as the investigations wore on and the media became increasingly hostile, he came to see it differently. "Talking to reporters had become useless," he says. "They had the story they wanted to tell, which was whatever story the Democrats and the intelligence leakers were feeding them. Coming to us for comment was just a formality, and what we said didn't matter anymore. They were no longer reporters, they were narrative pushers."

Langer began embedding critiques of the press's performance in his comments to the media. For instance, when CNN requested comment for one 2018 story involving the congressman, Langer fired back, "It's unsurprising to see the left-wing media spin Chairman Nunes's routine observations as some nefarious plot, since these same media outlets spent the last year and a half touting a nonexistent Russia collusion conspiracy."

Langer decided he needed a new communications strategy. "Number one, to hell with these guys," he says. "And number two, we have to push back."

Nunes had seen evidence of a real scandal: Obama officials had unmasked Trump associates and leaked their identities to the press. The leaks were criminal, abuses of power that violated the privacy rights of US citizens. Further, using national security surveillance programs to push a political operation risked provoking a popular backlash demanding an end to programs keeping Americans safe from terrorism. The leakers had put Americans into danger.

———————

The Democrats played to block by getting Nunes put under investigation. That amplified calls for the HPSCI chairman to hand over the reins of the Russia probe.

The campaign against him was financed by left-wing money. Three progressive activist groups, MoveOn, Citizens for Responsibility and Ethics in Washington (CREW), and Democracy 21, filed complaints with the Office of Congressional Ethics (OCE) accusing Nunes of having leaked classified information during the March 22 press briefing.

"Anyone can file a complaint with the OCE against any member of Congress," says Langer. "Some groups use that as a weapon. Others use it to puff themselves up by filing some frivolous complaint against congressmen they don't like so they can issue a press release. The OCE gets tons of complaints, and the vast majority of them probably never get a second look. There's no way they can handle all of these, but the House Ethics Committee picked up the complaint from OCE and decided to investigate it."

The investigation was politicized from the outset, he explains. "Before they announced they would take this complaint, four of the five Democrats on the Ethics Committee had publicly denounced Devin for his unmasking revelations. Some accused him of leaking classified information; others said he needed to be removed as chairman. That's clearly prejudgment, and those members should have recused themselves from the investigation. But that's not what happened."

On April 6, Nunes decided to step aside from leading the Russia investigation. "I had to," he recalls. "I was in the valley of death, and there was no other way out. They'd start sticking cameras in the faces of Republicans all over the Hill, demanding that I be forced out of the chairmanship."

Also, Nunes had seen evidence of a separate issue that would determine the course of HPSCI's work: the FBI had used the Steele Dossier to obtain the spy warrant on Carter Page. If he kept fighting the Russia investigation, he'd cut himself off from what he already understood was the real issue. He asked other Republican committee members to take over the investigation: Mike Conaway, Trey Gowdy, and Tom Rooney. "I thought it would be over soon," he says. "I was thinking that people were reasonable and there was no evidence of any wrongdoing, so this would be cleared up in two weeks, by the time the Easter break ended."

Conaway, on the other hand, remembers thinking that it was going to take some time. "I've served as chairman of the Ethics Committee, so I knew those things take forever," he tells me.

The eight-term congressman from Texas had been a military policeman in the army. Nonetheless, it was impossible to keep Adam Schiff in line. Conaway remembers his first meeting with HPSCI's top Democrat after he'd taken over the investigation. "I looked for Adam Schiff the next day and found him in the cloakroom," he says. "I said, 'Hey, Adam, I've been asked to take over the Russia investigation,' and he said, 'Great, let's work good together.' I said, 'Now, Adam, I am not going to go on TV, and I've asked my guys to not go on TV. Would you do the same? Would you and your guys get off TV and let's conduct this investigation the way it ought to be done, behind the scenes?' He looks at me incredulously and said, 'Well, I have to ask permission from Nancy Pelosi to do that.'"

Conaway was stunned. "It never occurred to me to ask Paul Ryan anything like that. I was relatively successful with myself. I was not on TV at all. I was totally unsuccessful with convincing Adam and his team to get off TV."

Schiff instead became the television face of the committee. He was a regular on CNN, forecasting nearly nightly that evidence of Trump-Russia collusion was just over the horizon.

Radio host John Batchelor came to refer to Schiff as "Pathfinder"—an advance scout illuminating the routes by which Trump might be impeached for collusion.

The nickname caught on with the Nunes team: "Pathfinder has found another path to collusion" became a regular quip among committee staffers every time Schiff stretched a new lie across the same worn bow.

The Left hung on every word that crossed Schiff's lips as he staged his campaign through the same media he fed with leaks and disinformation. Schiff was among those other figures—former Obama aides, Clinton operatives, corrupt law enforcement and intelligence officials, and the press—who poisoned the American public sphere with the collusion hoax.

There was so much going on during that March and early April period, says Langer, that he wasn't able to see how much had changed and how quickly. "It was just such rapid fire that I didn't really have time to take a step back and think about it," he says. "But after Devin stepped aside from leading the Russia investigation, I could look at it with some perspective. Then I put it all together in the same way Devin already had: they were using Russia to take down Trump."

Langer says that April period was a low point for the committee. Nonetheless, finding that the FBI had used the Steele Dossier to obtain the FISA warrant pointed HPSCI in a new direction.

"I couldn't have dreamed they'd be that dirty," says Nunes. "As soon as we saw they'd abused the FISA process, we opened up the investigation right away because the FISA issues bled into other matters, like how they started the whole investigation. It was all a setup."

It was then he realized he'd come across the biggest political scandal in US history. "They used the intelligence services and surveillance programs against American citizens," he says. "They spied on a presidential campaign and put it under a counterintelligence investigation so they could close it off and no one else would see what they were doing. They leaked classified intelligence again and again to prosecute a campaign against a sitting president. Ninety percent of the press was with them, and the attorney general was out of the picture."

That meant it was up to Nunes and his team to expose the hoax, get out the truth, and uphold the rule of law. Any offense they devised would involve going against the top levels of the DOJ and FBI, congressional opponents, the media, and the more than half of the country that had swallowed the collusion narrative.

Strangely, Nunes's team liked their odds. Help was on the way. At the end of March, the HPSCI chair met with a former public defender and onetime DOJ prosecutor and offered him a job. With Kashyap "Kash" Patel on board, the momentum would shift. Objective Medusa was about to begin.

PART TWO

INVESTIGATING THE INVESTIGATORS

Chapter 13

OBJECTIVE MEDUSA ON OFFENSE

THERE WAS AN UPSIDE, says Nunes, to stepping away from leading HPSCI's Russia investigation. "Knowing that there was no collusion, nothing on Trump, I could focus on the other things we'd started to find, like the unmaskings, FISA abuse, and other related matters."

On March 8, Nunes had written the Justice Department asking for copies of any applications submitted to the Foreign Intelligence Surveillance Court. "We were doing due diligence for the Russia investigation," he says, "and we wanted any documents we thought might exist regarding a counterintelligence investigation."

There was a FISA warrant on Carter Page. Nunes was briefed on it in mid-March. That was thanks partly to the efforts of Iowa Senator Chuck Grassley. The chairman of the Senate Judiciary Committee and his staff would come to play an important role in uncovering FBI and DOJ crimes and abuses. The work of Grassley and his staff reinforced the work of Nunes and his team.

The Senate Judiciary Committee had long been accustomed to looking at irregularities at the Department of Justice and the FBI.

Grassley made sure HPSCI saw the FISA warrant. Grassley knew how to pressure DOJ. "Senator Grassley made it clear that his committee wouldn't confirm Rod Rosenstein as deputy attorney general unless he saw the FISA," says Nunes. "Since we'd been asking for it, Grassley made sure we saw it as well."

They saw that the FBI had used the Steele Dossier to obtain a warrant to spy on a US citizen. Not being able to say anything about it, while the media launched false allegations of collusion against the Trump administration daily, caused heartache for HPSCI Republicans. "All the members wanted to disclose it," remembers Nunes. "We're the ones with the sole jurisdiction for oversight of the intelligence community. So it was our responsibility, and Congress is counting on us when red flags pop up."

But they couldn't say anything, not to the US public, not even to fellow members of Congress. The FBI and DOJ had buried it, like so much of the anti-Trump operation, under the heading of classified intelligence.

Then an April 11, 2017, *Washington Post* story disclosed news of the FISA warrant on Page. The story, written by Ellen Nakashima, Devlin Barrett, and Adam Entous, was meant to further bolster the narrative that the Trump team had coordinated with Russia. The FBI had been so worried about signs of the Trump team's friendliness toward Russia that it had used its most intrusive form of intelligence collection to monitor a US citizen.

But for the anti-Trump conspirators across the US government and in the press, it was just a means of building the momentum necessary to take down the president.

Just a few days later, Kashyap Patel joined Nunes's team. HPSCI staff director Damon Nelson asked the chairman why he hadn't gone through the normal hiring process. It was a decision Nunes had made on the spot. "I wanted him," says Nunes, "and we needed him."

Nelson named the new hire the lead investigator. Patel helped take back the initiative after the ethics complaint pushed Nunes off leading the Russia investigation.

At first Patel's new colleagues didn't know what to make of him. As a former prosecutor, he was always looking for the win. That didn't comport well with the give-and-take that had previously governed HPSCI's bipartisan ethos. The committee's job was to pass legislation helping the intelligence community and provide constitutionally mandated oversight.

But now the committee was returning to its original purpose when it had been established in the wake of the scandals that had rocked the intelligence community in the 1970s: to investigate crimes and abuses of an out-of-control intelligence community violating the rights of US citizens.

As a New Yorker, Patel's style sometimes clashed with those of the easygoing Californians, southerners, and midwesterners who made up the HPSCI staff. And his colleagues didn't know what to make of what he was saying about the upper echelons in federal law enforcement.

"He was always going on about the top people at DOJ and FBI," says a former Army Special Operations officer on Nunes's team, "and at one point I turned to him and told him, 'Give it a rest.' But Kash was right."

Nunes told his team he trusted Patel. "I wanted Kash to lead, and I wanted them to follow his lead," he says. "I hired him to bust doors down and didn't want them to get in his way."

Another HPSCI staffer remembers being skeptical at first. "Kash proposed a heroic quest," says Patel's investigative partner, "Jim," who asks that his real name not be used.

Together, their diverse temperaments, legal training, professional experience, and physical appearance were a study in contrasts, like something scripted for a police drama. Patel went in headfirst, while his investigative partner was more reserved, more cerebral.

"Kash had a grand vision for the investigation," says Jim. "We said, 'We'll believe it when we see it.'"

———————————

Patel likes to mix it up in the corners. He's a lifelong hockey fanatic. He coaches youth hockey in the Washington, DC, area and skates defense for the nationally renowned Dons, an amateur team named after the hockey commentator and fashion legend Don Cherry.

Patel grew up on Long Island cheering for his local franchise, the New York Islanders, and was born in Queens, like the forty-fifth president. He says he knew Trump was going to win the moment he came down the escalator. "One, he's from New York and doesn't like to lose. He plans everything. Two, no one dominates the media like that guy. So everyone calls me crazy for eighteen months, but I was right."

We're sitting in one of the few remaining Washington, DC, bars where smoking cigars is permitted. Patel hands me a Gurkha, made by a friend in Miami, Kaizad Hansotia, and lights it. He says he was expecting that there would be irregularities with the FBI's Russia investigation. He knew the Crossfire Hurricane group: McCabe, Strzok, Page. "They're really good agents and really good lawyers," he says.

The problem, he says, was that there was no accountability in significant parts of Obama's Justice Department, often even when dealing with high-profile cases. "We had great terrorism cases just sitting on the shelves at DOJ and no one would approve them, because the bureaucracy was so bad. I joked that if you want to move quickly through DOJ, keep screwing up. Everyone who's implicated in your mistakes has an interest in covering it up, so they'll promote you."

There seemed to be no rhyme or reason to the way the upper echelons worked. It was out of the ordinary, Patel thought, that Comey had never investigated the DNC's servers after the alleged hack. "Instead, Comey just accepted CrowdStrike's assessment," he says. "Some random outside company that happened to be retained by Perkins Coie, the campaign's lawyers. I never worked a case involving cyber where the FBI said, 'Let's not use our own people on this one.' You're supposed to do it yourself, you're the FBI."

For Patel, Comey's exoneration of Clinton was a stark illustration of everything that was wrong at DOJ. "He hijacked the Clinton investigation," he says. "That was not his call to make. You don't go on TV and say, 'I, the FBI director, am deciding what is a prosecutor's decision.' And by the way, all my colleagues in the national security division, all truly apolitical, every one of us would have taken the Clinton case to a grand jury."

Patel had had enough. "I was at the doctor's that day, and he asked why my blood pressure was running so high. I told him it was Comey's speech. All that just added up over time, and I was thinking 'I got to get out of here.'"

When Patel accepted the job with Nunes's team in April 2017, he didn't know much about Congress or the Intelligence Committee. "But I was prepared to know who I would be dealing with in DOJ when I came on. I told Devin that we will find that the people running the Russia investigation will have done inappropriate things. That was my experience, having worked with them and seeing it occur. No one believed me. Maybe from an outsider's view looking in, I might have also called myself crazy for saying that. Because it's supposed to be DOJ."

Still, he told Nunes that if they really found something on Trump's working with the Russians, they'd have to follow it no matter where it led. "I needed to have assurances of accountability," he says.

Nunes and Nelson wanted to start interviewing people immediately. Patel put on the brakes. "I told them, 'No, not right away we don't. We do at some point, but witness interviews are window dressing. That's Investigation 101. What we need are all the documents.'"

Patel explains that as a public defender he learned that documents are the key to taking on DOJ. "You have much fewer resources as a public defender. Witness testimony is great but if we can get the government's own evidence to show X, Y, and Z, then you've got them."

The first document was the Steele Dossier. "Did these people named in the dossier actually do the things they're alleged to have done? I told Devin if they did, then the president's kind of screwed."

Patel read the dossier closely. "At first it looked laughable," he says. "I mean, I grew up in New York. I don't know Trump, but I grew up with the guy. Even for him I'm like 'This is ludicrous.' So I started by thinking that there were things in it that were either true or not—like did Trump's lawyer Michael Cohen go to Prague. If he didn't, then that's a problem proving the dossier is real."

But the centerpiece of the dossier, says Patel, is Carter Page. "If Page really did what the dossier claims, then that's bad. That's what you get a FISA for: a US person who is believed to be acting as a foreign agent and commits a crime."

Page first appears in the dossier in two memos from the mid-July period. Report 94, dated July 19, alleges that Page met secretly with Rosneft CEO Igor Sechin during his trip to Moscow in early July. According to Steele, they discussed dropping sanctions in exchange for bilateral energy cooperation. Page has denied the allegations since they were first relayed to him in late July 2016.

What the FBI knew about Page, however, made him a more attractive target for a FISA warrant. In 2013, Russian operatives working out of the Russian UN Consulate in New York had tried, unsuccessfully, to recruit Page. The former navy officer had helped the FBI make its case against the spies, but he was in the system for a Russia-related espionage matter. The FBI twisted that information to mislead the secret court to obtain the warrant.

"The biggest tool for counterintelligence investigations is a FISA," says Patel. "So once an investigation is opened, you pick the easiest target to get a FISA on, even if it's not the actual person you want."

Page was the point of entry to gain access to the communications of the Trump team. The dossier, synchronized with Fusion GPS's media narrative around Page, was what the Crossfire Hurricane team used to jimmy the lock.

The July 19 Steele report alleging that Page had had a "secret meeting" with Sechin checked off an important box for the FISA application process. A warrant is granted to find out about the target's clandestine activities on behalf of a foreign power. To obtain a FISA on a US citizen also requires showing probable cause that those clandestine activities involve or may involve a crime. There is no crime alleged in the July 19 memo. The substance of Page's supposed meeting is not criminal. Removing sanctions on Russia in exchange for bilateral energy cooperation would be a matter of policy.

The criminal predicate for the FISA warrant was introduced subsequently, in a memo, Report 134, dated almost exactly three months later, October 18. Report 134 is a revision of the July 19 memo that was directed by someone who knew the requirements for obtaining a FISA. The October 18 version described the same meeting in early July and appears to be related by the same "intimate" of Sechin's who had reported the meeting to Steele's intermediary in July.

This time, however, Sechin's "close associate" provided a different account. Instead of offering bilateral energy cooperation in exchange for convincing Trump to relieve sanctions, Sechin tells Page that he will profit personally. According to the memo, Page was offered "the brokerage of up to a 19% (privatised) stake in Rosneft in return."

That's bribery. The scheme would have made Page a wealthy man. The brokerage fee would have amounted to at least tens of millions of dollars as a percentage of a deal worth more than $10 billion.

Adam Schiff and media pundits claimed that Rosneft's eventual sale of a 19 percent stake proved the veracity of the dossier. However, the 19 percent figure would have been easy to pull off the internet. By spring 2016, it was widely reported that Russia was looking to sell off between 19 and 19.5 percent of Rosneft. Nevertheless, the figure may have proved persuasive to the FISA court; a specific number is more persuasive than vague allegations of a bag of cash.

The Trump adviser, according to Steele, "expressed interest and confirmed that were Trump elected US president, then sanctions on Russia would be lifted." The memo tied Page's potentially criminal actions to Trump himself. According to Steele's source, Page was "speaking with the Republican candidate's authority."

The July 19 memo regarding Sechin and Page's meeting is documented word for word, as if it had been cut and pasted from the dossier into the FISA application. The allegations are repeated in the three subsequent FISA application renewals. However, the revised October 18 memo alleging bribery is not apparent in any of the four applications.

Since it is the later memo, alleging a potential crime in connection with clandestine intelligence activities, that fulfills the requirements of a FISA warrant, it is likely that the information is under redaction. It is not hard to see why the FBI and DOJ would seek to conceal the fact that a falsified document dated October 18 was used to obtain a secret surveillance warrant three days later, October 21.

Patel says the money that Page was supposed to have collected from the deal with Sechin was another aspect of the dossier that could be found to be true or false. "It's hundreds of millions of dollars," he says. "You could find out if Page has that kind of money. We called him in and spoke with him. He obviously didn't have that kind of money. It was clear the story in the dossier was nonsense."

The purpose of HPSCI's Russia collusion investigation was to find out if anyone in the Trump campaign had really made deals with the Russians. But if the supposed linchpin of the Trump-Russia collusion scheme was innocent, what was the evidence?

Patel's next step was to collect all the investigative documents surrounding Crossfire Hurricane. "I knew I had to get the documents leading to the production of the FISA," he says. "I wanted to know what the government knew, when they knew it, and if there were any material omissions in the FISA application."

Once they secured the documents from the FBI, Patel and the Intelligence Committee moved to interviews to get people on the record. Did anyone have proof that the Trump team had colluded with Russia?

"I had to tell a lot of people that collusion isn't a crime," says Patel. "It sounds bad, but it doesn't exist, it's a legal fiction. But I was like, okay, we've got to use that because it's in the media and everybody's already using it."

The important thing was to determine if there had been any criminal activity. Patel, along with HPSCI members Trey Gowdy, Tom Rooney, and Mike Conaway, and their staff came up with the "three Cs": collude, conspire, coordinate.

"Conspiracy is a real crime," says Jim. "Coordination isn't a crime, but it was a way to explain in layman's terms a predicate for conspiracy. So did anyone see any coordination between the Trump team and Russia?"

Nunes's committee interviewed officials from the Obama administration, the law enforcement and intelligence communities, and the Trump campaign. It was the same line of questioning for all of them.

"We asked them the three Cs straight up," says Patel.

He runs down a partial list:

"'Do you, Attorney General Loretta Lynch, have evidence of the three Cs?'

"'No, I don't.'

"'Do you, Deputy Attorney General Sally Yates?'

"'No.'

"'Do you, Jim Comey?'

"'No.'

"'Do you, Andy McCabe?'

"'No.'

"'Do you, John Podesta?'

"'No.'

"'Do you, Glenn Simpson of Fusion GPS?'

"'No.'"

A number of witnesses tried to sidestep Patel's line of questioning.

"And I said, 'Hang on. I'm not asking if you thought it happened or if you heard it happened,'" Patel says. "I said, 'Do you have information that exactly addresses this issue? If you tell me it exists, we'll go get the documents, we'll go get the people, we'll use subpoenas.' We weren't hired to clear Donald Trump. We were charged with figuring out what happened."

The investigation, he says, was going to reveal whether there was collusion or not. "It's a finite question. We weren't trying to solve an unsolvable murder. Donald Trump got elected. We knew the Russians definitely did some squirrely stuff, hacked some things and whatnot. The issue was, was there evidence that anyone from the Trump campaign said anything to the Russians like 'Trump wants to be president, you help him, he'll help you down the road'? We asked every single person we interviewed, and not a single person answered affirmatively to that question."

There was nothing.

"So if no one had any evidence," says Patel, "including the principals that were running the investigation, then maybe it didn't happen. It became evident that the answer was no across the board. I didn't expect to find that clean of an answer. But we did."

If there was no evidence of collusion, conspiracy, or coordination, what had happened? The FBI had opened an investigation on the Trump campaign and had obtained a surveillance warrant without any real evidence. Something was very wrong.

Patel had already warned Nunes and the staff that they were going to find irregularities in what the FBI and DOJ had done. "Once we discovered bad action by FBI and DOJ, our driving force became proving what they knew and when they knew it, especially when it came to the Carter Page FISA," he says. "Misleading the Foreign Intelligence Surveillance Court is a seriously grave offense for which there must be accountability. And we felt the evidence would speak for itself; the fight was obtaining it for the public to see.

"I said from the beginning that Jim Comey and Andy McCabe are not squared away guys," he adds. "I knew that something was up."

Not everyone saw it that way, says Patel's investigative partner. "Many of these people coming from the IC, especially Comey, had gotten a lot of mileage out of being the source of disclosures to members and had given the appearance of candor. This is the guy who comes and tells us secret stuff," says Jim. "The inclination was to trust him."

But Patel had worked with Comey and the others. "You cannot put on paper the value of sitting in a room with people," he says. "My job has always been to read people. I was a trial lawyer. I had to read juries. I was pretty good at being able to read people and find their biases. I said the same thing when I was running this investigation: 'I know these guys, I know their biases. I've been in a room with them. They present well. But they have agendas. And they tailor their investigations to reflect those agendas, at least the high-profile ones.'"

The fundamental problem with the Crossfire Hurricane investigation was the Crossfire Hurricane group. Now it was time for the Nunes team to pivot; they were going to investigate the investigators.

"I told Devin that our investigation is going to be a thing," says Patel. "I told him we needed a name. It's going to be big."

HPSCI was investigating Russia collusion, but now it was turning its attention to what law enforcement authorities might have done during the course of Crossfire Hurricane: unmasking, FISA abuses, and other related matters.

"There are so many parts to this," Patel remembers telling Nunes. "There were so many snakes on one head. I told Devin, 'We need to cut off the head, like Medusa.' So that's what I called it: 'Objective Medusa.' It was our thing."

Chapter 14

THE PAPER COUP

PATEL'S WARNINGS about the FBI's top echelon were starting to make an impact. Nunes had had his suspicions about Comey and McCabe previously, but his awakening came soon after Patel joined.

"I expressed my concerns about the unmaskings in March," Nunes remembers. "I wanted to speak to the FBI director and called him repeatedly. A month later I see Comey coming in for an informational meeting on Russia, and I told him I'd been trying to get ahold of him to look into the unmasking."

The FBI director lied to him. "Comey says, 'Oh, if I'd only known, Mr. Chairman, I'd have called right away.' So that's when I knew he was crooked. He wouldn't meet me to discuss unmasking because clearly his guys are involved in it. He's a liar and a con man."

Patel acknowledges that his perspective on the FBI's top two officials went against the grain. The FBI is a respected institution, and Comey had cultivated a following not only in the law enforcement community but also among the press and bureaucracy intellectuals, such as Benjamin Wittes, a fellow at the Brookings Institution and editor in chief of Lawfare, a national security blog. Wittes played a large role in pushing the collusion narrative through his blog and on Twitter, where he posted images of cannon going off—Boom!—every time a new leak promised to topple Trump. He continued to promote his friends in law enforcement even after the scale of their abuses and crimes became clear.

Patel says he understands why so many of his new colleagues initially defended Comey and McCabe: "Comey's the director of the FBI and McCabe's his deputy. They must be as good as they say they are."

Patel stipulates that they were good lawyers and good agents, but there was something wrong with the self-images they'd created. The problem was more than vanity, it was hubris.

Virtually every meeting room in Washington is packed with men and women who are vying to be smartest in the room. What made Comey and McCabe different was the power they had at their disposal to arrange the world in accordance with their preferences. They could shape reality. They could destroy the president with an investigation. Imagine what they could do to anyone else who got into their crosshairs.

"They'd inverted the principles of constitutional democracy," says Patel's investigative partner, Jim. "In their view, elected officials were accountable to unaccountable bureaucrats."

Comey and the Crossfire Hurricane team thought they could decide an election. "Comey sees himself as the protector of America," says Patel. "He has an ego that can't fit on planet Earth. McCabe was his protégé, and they thought the world of each other, and they would say that publicly every chance they got."

Patel saw something else: "McCabe was overseeing the Clinton investigation after his wife got nearly seven hundred thousand dollars from Clinton allies for her run at a state senate seat. That's a lot of money. And they never thought that was a problem. McCabe didn't think to recuse himself from the email investigation."

Instead, says Jim, "McCabe fought recusal tooth and nail. He thought he was above reproach because his boss did."

"Comey said they weren't going to prosecute Hillary for leaks of classified information, when the whole world knew that she'd leaked classified information," says Patel. "And they went back and forth on whether or not she intended to leak it. It was a total fabrication, because the statute requires no intent. And so I thought, if they did it there, and knowing how they operate, it's possible they did something here, too, while investigating another presidential campaign."

That fact alone still brings Patel up short. "Comey had both presidential candidates under investigation. That's J. Edgar Hoover style."

Nunes had become convinced that Comey was a con man after he'd lied to his face in April. But he knew there was something wrong with FBI director Comey's March 20 testimony in front of HPSCI. "We'd been hearing since the election about Trump and Russia," he says. "It's everywhere in the press. I wanted to get his testimony because I wanted to do as much in public as possible to force them to say they didn't have anything. I thought Comey would be a calming influence. I thought he would answer questions and say, 'Okay, we're interviewing a few people, but this is not about the president.'"

But because the Crossfire Hurricane team had nothing on Trump and because of all the evidence of their own wrongdoings, Comey had to stay on offense.

"The March 20 hearing was to give the FBI a chance to come clean," says Nunes. "'Okay, what do you have? You got nothing, and we know it because you never showed it to us.' We were calling his bluff," says Nunes. "And Comey doubled down."

After the chairman made a brief introduction, ranking member Adam Schiff took the microphone. Allocated five minutes, Schiff spent nearly twenty legitimizing a conspiracy theory by reading the dossier into the *Congressional Record* and parceling out other parts of the dossier to Democratic members. He cited Steele, whose "Russian sources tell him that [Carter] Page has also had a secret meeting with Igor Sechin." Further, said Schiff, "according to Steele, it was Manafort who chose Page to serve as a go-between for the Trump campaign and Russian interests." He then set the stage for Comey's big revelation: the FBI director, he said, "may or may not be willing to disclose even whether there is an investigation."

Comey thanked the committee, then made his move:

> *I have been authorized by the Department of Justice to confirm that the FBI, as part of our counterintelligence mission, is investigating the Russian government's efforts to interfere in the 2016 presidential election and that includes investigating the nature of any links between individuals associated with the Trump campaign and the Russian government and whether there was any coordination between the campaign and Russia's efforts.*

Nunes was surprised. "I had no idea he was going to pull that stunt," says the congressman. "Comey leaves the whole world with the impression they were investigating Trump while playing word games that they were only investigating the campaign."

Nunes later came to realize that Comey's testimony had drawn a larger circle around the anti-Trump operation. "At the time we didn't know the FBI was in on it," he says. "We knew Obama people were, because of Obama's dossier. But we thought the FBI was clean."

The FBI had been investigating Trump and his associates since winter 2015–2016. It had been monitoring Carter Page's communications for five months at that point and still had nothing to tie Trump to the Kremlin. If the conspirators were going to topple Trump, they needed another instrument. Comey supplied it.

In announcing the investigation, Comey set a trap: if Trump fired him, he'd become vulnerable to charges of obstructing an ongoing investigation.

It was the first in a series of obstruction traps designed to hem in the president. Any attempt at self-preservation, to flush out the conspirators who were determined to end his presidency, would only put him in further danger.

The plotters were counting on the apprentice chief executive to make a mistake. In the meantime, they'd buy themselves enough time and maybe find something else they could use to remove him from the White House. He wasn't their president, so he wasn't really the president at all.

"A successful coup," says Edward Luttwak, the author of *Coup d'État: A Practical Handbook*, "requires the conspirators to take over a small but sufficient part of the government apparatus. For instance, if the country has a million soldiers but they are on remote fronts, a garrison of three thousand men in the capital can make and unmake governments."

Imagine that the top military brass is plotting to overthrow the commander in chief. Now move them out of the Pentagon and drop them into the same high-level posts—number ones, their deputies, deputy assistants, and so on—at the Justice Department and Federal Bureau of Investigation. It would be a bloodless uprising, not a military putsch. They'd encircle the White House not with tanks but with paper: memos, letters, and legal documents as well as falsified reports, such as the Steele Dossier.

Also news stories. The media, as Luttwak wrote in his 1968 book, are central to the success of any coup: "Control over the mass media emanating from the political center will still be our most important weapon in establishing our authority after the coup."

In this case, the conspirators already had access to as much media as they needed. They'd been feeding Trump-Russia propaganda to their accomplices in the press corps for more than a year.

"The anti-Trump operation," says Luttwak today, "was a very American coup, with TV denunciations by seemingly authoritative figures as a key instrument."

The plot against Trump was a bureaucratic insurgency waged almost entirely through the printed word. It was the "Paper Coup."

The earliest evidence of the operation was in print: the press reports alleging the Trump circle's ties to Russia. The dossier, more paper, moved in tandem with the espionage campaign, dispatching operatives to dirty the Trump team with promises of information damaging to Clinton.

Even their dangles were documents: Clinton emails, specifically. Press accounts were used to secure more paper, a FISA warrant, that magnified the Crossfire Hurricane team's surveillance powers.

After Trump's election, Obama ordered the intelligence community assessment, an official document that produced more media reports and legitimized more spying on the Trump administration. News reports of the dossier opened up more channels for the Crossfire Hurricane team to spy on the Trump presidency.

And now Comey's testimony would engender more paperwork: memos, reports, testimony, leaks of classified information, legal strategies, more news stories. In the hands of the conspirators, veterans of countless bureaucratic wars, it was all the ammunition they needed.

———————

Senate Democrats, led by Judiciary Committee ranking member Dianne Feinstein, had been clamoring for a special counsel to oversee the Russia probe since Sessions had recused himself on March 2. Judiciary Committee chairman Chuck Grassley recommended that the decision be left to Trump's nominee for deputy attorney general, Rod Rosenstein. "Once confirmed, Mr. Rosenstein can decide how to handle it," said Grassley. "I know of no reason to question his judgment, integrity, or impartiality."

Trump was eagerly waiting confirmation of his new deputy attorney general. With Sessions out of the picture and DOJ still controlled by Obama appointees, he didn't dare move against Comey. But he was losing his patience.

In a March 30 phone call, Trump had asked Comey about his testimony ten days before. The president said it would be great if Comey could say publicly that he wasn't himself under investigation. He asked the FBI director several times to find a way to get that out.

Comey reminded Trump that he had already told him he wasn't being investigated. He'd said so during the January 6 briefing about the dossier. Again in April, the president asked if Comey could say that he personally wasn't under investigation. Comey told him to go speak to DOJ about it.

Comey was brushing off the president, just as he had ignored Nunes's requests to speak about the unmaskings. And, like the HPSCI chair, Trump came to understand that Comey, as Patel put it, wasn't a squared-away guy.

If the president wasn't under investigation but his subordinates or associates were, why didn't the FBI provide him a defensive briefing to warn him of who might be compromised? It seems that everyone in the White House was getting defensive briefings about attempts to compromise the administration except the president.

A memo that Comey wrote to document his conversations with Trump records that two FBI agents gave defensive briefings to someone on the White House staff on February 8. On February 10, McCabe provided a defensive briefing to the vice president's staff. What was going on? Strzok and Page had texted each other about using defensive briefings as a pretext to collect intelligence on Trump.

Comey kept Trump in the dark. Trump had asked for his FBI director's loyalty, and Comey was instead working against him. Comey would have to go.

Soon after taking his post on April 26, Rosenstein wrote a memo that would justify cutting the FBI chief loose. Trump attached the memo to his own letter thanking Comey for "informing me, on three separate occasions, that I am not under investigation." Rosenstein's memo focused on procedure. "The Director was wrong," he wrote, "to usurp the Attorney General's authority" in announcing that the investigation of Hillary Clinton's server "should be closed without prosecution."

Rosenstein was absolutely right, says Patel. "That's the call of the prosecutor, not the agents." That was the last time Objective Medusa's lead investigator agreed with the new deputy attorney general, who was a gifted bureaucrat but temperamentally ill suited to the highly politicized environment of the moment.

Democrats criticized Rosenstein for supplying the rationale to oust Comey. He didn't understand why he was being blamed, and he lost his bearings.

"He did the right thing," says Nunes. "But he couldn't handle the pressure coming at him from the Democrats, the anti-Trump Republicans, and the press, so he panicked."

Comey's firing initiated what has come to be known as the "Nine Days in May." It's a reference to John Frankenheimer's *Seven Days in May*, the 1964 film about US military and political officials intending to stage a coup in a week's time.

In Trump's case, the nine days constituted the critical period from May 9 to 17, during which the highest levels of US law enforcement deliberated over how best to seize power from the president.

One option was to strike quickly.

Rosenstein, reportedly dejected and isolated from his peers, was eager to regain the favor of the colleagues whose boss he'd fired. He raised with McCabe and others the possibility of recording Trump.

The aim was to gather evidence to convince administration principals to invoke the Twenty-fifth Amendment, stipulating that the president may be removed from office when the vice president and a majority of the cabinet declare that he or she is unable to discharge his duties.

Rosenstein also suggested that McCabe and other FBI officials interviewing for the now-vacant director's job might record Trump. How? Rosenstein said that the White House never checked his phone for meetings there.

Rosenstein thought he could get at least two cabinet members to agree to remove Trump. That option was discarded as too impractical. Instead, the conspirators took the path that Comey had laid out by testifying before HPSCI: to tie up Trump with an investigation and set him up for an obstruction of justice charge.

Even after having been involuntarily returned to private life, Comey played an important role in the Paper Coup. Hours after he was fired, Strzok texted Page: "We need to open the case we've been waiting on now while Andy is acting."

Thus McCabe opened an investigation on Trump after Comey was let go for failing to state publicly that Trump was not under investigation. The acting FBI director said he had been worried about what might happen to the Russia case if he were removed. "Was the work," McCabe asked himself, "on solid ground?" He said he "wanted to protect the Russia investigation in such a way that whoever came after [him] could not just make it go away."

McCabe knew that Trump was unlikely to choose him to replace Comey. And it was possible that the next FBI director would deprioritize or even discontinue the investigation. To lock it in, he urged Rosenstein to name a special counsel. Even if Trump hired a loyalist for the director's job or McCabe was fired, the investigation would continue.

Appointed by the Department of Justice, the special counsel would now be under the control of the official overseeing the Russia probe, Rod Rosenstein. The deputy attorney general would now fulfill his promises of goodwill to the Crossfire Hurricane team.

The strategy required an assist from Comey himself. He said he had asked a friend to leak to the *New York Times* his memos, including one commemorating "the president's February 14 direction that I drop the Flynn investigation." Comey said he had been sure that that would get a special counsel named to the case.

On May 16, the *Times* published Michael Schmidt's story sourced to Comey's leak of classified information. The next day,

Rosenstein wrote a memo appointing former FBI director Robert Mueller III special counsel.

Comey's predecessor at the FBI would continue Comey's investigation. From paper to paper to paper, McCabe, Comey, Rosenstein, and Mueller had put the Paper Coup onto solid ground.

At that point nearly any attempt by Trump to discharge his duties as commander in chief—by firing Mueller, for instance— would have led to obstruction of justice charges. Even though DOJ protocol forbids prosecuting a sitting president, Congress could use Mueller's finding as the basis for impeachment proceedings and continued investigations of Trump through the framework of alleged obstruction.

Comey's memos of his conversations with Trump unintentionally draw a sympathetic portrait of a Beltway novice who was trying to find his footing in the White House and sought advice from experienced bureaucrats.

Trump didn't realize at first that they were out to humiliate him, then depose him. He invited Comey to bring his family to dinner at the White House. The FBI director left an awkward silence for the commander in chief to fill. "Or a tour," said Trump, "whatever you think is appropriate."

Trump complained about the leaked transcripts of his conversations with the leaders of Australia and Mexico. "It makes us look terrible to have these things leaking," he said. He talked about the leak of Flynn's conversation with the Russian ambassador. He said that Flynn hadn't said anything wrong while speaking to Kislyak. He told Comey that he *hoped* he could let it go. The wording was inherently nonobstructive; the president could have *directed* Comey to let it go.

Trump told Comey that he was upset about the "golden shower" story, especially how it had made his wife feel. He said "it bothered him if his wife thought there was even a one percent chance it was true in any respect." He confided to Comey, "It has been very painful."

He asked Comey if the FBI should investigate the Steele Dossier. Comey discouraged him, saying it "would create a narrative that we were investigating him personally."

Comey was lying. The FBI had in fact used the dossier as the road map in its nearly yearlong investigation of Trump. Comey was protecting himself and the Crossfire Hurricane team. A genuine investigation of how the dossier had been funded and assembled would have cleared Trump—and revealed the nature of the Clinton-sponsored operation against him.

That's why the work of the Objective Medusa team was essential: Comey's FBI was crooked.

Trump asked Comey to say he wasn't being investigated. It was bad for everyone. He said "he was trying to make deals for the country, the cloud was hurting him." He assumed that Comey wanted the same for America and implored him to help by getting out word that the president wasn't under investigation. Trump was insistent—it was hurting his ability to serve Americans. He was trying, he said, "to do work for the country, visit with foreign leaders, and any cloud, even a little cloud, gets in the way of that."

Finally, he understood that Comey didn't see things that way. Comey saw him not as the president but as a target. "There's no way in their minds that Jim Comey and Andy McCabe's United States of America would elect this guy to be the president," says Patel.

Trump wasn't their president. And the America that had elected him was beneath contempt. They were keen to impose their perverted fantasies on the public consciousness and show

Trump supporters that the president they had chosen was a man who hired prostitutes to urinate on a hotel bed.

"The Russia investigation gave them everything they needed to delegitimize the election of Donald Trump," says Patel. "As soon as he was elected, as soon as this stuff started coming out, they're like 'Okay, we knew he didn't win fairly. Now we have our angle.'"

I ask the Operation Medusa investigators if it's possible that the DOJ and FBI really believed Trump was a Russian spy.

"They could believe Trump is a Russian spy," says Jim. "That was within the realm of the believable. What they couldn't believe was that he could win the presidency."

Did Patel also believe that was true of some of his former DOJ colleagues? "All the people involved did," says Patel. "They banked on finding Donald Trump in league with Putin. Absolutely. They thought it's just a matter of time until we find it. They had to believe it. This is how they think. They ran with it to the media, and they all thought they were going to find the equivalent of the Watergate tapes. It was just a matter of time."

But Trump had worked in New York City for forty years. His businesses—real estate and casinos—must have attracted the attention of the FBI's New York field office, as well as the New York Police Department. If there had been anything there, the FBI would have known long before.

"The FBI guys out in the field every day aren't running the show," says Patel. "It's James Comey, Andrew McCabe, Peter Strzok, Lisa Page. I worked with these people. I know their methodology."

The Greeks believed that Hubris begets Nemesis, the goddess of retribution. She settles scores with the arrogant, those who relish the public degradation, the shame they bring on others. It wasn't just Trump who was dragged through the mud to delegitimize his presidency but his supporters as well, half the country.

Yet it was all of America that paid the cost Comey and the Crossfire Hurricane team incurred. "After weeks and months, as they realized they had nothing on Trump and Russia," says Patel, "they told themselves, 'Okay, we probably misfired on this one, but we're going to keep running with this narrative because half of America believes it anyway.' And that's what split America apart."

Chapter 15

DIRTY COPS

ON MAY 17, Rod Rosenstein and Andrew McCabe called for a Gang of Eight briefing in a secure facility at the Capitol. When Nunes arrived, McCabe told Rosenstein he was worried that the briefing was going to get back to Trump. The acting FBI director wanted the chairman of the House Intelligence Committee gone from the room and prompted the deputy attorney general to act like a nightclub bouncer to keep him out.

Rosenstein asked Nunes to step outside. "He asked me if I could be in the room," says Nunes. "I said, 'Why can't I be in the room?' He insinuated that someone wanted me gone from the room. I said, 'I don't know who told you that, but whoever it is, they can get the hell out of the room.'"

Nunes saw what they were up to. "They were obstructing our congressional investigation into their abuses."

That was only the half of it. "McCabe said in his book he was worried about me leaking and reporting back to Trump," says Nunes. "McCabe was looking for a way to stick me in the middle of one of the obstruction traps they were setting for the president."

With Comey's March 20 testimony, the Crossfire Hurricane group put aside collusion and moved to setting obstruction of justice traps. Nunes figured out that they had seen him as bait for one of the snares they'd set for Trump.

"They were just waiting for me to talk to the president, but I never spoke with the president or any other White House staff about the Russia investigation. I limited my conversations with the White House to tax reform and San Joaquin Valley issues."

Nunes wasn't leaving the room.

Rosenstein briefed the congressional leaders on his decision to name Robert Mueller to lead the special counsel. It was a continuation of the investigation that Comey had announced in his HPSCI testimony two months before, Crossfire Hurricane.

McCabe told them that the FBI had opened an investigation on a sitting president. FBI leadership had determined Trump might be a Russian agent.

What evidence was there for such a sensational claim? Maybe, the Bureau's top men and women conjectured, Trump had fired Comey at the behest of the Russian government. Maybe it was something else. It didn't matter; it was part of the game plan to set as many obstruction traps as possible.

It was further evidence that there was something very wrong at the top levels of the FBI. "At that point we already know the Crossfire Hurricane team is dirty," says Nunes. "So when Mueller came on, we were thinking, Okay, now we have a grown-up to take charge."

Nunes's initial optimism soon soured. "I thought Mueller would say, 'Look, there was no collusion because there's no evidence of it.' And that would be the end of it. I thought the special counsel would get the politics out of the investigation. But instead Mueller made it even more political."

The premise of the special counsel investigation was political. There was no need to continue the counterintelligence investigation of Russian interference in the 2016 election if the January 2017 ICA had already determined that the Russians had interfered—and with the purpose of helping Trump. If the IC had been looking to hold the Russian government accountable, that would best have been done far from the spotlight, where US intelligence officials could most efficiently respond to the Kremlin's actions.

Nunes says he'd thought that Mueller would investigate the leaks—especially the ones that had led to Flynn's leaving the White House. Instead, the scores of lawyers and agents that the special counsel added to the original Crossfire Hurricane team increased by many times the possible sources of leaks.

An early and important Mueller-era leak went to the *Washington Post* for a June 14 article reporting that Mueller was investigating Trump for obstruction. According to the story—bylined by Devlin Barrett, Adam Entous, Ellen Nakashima, and Sari Horwitz—the special counsel was particularly interested in a March meeting between Trump and his newly named director of national intelligence, Daniel Coats.

That was sourced to a *Post* story based on a leak of a meeting between the president and an intelligence chief; Entous's June 9 story had reported that Trump had asked Coats to intervene with Comey to let Flynn alone.

The Nunes team soon saw that the special counsel was simply a continuation of the slow coup. It even included members of the Crossfire Hurricane team, including the FBI couple Peter Strzok and Lisa Page. But even Strzok privately admitted that the case was a wash. He'd hesitated to join the special counsel, as he texted Page, "because of my gut sense and concern there's no big there there."

The most important thing to know about the special counsel investigation is that by the time Mueller came on, the FBI had been monitoring Trump communications for seven months. Since October 21, it had been looking for just one email or phone call and had come up with nothing. Mueller could have wrapped up the collusion investigation on May 18. Instead, the anti-Trump operation marched on, with the same people and even more power and resources.

McCabe was now the acting director of the FBI. Christopher Steele was still around, too. Right after Comey had been fired, McCabe had reached out to him through Bruce Ohr.

The new funding source for the external operation was the Democracy Integrity Project (DIP), run by former Dianne Feinstein aide Daniel Jones. DIP paid Fusion GPS, which Jones called a "shadow media organization," at least $3.3 million to continue its work, while Steele received $250,000. Another Fusion GPS contractor for the Trump-Russia project, Edward Baumgartner, was paid $125,000.

The special counsel investigation was a show trial to punish Trump associates. It was conducted behind closed doors so that the Mueller team could shape the narrative through a continued campaign of leaks. With limitless resources, Mueller was accountable only to Rosenstein, the deputy attorney general whose actions were shaped by his fearful responses to the kind of "resistance" activists with whom Mueller had stacked the special counsel.

"It was a team of dirty cops," says Nunes. "Andrew Weissmann was the worst. He already had a history as a hard-core anti-Trump partisan."

Weissmann, a senior DOJ official, had made his political preferences clear by attending Clinton's ultimately disappointing election-night party. After Trump fired Deputy Attorney General

Sally Yates for refusing to defend the Muslim travel ban in court, Weissmann wrote her a congratulatory note. "I am so proud," he wrote in the subject line. "And in awe," he continued in the body of the email. "Thank you so much. All my deepest respects."

Weissmann knew about the Steele Dossier. Bruce Ohr had briefed him and Zainab Ahmad, another lawyer named to the special counsel investigation, in the summer of 2016 about Steele and Simpson's work.

The special counsel team was a hunting party of more than a dozen Clinton and Obama activists who'd accepted Mueller's invitation to shoot Trump associates in a barrel.

- Jeannie Rhee had donated more than $16,000 to Democrats since 2008. She'd defended Hillary Clinton in a 2015 lawsuit seeking access to her private emails. Rhee also represented the Clinton Foundation in a racketeering lawsuit and Ben Rhodes during the House Select Committee on Benghazi investigation.

  For a time, Rhee represented Clinton associates for HPSCI's Russia investigation. Her joining the special counsel was an obvious conflict of interest.
- Aaron Zebley, Mueller's former chief of staff at the FBI, represented Justin Cooper, a former Clinton aide who had helped set up Hillary's private email server and destroyed her electronic devices with a hammer.
- Greg Andres donated $2,700 to Senator Kirsten Gillibrand's 2018 campaign. Andres's wife, Ronnie Abrams, a US district judge in Manhattan, had been nominated to the bench in 2011 by Obama.
- Andrew Goldstein contributed a combined $3,300 to Obama's campaigns in 2008 and 2012.

- Kyle Freeny contributed a total of $500 to Obama's presidential campaigns and $250 to Hillary Clinton's.
- Rush Atkinson donated $200 to Clinton's 2016 campaign.
- Kevin Clinesmith was an FBI lawyer who'd worked on Crossfire Hurricane as well as Midyear Exam. His text exchanges with colleagues after Trump's election are indicative of the Mueller team's sensibility.

"I am numb," Clinesmith wrote after the election. "I am so stressed about what I could have done differently."

Everything he held most dear was at risk—which was what? The peace and security of his fellow Americans? Their fundamental liberties? The Constitution? No, the policies of the previous president.

"I just can't imagine the systematic disassembly of the progress we made over the last 8 years," he texted colleagues.

The work of law enforcement officials was to use the resources of the federal government to ensure that taxpayers didn't stand in the way of the progress of which they were too ignorant to be grateful.

"We have to fight this again," Clinesmith wrote. "Viva le resistance [sic]."

The special counsel investigation was the instrument he and his colleagues would use to rewrite history and undo an election.

For Mueller it was personal. If the job of the special counsel required covering up the abuses of power and subsequent crimes committed by US intelligence officials and the Obama administration, it was a small price to pay. As the father of the post-9/11 FBI, he had been partly responsible for the dominant culture of the FBI's upper echelon. He was protecting his legacy.

A week after Mueller started as FBI director on September 4, 2001, his job description abruptly changed. The post-9/11 FBI had to be able to prevent terrorist attacks, which meant, according to the Bureau's website, that it "needed to be more forward-leaning, more predictive, a step ahead of the next germinating threat."

Mueller set about transforming the United States' federal law enforcement organization into an intelligence agency.

Equally important, 9/11 further centralized the Bureau. A natural consequence of bulking up headquarters to coordinate with other agencies as well as foreign governments on counterterrorism operations was that the Bureau wielded more influence.

The FBI was the central piece not only protecting the national interest but also preventing the overriding worry of the political class—another massive terror attack on the homeland—from becoming reality. Power, money, and prestige flowed from throughout the Beltway to the Bureau.

Retired FBI agent Mark Wauck says the corporatization of the FBI was under way long before the 2001 attacks. "William Webster was appointed to run the Bureau in 1978," says Wauck, who joined the FBI the same year. "He was a federal judge who didn't know how to run a law enforcement agency, so he used a management model that IBM pioneered: management by objectives. This had an enormous effect on the FBI over the years."

The new model set goals and standards for achievement that had to be checked off before agents got promotions—e.g., subpoenas served, arrests, indictments, convictions. Further, explains Wauck, "the corporate model required agents to cycle back through headquarters every few years or so to advance their careers." Promotions flowed from FBI headquarters.

Wauck argues that 9/11 hastened the Bureau's entry into the intelligence community, but it had already been under way before Mueller took over. "The Hanssen thing started it," says Wauck. He's referring to FBI agent Robert Hanssen, who sold secrets to the Soviets, then the Russians, starting in 1979 until his apprehension in February 2001. "It was seen as a tremendous failure for the Bureau," adds Wauck, "and it was."

According to Wauck, the FBI had looked with disdain on the CIA after CIA officer Aldrich Ames had been arrested in 1994 for spying on behalf of Moscow. "The idea was that this was something Agency eggheads did," he says. "We at the FBI don't betray America. Then along comes Hanssen. It was a huge intelligence failure. We didn't know, and we kind of did."

Wauck knew, and he said something. It wasn't easy. Hanssen was his brother-in-law. Wauck prefers not to talk about the painful episode, except to note that his warnings were not heeded when he first identified Hanssen to his superiors as a potential problem in 1990.

Thus 9/11 echoed the Hanssen case. The 9/11 Commission Report faulted the FBI, the CIA, and the firewall that prevented them from sharing the intelligence with each other that might have saved American lives. In both cases, the information had been there but there had been no incentive to piece it together.

Thanks in part to the efforts of Mueller's FBI, there was no major catastrophic Islamic terror attack following 9/11. However, in its eagerness to prevent another major attack, the FBI became nearly fanatical in its pursuit of suspects.

Weeks after 9/11, anthrax mailed to various destinations killed five people and infected another seventeen, while shutting down Capitol Hill and Washington's mail system. *New York Times* columnist Nicholas Kristof published the ramblings of a conspiracy-minded college professor who identified a virologist named Steven Hatfill as the culprit.

Mueller told congressional leaders in January 2003 that bloodhounds trained to sniff anthrax had confirmed that Hatfill had been responsible for the letter attacks. He was wrong. Hatfill was cleared in 2008 and won a $5.8 million settlement from the US government. Having wasted millions of dollars of taxpayers' money without ever arresting the actual criminal, Mueller refused to admit that he or the FBI had erred.

Mueller was incapable of admitting he was wrong. In 2002, he directed his agents to oppose pardons for four wrongfully imprisoned Massachusetts men. They'd been framed by dirty FBI agents in order to protect one of their confidential sources, a Boston mobster who'd actually committed the murder for which the four men had been jailed. In 2006, the estates of the four men, two of whom had died in prison, were awarded $102 million for their wrongful decades-long imprisonment due to FBI misconduct.

Mueller was a zealot and his virtue a charity funded by the US public. Wauck remembers a talk he gave at Georgetown University a year after the former director left the FBI. "He said, 'I became a prosecutor because I like putting people in jail, and going through the trials,'" he recalls. "It's a remarkable statement. It shows a real detachment from other human beings. When I was dealing with criminals, even with what you might call lowlifes, I tried to see where they were coming from, at least that they were human beings. Most of them aren't monsters. Taking away someone's liberty is a big thing."

Mueller became a high priest of the Beltway bureaucracy. And the institution he led became a reflection of him, as well as the culture that had produced him.

"We do have a governing elite," says Wauck. "And it consists largely of lawyers. People who run executive agencies are lawyers, and the courts have taken an increasingly large role in determining how we live."

Wauck remembers the beginning of his law career and witnessing the change. "When I was in law school in the midseventies, they were proposing new theories of the law, even the concept of a trial," he says. "The traditional notion of a trial, the process of examination and cross-examination, was that it was the most powerful method for getting at the truth. But people started to scoff at that and the idea that there was any such thing as the truth."

That kind of relativism wasn't just in the law schools; it reflected larger trends in the entire country. "By the beginning of the twenty-first century, everyone had grown up with these ideas," says Wauck. "The bureaucracy mirrors where we are as a society."

Students who'd internalized those theories as undergrads found them reinforced in law school and were primed by the time they entered the workforce. Those who joined law enforcement seeded their values in the bureaucracy, US attorneys offices, Main Justice, and eventually the FBI.

"The Bureau was taken over by the legal elite," says Wauck. "Even a guy like McCabe is a lawyer. The FBI is run by former prosecutors: a Boston Republican, like Mueller, or guys from the Southern District of New York, like Comey."

But if prosecutions aren't for finding the truth, what was the point of going through with them, except as a statistic to be checked off before getting a promotion? "The law and law enforcement institutions became a tool for shaping the country according to the preferences of its governing elite," says Wauck.

This is how, explains Wauck, you get a figure like FBI lawyer Kevin Clinesmith worrying that the FBI hadn't done enough to protect Obama's policies. The special counsel was a team of legal activists using the law to advance the political inclinations and privileges of the United States' bureaucratic aristocracy. "The upper layers of the FBI," he says, "have become populated by people like that."

Mueller's show trials confirmed what many Americans already suspected: that in spite of all the fine rhetoric, we are not all equal under the law and the ruling class sees its own interests as being identical with the public good.

———————————

"DOJ is a great institution," says Patel. "Their one big problem is that they never admit they're wrong. And when you show them that they're wrong, they double down on it and it ends up screwing them. And that's how I won a lot of my federal public defender cases against the Justice Department. I'd find out what they did wrong and give them an out, and they wouldn't take it. And then the judge would be like 'You guys effed up. Kash, your clients can go home.'"

In midsummer, Patel was still looking for answers about Steele and his notorious reports. The lead Objective Medusa investigator saw an opportunity to learn more during a HPSCI staff trip to England.

Part of the committee's work under Nunes involved visiting sensitive intelligence sites around the world that were vital to the US intelligence community. "I went to England," says Patel, "with a former committee staff monitor, Doug Presley, to look into a topic that was very important to the committee."

Patel figured that as long as he was in Steele's vicinity, why not continue that work as well? He and Presley found a pleading in the British court system on behalf of Steele. He'd been sued for libel by Aleksej Gubarev, a Russian tech expert accused in a Steele memo of targeting DNC computer systems.

In the court filings, Steele had said he had briefed several news organizations—the *New York Times*, the *Washington Post*, CNN, *The New Yorker*, and Yahoo! News—in late summer to early fall 2016. Further, instead of attesting to the veracity of his Trump-Russia investigation, Steele had punted.

"His lawyers decided not to assert a truth defense," says Patel. "He said the intelligence he collected was raw and unverified. He had not put it through the process that he had learned as a professional, to analyze it, to run it against other things, tradecraft that you normally use to say whether this legit or not."

That was a significant admission, and Patel and Presley wanted to know more. They checked back at the home office to get the go-ahead to look into it. "I told Damon, 'Steele is represented by counsel,'" says Patel. "'So let's reach out to his lawyer and ask if Steele will participate in our Russia investigation since he and his dossier are central pieces of it.'"

Steele's lawyer was in London. On the day they were headed back to the United States, Patel and Presley stopped in at the lawyer's office. "We found she was unavailable and left contact information and asked if she could call us," says Patel. "We later found that we'd apparently upset her."

Langer steps in to explain how the story immediately began to circulate through the press, even as Patel was in midflight. "I started getting calls from multiple reporters at the same time, all with the same story," he says. "Patel and Presley flew to London to try to ambush Christopher Steele."

The point of the story was to show that the Nunes team was unethical because Patel and Presley had tried to approach Steele directly even though they knew he was represented by counsel. They later figured out how that particular piece of fake news had taken off. "Fusion GPS' attorney Joshua Levy was assisting Steele's lawyer," says Patel. "She called Levy, who started shopping the story, just making stuff up." Levy denies this.

Patel hit the ground to find himself in the middle of a manufactured story. "I land at Dulles, turn on my phone, and as I'm walking off the plane, my phone rings. 'Oh, hey, Kash, what's going on? This is Adam Goldman from the *New York Times*.' I've never talked with him before, and he says, 'Hey, what are you doing in London? I hear you're tracking down Steele.'"

Langer regrets that he wasn't able to keep Patel and the other HPSCI staff members out of the media storm. "It was my responsibility," he says. "It was my biggest regret that I couldn't protect my own guys. It's a hell of a thing for staffers to have their names splashed all over the media like Kash and Doug did. All they did was try to make contact with Steele's lawyer. But a lot like the Midnight Run story, it was spun as another example of the bizarre, out-of-control Nunes team."

He continues, "The press attacks on Kash were relentless. Not long after the London story appeared, The Daily Beast ran a piece quoting some anonymous source—obviously a HPSCI Democrat—calling Kash Nunes' 'Torquemada.'"

Patel's family and friends, as far away as India, wanted to know why he was the focus of so much negative press attention. "Every time they hit me with a manufactured story," says Patel. "I knew I was over the target."

He brushed it off and redoubled his efforts to get answers about Steele and his dossier. "After doing a lot of fraud cases and tracking terrorism finance networks at JSOC, I learned the easiest thing to do is go after the money," he says. "So I said, 'We have to find out who paid for this thing, because Steele didn't just do it and no one paid him. Maybe the government paid him or the Bureau paid him. Maybe the CIA paid him.' I was thinking of eighty-eight different possibilities. I was not thinking the DNC and the Hillary campaign paid him, because that was just insane."

HPSCI had previously tried to get Fusion GPS's records but without success. "We'd written letters to more than a hundred witnesses asking for documents, and many complied; a few did not, which was their right," Patel says. "When we got to Fusion GPS, they shut us down hard and fast immediately."

Patel decided to get Fusion GPS's financial records directly from its bank. But the committee was not accustomed to subpoenaing private, nongovernmental entities. Patel had to convince Nunes that it was the right way to go. He had two weeks of concentrated face time with the boss as they traveled together in the late summer.

Every August Nunes picks a part of the world to focus on as it relates to the committee's oversight duties. In the summer of 2017, he chose the Balkans. "We went to maybe ten countries," says Patel, "visiting with our folks, with foreign government officials, and seeing where we could assist further and what our guys on the ground needed. I spent every night for the entire two weeks, starting in Sarajevo, trying to convince Devin to issue a subpoena."

Nunes remembers that he and Patel were standing on the spot where Archduke Franz Ferdinand had been assassinated in 1914. "He's talking about this subpoena, and I looked at him and told him, 'Kash, you're going to get *me* shot.' If we were going to take a shot at them, we couldn't afford to miss."

Patel says he knew it was a pretty drastic step. "So I told him," Patel recalls, "'I think I know who paid for this thing, but I need a subpoena. If you give me this subpoena and I'm wrong, I'll tell you I was wrong, and you'll shut down this portion of the investigation, and I'll quit.'"

Nunes explains that he was enthusiastic about Patel's proposal but was calculating the political costs in case they misfired. "Kash had the legal stuff covered, but I had to think about the political dimensions," he says. "Any misstep we made could cost us the support we had from Republicans. Could you imagine if one time, one of these fake news stories were true?"

As the trip was winding down in northern Italy, Nunes gave Patel the green light. It was after a long day visiting the US Army Africa Command in Vicenza, a town just outside Venice, and the two Americans found themselves in an old-school Italian cafe on an empty square in the five-hundred-year-old town. "It looked like it was out of *The Godfather*," says Patel. "We're both drinking Negronis, and I realized it was a go with the subpoena. Devin looks at me and said, 'Okay, this makes sense. When we get back, we're going to do this.'"

Chapter 16

THE DEEP STATE DIGS IN

THE OBJECTIVE MEDUSA team scored its first big win in the fall of 2017. HPSCI litigated with Fusion GPS to get its bank records.

"That took months," says Patel. "We issued the subpoena, and finally the court called to say they were going to rule in our favor. The court said we were entitled to see the information, pursuant to our investigation."

Nunes was walking on the Capitol Hill grounds when he heard who had funded the dossier. "Jack called me to say it was the Clintons," he says. "And I said, 'Are you kidding me?' I was actually surprised they hadn't funded it through a super PAC, but they probably wanted to control it more directly."

Nunes thought that now that the dossier's funding had been made public, that would be the end of it, and their work was done. "You'd think that would have been the turning point," he says. "We showed how it had been paid for by Trump's political rivals, so obviously this thing couldn't be taken seriously anymore."

Nunes would be surprised several more times over the next year. No matter what he uncovered about the dossier and the anti-Trump operation, the Russiagate narrative lived on. In fact, the events of October were the first iteration of a pattern that was to be repeated frequently over the coming months.

First, as the Nunes team was zeroing in on a target, the press posted attacks from political operatives to delegitimize his committee's work—even before the media had a grasp of the details. After preemptive efforts to derail Objective Medusa investigators failed, the conspirators leaked details to the press in an effort to shape the news as favorably as possible. In that case, Nunes drew heat from congressional rivals immediately after issuing the subpoena for Fusion GPS's records. The HPSCI chairman, said one of the committee's Democrats, Eric Swalwell, was "trying to undermine the investigation."

Fusion GPS's lawyer took a shot, too. "This is a blatant attempt to undermine the reporting of the so-called 'dossier,'" said Joshua Levy, "even as its core conclusion of a broad campaign by the Russian government to influence the outcome of the 2016 presidential election has been confirmed by the US intelligence community and is now widely accepted as fact."

Shortly before the court's ruling, Fusion GPS broke the news via an anonymous, preemptive leak to the *Washington Post*'s Adam Entous, Devin Barrett, and Rosalind Helderman for an October 24 story.

The Hillary Clinton campaign and the Democratic National Committee helped fund research that resulted in a now-famous dossier containing allegations about President Trump's connections to Russia and possible coordination

*between his campaign and the Kremlin, people familiar
with the matter said.*

*Marc E. Elias, a lawyer representing the Clinton
campaign and the DNC, retained Fusion GPS, a Washington
firm, to conduct the research. . . .*

*Fusion GPS gave Steele's reports and other research
documents to Elias, the people familiar with the matter
said. It is unclear how or how much of that information
was shared with the campaign and the DNC and who in
those organizations was aware of the roles of Fusion GPS
and Steele. One person close to the matter said the campaign
and the DNC were not informed by the law firm of Fusion
GPS's role.*

In fact, Elias had briefed Clinton campaign manager Robby
Mook on the dossier. Further, the campaign had repeatedly released
statements timed to the release of articles sourced to Steele and
Fusion GPS's work.

For instance, there was the September 23, 2016, press release
posted shortly after Isikoff's story about Carter Page. Echoing
Steele, the Clinton campaign claimed that "Page met with a
sanctioned top Russian official to discuss the possibility of ending
U.S. sanctions against Russia under a Trump presidency."

An October 19 campaign press release repeated Steele's claims
about Page, rehearsed Fusion GPS talking points about Flynn at the
RT dinner, and even threw in a handful of names from the May 20
protodossier, such as Felix Sater.

The *Post* story caused some anxiety among media friends of
Fusion GPS who wondered why they hadn't been given the leak.
"Folks involved in funding this lied about it, and with sanctimony,

for a year," *New York Times* reporter Maggie Haberman complained on twitter.

"When I tried to report this story," tweeted her *Times* colleague Kenneth Vogel, "Clinton campaign lawyer [Marc Elias] pushed back vigorously, saying 'You (or your sources) are wrong.'"

In other words, even though major press organizations had known for more than a year that the dossier had been funded by the Clintons—but couldn't get it confirmed—they still wrote about it as though it were a genuine intelligence report.

Though the story upset rivalrous media operatives, the revelation of the funding source galvanized support on the right. "It wasn't that my colleagues were against me before that," says Nunes. "They figured after I came out about the unmasking that Obama officials had done something bad. But it wasn't easy to back me when the Left had me under an ethics cloud."

Now Republicans became more vocal. "But our eye was on the entire country," says Nunes. "We still couldn't get to critical mass— fifty percent of America plus one. If you have public opinion on your side, you can bust a whole bunch of things open. We weren't there."

In retrospect, it's easy to see why the anti-Trump operation couldn't stop. There were too many institutions invested in the enterprise to walk away. Chief among them were the Democratic Party and its corporate infrastructure, the press, and the Department of Justice.

———————————

Bank records showed that between May 24, 2016, and December 28, 2016, Perkins Coie paid Fusion GPS $1,024,408. "But they weren't the only law firm that was giving Fusion GPS money," says Patel.

Between March 7, 2016, and October 31, 2016, BakerHostetler paid Fusion $523,651 for its work with Russian lawyer Natalia Veselnitskaya.

The bank records showed that eight other law firms were also paying Fusion GPS. HPSCI's arrangement with the court prohibited the committee from releasing confidential information contained in the records.

Three journalists, their names were not released, who reported on Trump-Russia matters had been paid by Fusion GPS. Equally, if not more, significant were the journalists and media organizations that had paid Fusion GPS for information. "Lots of media entities and writers and authors were giving them money," says Patel. "Individual writers were paying Fusion GPS."

Fusion GPS was double dipping, charging media companies for the content that law firms were paying them to disseminate. Why not? Media organizations couldn't produce their own content, so they paid for material.

"Fusion GPS very successfully marketed itself as an information-gathering entity," says Patel. "And prior to this they kept below the radar, which is another talent of theirs. They didn't divulge their clientele." Further, he says, "they had a good network of contacts at high-end publications to whom they could offer their own network, like Christopher Steele or Bruce Ohr."

Both Steele and Ohr were on Fusion GPS's payroll. "Formally they were paying his wife, Nellie," says Patel. "But by extension they were paying the number four guy at DOJ."

———————————

The bank records showed that Nellie Ohr was one of Fusion GPS's contractors. She came on in October 2015 and was employed until

September 2016. She was paid $55 per hour for a total of $44,000—more than fair compensation for twenty weeks of part-time work.

Patel recalls that his partner was searching the internet for information about her and found a picture.

"Here's Nellie Ohr with her husband," Jim said aloud. "Bruce Ohr."

Patel jumped up from his seat and stared at the photo of the two together. "I said, 'What the hell?' I know Bruce, not personally but as the assistant deputy attorney general for organized crime," he says. "When I was a federal public defender, I had cases against his office. So we found online a photo of them together and an article and we're like 'What the hell?'"

The upper echelons at Justice hated Trump, says the former prosecutor. "If Nellie Ohr was working on this anti-Trump project, then I knew Bruce must be involved, too. It was one of those green-light moments."

Patel took his discovery to Nunes. "I said, 'Hey, by the way, the number four at the Justice Department is running this side investigation. Devin says, 'Okay, get out of my office if you're going to be drinking early.' I was like 'I'm telling you, sir. I'm right. I know these guys.'"

Patel knew where to look to get the proof. In the fall, Nunes had started to take him to meetings with Rosenstein and his senior staff at DOJ. Even though HPSCI had subpoenaed DOJ in August 2017 for material on Steele, the dossier, and the FISA warrant, Rosenstein hadn't been paying much attention. "Once we get into October, he starts to pay attention," says Patel.

Rosenstein had come to recognize that there were serious problems with the FBI's investigation of Trump, and now he was in the middle of it. He indicated that he hadn't actually read the spy warrant on Page before he had signed the final renewal in

June 2017. If so, it was a damning failure. It meant that the deputy attorney general had put his name onto a document that allowed the special counsel he had appointed to spy on the White House based on Clinton-funded dirt.

Patel asked Rosenstein to what extent the FISA on Carter Page had been verified. "I asked him about the Woods file, and he says, 'I don't know what that is,'" says Patel. "I'm thinking, he was the United States attorney for Maryland and a federal prosecutor, and he doesn't know what a Woods file is. Is this guy being coy, or does he really not know? So I explained it to him, in front of his senior staff."

The Woods procedures were designed to minimize factual inaccuracies in FISA applications. A Woods file holds the documents proving assertions of fact. "It's a verification file," says Patel. "So every time you assert a fact before the FISA court, there's a document in a binder, the Woods file, that supports it."

Rosenstein's ignorance of standard DOJ procedures suggested to Patel that the deputy attorney general had really not read the warrant. "That was about the time Rosenstein really started to dislike me," he says.

In a subsequent meeting at DOJ, Patel added another item to the list of documents he wanted: the records of every FBI interview, known as a 302, with Bruce Ohr. "I told Rosenstein that I wanted all the Ohr 302s. And he says, 'None of these exist. You don't know what you're talking about. If you think my ADAG was out there running this side investigation, you're crazy.'"

Patel's hunch was right. "Not forty-eight hours after that meeting, I get a call from a guy on Rosenstein's senior staff who tells me that twelve Bruce Ohr 302s came in," he says. "So then we went over there and read them—jackpot."

The twelve 302s documenting Ohr's meetings with the FBI start on November 22, 2016. However, they memorialize all of Ohr's interactions with Simpson and Steele, which began in January 2016 at the latest.

Those meetings, conversations, and exchanges are crucial to understanding what the FBI and DOJ knew and when they knew it. For instance, it was September 2016, a month before the Page FISA was obtained, when Steele told Ohr that he was "desperate that Donald Trump not get elected and was passionate about him not being president."

Patel filed that away. "The FBI and DOJ knew their main source had a tremendous bias against a target of their investigation, and they intentionally failed to disclose this fact to the FISC," he says.

Ohr and Steele had known each other since 2007. They'd worked on the FIFA case together and had been in steady communication about Oleg Deripaska and other matters since January 2016. Yet according to Nellie Ohr, neither she nor her husband had known that Glenn Simpson had hired both her and Steele to investigate Trump's Russia connections until they met for breakfast on July 30, 2016.

The story was not credible, according to an Objective Medusa investigator who believes Nellie Ohr lied to Congress.

Soon after the breakfast, likely in early August, Bruce Ohr met with Andrew McCabe and Lisa Page. Ohr knew them. He'd worked with McCabe when the FBI man had led the Eurasian organized crime task force in New York City. Ohr had been Page's supervisor when she had been a DOJ trial attorney in the Organized Crime and Racketeering Section.

The FBI had activated Steele as a confidential human source in February, but now Ohr was briefing the Bureau's deputy director about what its own informant had come up with on Trump and Russia in his Clinton-funded research.

Ohr met with Lisa Page again later, in August 2016. They were joined by Peter Strzok and several DOJ officials, Bruce Swartz, Zainab Ahmad, and Andrew Weissman. The last two DOJ officials later joined the Mueller team.

On August 22, Ohr met with Glenn Simpson, who talked about Carter Page, Paul Manafort, and Trump's lawyer Michael Cohen. Ohr relayed to the FBI what his wife's boss had told him.

Ohr also passed on his wife's Fusion GPS work to the FBI. In the fall, she gave him a thumb drive with her work on it, and he handed it off to the Bureau.

Ohr stayed in contact with Steele throughout the fall of 2016. In September, they met in Washington for breakfast. Steele texted him often. On October 18, he texted: "I have something quite urgent I would like to discuss with you."

October 18 was the date of the Steele memo alleging that Carter Page had been offered a bribe—the memo that had helped obtain the spy warrant on Page granted three days later.

"When I got a call from Chris Steele and he provided information, if it seemed like it was significant, I would provide it to the FBI," said Ohr. He revered the former British spy. "When I receive information from Chris Steele, I'm not going to sit on it," he said. "I've got to give it to the FBI."

On November 1, 2016, Steele was fired by the FBI for speaking to the press. Ohr became his back channel to the FBI. Ohr first met with FBI agent Joe Pientka, who became his handler. Ohr's November 21 meeting with Pientka was documented in the first 302.

Now Bruce Ohr was servicing his wife, his wife's colleague, and his wife's boss.

Ohr met with Simpson again in December. Simpson gave him a thumb drive that contained what became known as the Steele Dossier, which the DOJ lawyer handed over to the FBI.

Shortly after Comey was fired on May 9, McCabe asked Ohr to reach out to Steele.

The twelfth Ohr 302 is dated May 15, 2017.

After the special counsel was named May 17, Steele told Ohr he wanted to speak with the Mueller team.

Ohr continued to meet with the FBI at the Bureau's request, as Steele's cutout, until late November 2017. The 302s of the post–May 2017 meetings were held in the custody of the special counsel and never disclosed to Congress.

Ohr said he had warned his DOJ and FBI colleagues prior to the FISA application that Steele had it out for Trump. Nonetheless, for more than a year, the DOJ senior official ran errands for anti-Trump political operatives: Steele, Simpson, and his wife, Nellie.

The term "Deep State" originated in the Middle East, describing the human bedrock of hard-security regimes, such as those of Turkey, Egypt, and Pakistan, managed by an entrenched network in which the military and security establishment intersect with political and corporate interests.

That's also true of Washington's permanent bureaucracy, the men and women behind the attempted anti-Trump coup. But the character of the US Deep State is different, the men and women softer.

They're educated suburbanites, many with law degrees. They exchange tips about curing and grilling meat, drink craft beers, and text their girlfriends on their way home to put their children to bed and kiss their wives good night. They share state secrets with journalists in exchange for basketball tickets.

Those involved in the attempted anti-Trump coup didn't risk capture, torture, and execution for plotting against the head of state. Nor did they have to arrange in secret for troop movements to surround the presidential residence. Uniquely, this coup, the Paper Coup, was conducted openly. The journalists who could have exposed the plot went to the same parties as the spies.

Everyone talked about it all the time. Strzok and Page texted each other like teenage girls. They texted about leaking information to journalists. They texted about planning a cocktail party for the judge who had handled the Flynn case, Rudolph Contreras.

When the Ohrs met with Steele and his associate for breakfast on July 30, it wasn't in some empty lot or field but in a hotel restaurant named after J. Edgar Hoover. Ohr walked into government buildings and briefed officials on the progress of the coup. FBI and State Department officials documented their conversations with the DOJ lawyer.

But like third-world coups, this one was a function of intersecting networks. One was a specialized professional network that cut across the various US government institutions and numerous fields: law enforcement, academia, and the media.

Nellie Ohr, for instance, said that she views herself "as part of a community of people who are interested in Russia." The Russia community was one of the networks at the center of the coup. The fifty-eight-year-old Ohr got her PhD in Russian history from Stanford and taught at Vassar in the 1990s.

"Chris Steele," said Mrs. Ohr, "was part of that community." There were many others in the Russia community, such as Edward Baumgartner, the other Russian linguist Fusion GPS contracted for the Trump project. He graduated from Vassar in 1995, while Nellie Ohr was teaching there.

Bruce Ohr had targeted Russian gangsters as chief of the DOJ's Organized Crime and Racketeering Section. Andrew McCabe had been in charge of the Eurasian organized crime task force in New York City, also going after Russian criminals.

Glenn Simpson had first become fascinated with Russian organized crime while he was a journalist at the *Wall Street Journal*. "We had a shared interest in that topic," Nellie Ohr said of her former employer.

The Russia community in Washington was extensive, with many playing roles in the coup. David Kramer, a longtime aide of John McCain, worked on Russia issues at the State Department. At the late senator's request, after the election, Kramer flew to England to meet with Steele at his home, where the former MI6 man gave him what would become known as the Steele Dossier. When he returned to the Beltway, Kramer met with Simpson, who also handed him pieces of the dossier. Kramer then gave the dossier to McCain, who gave it to Comey. He also passed on Steele's reporting to Carl Bernstein at CNN, Rosalind Helderman, and Tom Hamburger at the *Washington Post*, Julian Borger at *The Guardian*, David Corn at *Mother Jones*, Peter Stone at McClatchy, and Ken Bensinger at BuzzFeed, which published it on January 10, 2017.

Like Kramer, former Obama ambassador to Russia Michael McFaul frequently provided quotes critical of Trump for Fusion GPS-generated Trump-Russia stories. Kathleen Kavalec was a Russianist at the State Department who spoke with Steele in October 2016 and Ohr a month later. She thanked the DOJ official for stopping by and sent him the link to a *Financial Times* article about the Trump team's alleged ties to Russia. The story was based on his wife's reporting for Fusion GPS.

The Russia network was a self-generated echo chamber. Everyone believed the same things about Russia and Trump because all they knew was one another's work, which they transmitted to others in the network.

Victoria Nuland was another Russianiast at the State Department, where she was Assistant Secretary of State for European and Eurasian Affairs. According to Bruce Ohr, Glenn Simpson was meeting with her in the fall of 2016.

Jonathan Winer worked at the State Department with Nuland and Kavalec. Winer had been working on Russia affairs since the late 1990s, when he met Bruce Ohr.

Nunes's announcement in February 2018 that he was looking into the State Department's role in the FBI's Russia investigation prompted Winer to explain himself.

He wrote in a February 8, 2018 *Washington Post* article that he had first met Steele in 2009 and had become his main contact in the Obama State Department. Steele shared his Trump-Russia reports with Winer in September 2016.

Winer wrote that he'd given a summary of Steele's reports to Nuland, who said secretary of state John Kerry needed to be made aware of Steele's material.

Nuland and Winer's stories didn't match. She claimed that she'd heard about Steele's work months before, in late June or early July. She said she'd believed it wasn't in the State Department's "purview" but was rather the FBI's business, and gave the ok for FBI agent Michael Gaeta to meet with Steele in London.

Winer wrote in the *Post* that he was an old friend of Sidney Blumenthal, who in late September gave him the Trump-Russia reporting he and fellow Clinton operative Cody Shearer had compiled. Winer passed the Shearer-Blumenthal work to Steele.

Winer also spoke with Simpson at the time. The State Department official was a source for the stories that Isikoff and Corn sourced to Steele. Winer vouched for Steele's reputation. He arranged for Steele to meet Kavalec a month before the election.

Evelyn Farkas was a Russianist at the Pentagon. In March 2016, she described how she had encouraged her former administration colleagues to disseminate intelligence on Trump-Russia throughout the government. That process increased the likelihood of leaks to the press.

Washington Post columnist Anne Applebaum was another member of the community of Beltway insiders interested in Russia. Her husband, Radosław "Radek" Sikorski, had held high-level posts in the Polish government. Starting in July 2016, Applebaum wrote dozens of columns based on Fusion GPS's conspiracy theory.

Stefan Halper was also part of the Russia community, having written studies for the Pentagon that dealt with Russia.

————————————

The professional networks intersected with smaller, more intimate units: couples, people in love, or people yoked together through some sort of shared interest or conviction.

The Ohrs were an important couple, one of the coup's nodes. The operation passed back and forth between them, with Fusion GPS and FBI as the two terminal points.

There were other Fusion GPS pairings as well, including Christopher Steele and his wife, Katherine, a former British government official, who defended her husband on social media.

So did Glenn Simpson's wife, Mary Jacoby. Also a former *Wall Street Journal* reporter, Jacoby felt her husband hadn't gotten enough credit for the coup. "It's come to my attention that some people still don't realize what Glenn's role was in exposing Putin's control of Donald Trump," she wrote in a Facebook post. "Let's be clear. Glenn conducted the investigation. Glenn hired Chris Steele. Chris Steele worked for Glenn."

Patel agrees. "Simpson ran a lot of the operation," says the lead Objective Medusa investigator. "Fusion GPS ran the media operation, and they ran both Steele and Bruce Ohr, aided by his wife."

But Simpson had also inadvertently given away the operation. He lied about his encounters with Ohr. He told Congress that he and Ohr had met only after the election. Patel knew otherwise based on FBI interviews. In November 2017, Simpson appeared before HPSCI. Unlike his Fusion GPS colleagues Peter Fritsch and Thomas Catan, who had invoked the Fifth Amendment, he talked.

"He couldn't help himself," says Patel. He asked Simpson if he'd ever been in contact with the FBI or DOJ.

"After the election," said Simpson. "During the election, no." He said that Steele had suggested he give some information to "a prosecutor named Bruce Ohr." Simpson said it "was sometime after Thanksgiving."

But Patel knew that Simpson and Ohr had met before the election, too.

Once Simpson lied in his congressional testimony, Patel was done. "I didn't want him to have a chance to change his story," says the former prosecutor. Patel believed that Simpson had committed a felony.

There were other Fusion GPS couples, such as Neil King, Jr., another former *Wall Street Journal* reporter brought on by his onetime colleagues Simpson and Fritsch. King's wife, Shailagh Murray, had also once worked as a journalist. She had become Vice President Joe Biden's communications director in 2011. She had been named a senior adviser to Obama in March 2015, in time to push the Iran deal to the echo chamber.

Most notoriously, there were Peter Strzok and Lisa Page. At the same time Patel uncovered the Ohrs' role, he also found out the FBI couple's secret. "We learned that Strzok had been reassigned to human resources," says Patel. "Having worked with tons of FBI folks, I knew what happened. I told my guys that if you're running high-level investigations, like big counterintelligence investigations, you only get reassigned to HR if you're sleeping with someone in the building or doing something else you shouldn't have been doing."

Nunes and Patel asked for all the documents regarding Strzok's reassignment. The text messages that the FBI and DOJ tried to hide from Objective Medusa investigators would tell an important part of the story.

Chapter 17

THE DECOY

WITHOUT THE BIG TITLES and the national security bureaucracy's legalistic self-defense mechanisms, the story was pretty straightforward: The Clintons hired a bunch of con men who got their dirty cop friends to frame Trump. The press and a corrupt prosecutor handled the cover-up.

The details mattered because the lawmen had used programs designed to keep Americans safe from terrorism as the centerpiece of the sting. The Objective Medusa team was fighting to get the details to the public.

HPSCI had its briefing, what came to be called the "Nunes Memo," ready by November but was still looking to fill it out with more details. The Objective Medusa team got an unexpected boost in December 2017 when McCabe, then the FBI acting director, testified before the committee that no surveillance warrant would have been sought from the secret court without the Steele Dossier's information.

For nearly a year, the dossier had been celebrated not just as an account of Trump's corruption but also as a gift from the future promising his doom. If Mueller was the Paper Coup's high priest, the dossier was its scripture.

"Up until then, everybody's saying how the dossier was the greatest thing since sliced bread," says Patel. "And then we started peeling it back and showed it was not credible. And now we have the acting director under oath saying 'No Steele Dossier, no FISA.'"

The Crossfire Hurricane team countered. They deflected attention away from the dossier by substituting it with a new origin story for the investigation. They tapped the paper of record to take dictation.

A December 30, 2017, *New York Times* story—"How the Russia Inquiry Began: A Campaign Aide, Drinks and Talk of Political Dirt" by Sharon LaFraniere, Mark Mazzetti, and Matt Apuzzo— explained how Nunes had gotten it wrong.

What had compelled the FBI to investigate the Trump campaign was not, according to the *Times*, "a dossier compiled by a former British spy hired by a rival campaign. Instead, it was firsthand information from one of America's closest intelligence allies."

Langer was hardly surprised that the Crossfire Hurricane team was switching streams. "It's exactly what you would expect them to do with the dossier hemorrhaging credibility," says Nunes's communications director. "Conveniently, the *New York Times* comes along to save the day. Even if everything in the dossier was false, it no longer matters because suddenly the dossier is irrelevant. So just forget thousands of press stories touting its claims, forget TV pundits going hysterical over it for a full year, forget Schiff reading dossier allegations into the *Congressional Record*, and forget that the FBI used it to get a FISA to spy on Americans. None of that matters because now the investigation is actually all about George Papadopoulos."

In April 2016, the Trump campaign volunteer had met with Maltese academic Joseph Mifsud, who'd said that the Russians had "dirt" on Clinton in the form of "thousands of emails."

"During a night of heavy drinking at an upscale London bar in May 2016," the *Times* claimed, Papadopoulos had relayed to Australian diplomat Alexander Downer that "Russia had political dirt on Hillary Clinton." On July 31, the FBI opened its investigation.

The story made no sense. If Downer was so concerned about Papadopoulos's revelation, why had he, a senior diplomat of an allied country, waited two months to report it?

Further, Downer, a former Australian foreign minister, was an ally of the Clintons. He had pledged $25 million to the Clinton Global Initiative. Why had he sat on information that might protect Hillary Clinton's candidacy? Because, claimed the *Times*, WikiLeaks had started leaking DNC emails in July. Then "Australian officials passed the information about Mr. Papadopoulos to their American counterparts."

The United States, Australia, Canada, the United Kingdom, and New Zealand are part of an intelligence-gathering and -sharing arrangement among the five English-speaking powers called "Five Eyes." The intelligence agencies of the five countries go through an established process before passing information to one another through official channels.

The issue, as Nunes said publicly, is that there was no official Five Eyes intelligence in the investigation's originating document. "They were eager to open the investigation," he says. "And Papadopoulos was the logical choice. They justified opening a broad investigation because they said they got their information from a Five Eyes partner. They didn't."

The investigation did officially open on July 31. But as Nunes and Patel explained, that was an arbitrary date that the FBI had provided in order to conceal everything else it had done previously.

The *Times* story, leaking details of a counterintelligence investigation, served the same purpose by trying to obscure the role the dossier had played. What really mattered, according to the *Times* story, was that Papadopoulos had drunkenly admitted to the inebriated Downer that he had inside information about how the Russians had dirt on Clinton.

Both Papadopoulos and Downer later denied that they'd been drinking heavily. It was another false detail planted by law enforcement sources, just like the suggestion that Papadopoulos had relayed Mifsud's information about Clinton's emails to Downer. Both Downer and Papadopoulos said that the Trump adviser had never mentioned emails.

The story also omitted a key detail: To get the Papadopoulos information into the system, the Crossfire Hurricane team and its partners had purposefully circumvented the normal processes for exchanging intelligence among the Five Eyes partners. It was a career foreign service officer at the US Embassy in London, Elizabeth Dibble, who had passed Downer's information to the FBI.

"They opened their investigation of the Trump campaign on what genuine intelligence officers call RUMINT," says Nunes. "That's rumor intelligence. It means it's not to be taken seriously. By calling it Five Eyes, they tried to make it sound official."

Patel agrees. "We'd come to learn that the facts alleged by the FBI were incomplete and misleading."

The urgency with which the FBI reportedly regarded Downer's tip—US officials, claimed the *Times*, were "alarmed"—is incompatible with the timeline.

After the investigation opened, the FBI waited nearly six months before it interviewed Papadopoulos. In the meantime, it obtained a FISA warrant on Carter Page instead of Papadopoulos, the ostensible collusion lynchpin.

The FBI told congressional leaders in January 2017 that it was searching furiously for the mysterious figure who would finally vindicate the Russia collusion narrative. But Papadopoulos was easy to find in Chicago. He spoke voluntarily with FBI agents.

Months passed, and Mueller's team allowed the former Trump adviser to travel abroad. The FBI arrested him as he reentered the country at Dulles airport in July. He had lied in his January 2017 interview, they said. Nearly six months had passed since then, but the important timeline was Mueller's.

The special counsel had been appointed in May 2017 and needed points on the board. Papadopoulos was an easy win. He pled guilty, and the statement of the offense was unsealed at the end of October. It read:

> *Defendant PAPADOPOULOS further told the investigating agents that the professor was "a nothing" and "just a guy talk[ing] up connections or something." In truth and in fact, however, defendant PAPADOPOULOS understood that the professor had substantial connections to Russian government officials.*

So did Papadopoulos think that Mifsud was just a big talker? Or did he understand that he was connected to Russian officials?

Mueller was walking a thin line. He needed to tie the arrest to his mandate. Rosenstein had tasked him to investigate "any links/ coordination between the Russian government and individuals associated with the campaign of Donald Trump." To make the arrest resonate with the Trump-Russia narrative, there had to be Russian-related activities.

So why didn't Mueller just say, as Adam Schiff had, that Mifsud was "Kremlin-linked"? Because there was no evidence for it. Making false allegations in court documents would have put the special counsel at legal risk. The only place where the Mueller team could safely indicate that Mifsud was tied to the Moscow government was in the head of George Papadopoulos— who *understood* that Mifsud had substantial connections to Russia.

In the real world, the evidence showed something else. The mysterious professor's closest public links were to Western governments, politicians, and institutions, including the British and Italian intelligence services, as well as the CIA and FBI.

British political analyst Chris Blackburn wonders why the FBI appeared to ignore Mifsud's professional networks. "When Peter Strzok got to London in early August to look into the Papadopoulos meeting with Mifsud," he says, "he would've found that the professor's most notable contacts were with high-ranking Western officials."

Blackburn's shaking off a midwinter cold and washing down a plate of fish and chips with a beer. The thirty-five-year-old researcher has taken the train down from northern England for a day to walk with me around the London neighborhood where the central scenes of the Papadopoulos drama unfolded—like the hotel where Mifsud told the Trump adviser about the Russians having Clinton emails and where Papadopoulos is supposed to have passed that information to Downer.

Blackburn's previous research focused on Islamist terror groups, putting him in touch with senior leaders of global intelligence agencies. He became interested in the Papadopoulos case when he noticed that the photographs of Mifsud he found online were of the former Maltese diplomat posing with Western political, diplomatic, and intelligence figures.

Why wouldn't a trained intelligence officer like Strzok find the same? "Maybe the FBI doesn't know how to use Google," says Blackburn, laughing huskily.

Mifsud had told Papadopoulos he had important friends around the world, and indeed he traveled anywhere for the chance to rub elbows with policy luminaries from around the world. At a 2009 conference sponsored by the Italian Foreign Ministry and the Brookings Institution, Mifsud had appeared alongside US foreign policy experts, including former Clinton administration Deputy Secretary of State Strobe Talbott.

Blackburn shows me a portfolio from the 2016 Doha Forum, a conference in the Qatari capital that gathers some of the world's most famous statesmen. Mifsud had chaired a panel including a former prime minister of France, Dominique de Villepin; the foreign minister of Norway, Børge Brende; a former foreign minister of Spain, Miguel Ángel Moratinos; and a former foreign minister of Italy, Franco Frattini.

If Mifsud really is "Kremlin-linked," the Doha panel alone compromised four senior European diplomats whose colleagues in their countries' intelligence services didn't know the moderator was a Russian spy.

"If Mifsud is truly a Russian spy," says Blackburn, "he'll go down as one of the most successful agents in history. He'd have penetrated the inner sanctum of European politics, diplomacy, and intelligence."

One of Mifsud's most notable contacts, says Blackburn, is prominent former UK diplomat Claire Smith. "She worked with

Mifsud at three different institutions: the London Academy of Diplomacy, University of Stirling, and Link Campus University in Rome." Her long professional relationship with Mifsud is a significant piece of evidence. "She was on the United Kingdom's Joint Intelligence Committee," says Blackburn. "It's a very significant institution in the UK's intelligence community, answering directly to the prime minister."

Smith also served on the Security Vetting Appeals Panel. "She was vetting UK government employees," says Blackburn. "So how could she have missed that her colleague was actually a Russian spy?"

Blackburn shows me a picture of Mifsud standing next to Smith at Link Campus University in Rome, surrounded by the Italian police officers they taught. Link's president is Vincenzo Scotti, who's held ministerial posts, including as interior minister responsible for domestic intelligence, in several Italian governments. Scotti is one of the kingmakers of Italy's current coalition government. In June 2018 he positioned a former Link professor, Elisabetta Trenta, for the job of defense minister. "That was one of Mifsud's colleagues," says Blackburn. "So I guess that's one more senior Western official compromised by Mifsud."

So were US intelligence agencies and officers. The CIA held events at Link Campus University, and former National Security Agency and Central Intelligence Agency officials taught there regularly. So did FBI officials. In September 2016, the FBI's legal attaché at the US Embassy in Rome sent Special Agent Preston Ackerman to conduct a seminar at Link. It was two months after the FBI opened Crossfire Hurricane. He worked in the same office as Christopher Steele's handler, Michael Gaeta.

If the FBI thought Mifsud was a Russian agent, why did it continue to send agents to teach at an institution with which Mifsud was affiliated?

It was at Link that Papadopoulos was first introduced to Mifsud, when the Trump adviser was part of a delegation visiting Rome in March 2016. They struck up an acquaintance and met several times in London over the course of the next few months. Mifsud emailed Papadopoulos from a policy conference in Moscow to say that he was arranging meetings for him with Russian officials. On his return, Mifsud told him that the Russians had Clinton emails.

"I never heard the words 'DNC,'" said Papadopoulos. "I just heard 'The Russians have thousands of Hillary Clinton's emails.'"

The Clinton campaign was concerned about potentially compromising material that might be revealed in the candidate's emails.

Two weeks after Mifsud told him about the emails, Papadopoulos was contacted by Downer. He thought it was strange that Australia's highest-ranking diplomat in the United Kingdom, a former foreign minister, was reaching out to a then-twenty-eight-year-old Trump campaign volunteer.

Papadopoulos said there had been no conversation about Clinton or emails. "I don't remember actually ever sharing that information with this person."

Downer said the Trump volunteer had never mentioned emails. He remembered his saying that the Russians had material that could be damaging to Clinton.

"The FBI opened a full investigation on a presidential campaign," says Nunes. "It's unprecedented. And the investigation is based on RUMINT about Clinton emails. Remember that at the time, everyone is whispering about Clinton's deleted emails. Republicans in Congress are looking for them. It's normal. And yet the FBI opens an investigation on someone talking about Clinton emails.

But as it turns out, it's not even about emails because Downer said Papadopoulos never said anything about Clinton's emails."

Papadopoulos said that Downer had appeared to be recording him with his phone.

Months later, another, older figure from the foreign policy community contacted Papadopoulos. Stefan Halper offered him $3,000 to write a paper on Mediterranean energy issues. He arranged for Papadopoulos's plane trip to London and his lodgings.

In September 2016, Halper met with the Trump adviser in the British capital. The Cambridge academic brought with him a woman he introduced as his graduate assistant, Azra Turk. Like Halper, she was a spy. The pair asked Papadopoulos if the Trump campaign had softened the GOP platform on Ukraine to appease Putin. They also wanted him to admit that he knew that Russia had Clinton's emails. Papadopoulos said he had no idea what they were talking about. He said that what they were suggesting amounted to treason.

In January 2017, FBI agents interviewed Papadopoulos. They asked if anyone had ever told him that the Russian government planned to release information on Clinton.

"No," said Papadopoulos.

"No?" the agents asked.

They already knew—just as Halper had known to ask Papadopoulos about emails. The FBI was trying, as Halper had, to draw a positive answer out of him.

It wasn't until after the agents raised the matter that Papadopoulos identified Mifsud and admitted that the professor had told him that "the Russians had emails of Clinton."

"Everyone is asking Papadopoulos about emails," says Nunes. "Why? Does Papadopoulos look like a guy that knows about emails?

So how did the FBI know to ask him about the emails on multiple occasions throughout 2016 and 2017 before having interviewed Mifsud, unless the FBI already received this information directly or indirectly from Mifsud?"

The FBI interviewed Mifsud in February, a few weeks after it set up Papadopoulos. Mifsud was in Washington, DC, for a policy conference at the Capitol. FBI agents spoke with him in his hotel lobby and let him go. The agents said they hadn't known what to ask him because Papadopoulos had lied to them. Papadapoulos, according to the special counsel's sentencing guidelines,

> *substantially hindered investigators' ability to effectively question the Professor when the FBI located him in Washington, D.C. approximately two weeks after the defendant's January 27, 2017 interview. The defendant's lies undermined investigators' ability to challenge the Professor or potentially detain or arrest him while he was still in the United States. The government understands that the Professor left the United States on February 11, 2017 and he has not returned to the United States since then.*

Why couldn't the FBI locate Mifsud for a follow-up interview? The press knew how to find him.

"Mifsud," according to an October 30, 2017, article by *Washington Post* reporters Rosalind Helderman and Thomas Hamburger, "told *The Post* in an email in August that he had 'absolutely no contact with the Russian government' and said his only ties to Russia were through academic links."

August was a month after Papadopoulos was arrested and two months before his plea deal was unsealed.

"I want to know how the *Post* reporters got Mifsud's name," says Nunes. "If it's not from the FBI or the Mueller team, how did they get it?"

Presumably, if Mifsud had been a secret Kremlin-linked operative, he'd have disappeared once reporters started asking questions about his connections to Russia. But the professor was still on the loose in Europe.

If Mifsud was a Russian spy, why didn't the FBI warn US allies about him?

Two weeks after Papadopoulos's guilty plea in October 2017, Mifsud was photographed at a London fund-raiser next to the future prime minster of the United Kingdom, Boris Johnson, then foreign secretary, responsible for the United Kingdom's foreign intelligence services.

The FBI opened the case because of Papadopoulos's meetings in the British capital in spring 2016. But nearly a year and a half later, the Bureau continued to keep the United States' closest partners in the dark about the "Kremlin-linked" professor, even if it risked compromising senior UK officials. It makes no sense.

But apparently the FBI said nothing to the Italians about the "Kremlin-linked" professor, either, because Mifsud was in Rome, too, where he gave interviews to the Italian press, even after his name went public at the end of October.

On November 1, 2017, nearly nine months after the FBI had spoken with him in Washington, Mifsud finally went into hiding.

If Mifsud is really a Russian spy, the United States and its NATO partners will be doing damage assessments for years. But neither the FBI nor the special counsel ever provided any evidence to prove that the mysterious professor is linked to the Kremlin.

Chapter 18

THE NUNES MEMO

"WE WERE CONTINUALLY finding things that shouldn't have been classified but were," says Nunes. "None of it was national security information. The FBI was just hiding what they'd done."

The Crossfire Hurricane team had buried what they'd done under classified intelligence, a classified counterintelligence investigation, and a secret court. The intelligence bureaucracy had written the rules, so they knew how to get around them and how to use them to keep anyone from connecting the dots, at least in public.

"Our committee members were increasingly uncomfortable having to sit on what we knew about FISA abuse and other matters," says Nunes. "We had to get it to the rest of the House members and then ultimately to the American public."

He wanted a way to get the information into the light. "But I kept getting a hundred and one ways to 'No,'" says Nunes. "I wanted a hundred and one ways to 'Yes.'"

One possibility was to put it to a full House vote on the floor. "That wasn't politically appealing to leadership," says Patel. "Then one of my colleagues found a relatively obscure committee rule stipulating that HPSCI can vote to declassify something if 'the public interest would be served by such disclosure.'"

The rule had been created when the committee was first established in the late 1970s. "The idea they probably had in mind was to stop someone like Nixon from secretly spying on Congress," says Nunes. "They would have never imagined it would be used to uncover a Deep State operation working with the losing political campaign to put the current president under investigation, leaving HPSCI as the only body that could see it happening and then disclose it."

In the late fall, Nunes went to meet with Speaker of the House Paul Ryan to discuss the memorandum his staff was writing to make the information public.

"The document was nearly finished by Thanksgiving," says Nunes. "I called the speaker and asked to meet with him. I wanted to brief committee members next morning on the plan before Thanksgiving recess. Ryan said his schedule was full all day and asked if I could meet him in his office at night. He pulled out a couple of local Wisconsin beers, and I told him that we're going to use this rule to get the information out."

Ryan supported the plan and wanted to make sure that HPSCI's case was solid. "There was more information that we wanted," says Nunes, "and the speaker wanted us to get whatever we wanted to make our case."

The press knew that HPSCI was up to something. "They were trying to piece together what we were doing," says Nunes, "which was the memo. They couldn't figure it out because we're so closely held."

A December 31, 2017, *Washington Post* article by Karoun Demirjian reported that Nunes was "convening a group of

Intelligence Committee Republicans to draft a likely report on 'corruption' among the investigators working for the special counsel."

The story was evidence that the press didn't know what was going on—and that they were trying to split Republicans. "It's supposed to be a story about Nunes on the ropes," says Nunes. "They manufactured the story, including fake quotes from Gowdy."

According to the *Post*, then South Carolina Congressman Trey Gowdy was referring to Nunes when he said "I'm interested in getting access to the information and not the drama."

"Gowdy called me later to say the quotes were fake," says Nunes. "The reporter was shouting questions at him about a different issue as he was walking down the hall, and they used those quotes to make it look like we were divided."

The *Post* story served the purposes of Rosenstein and the new FBI director, Christopher Wray, who didn't want to give HPSCI the documents it had requested. The article showed that Nunes was reckless, which was the message the two bureaucrats took to their meeting with Ryan right after the new year.

The senior law enforcement officials recited what had become a familiar refrain. "They told Ryan it's going to do irreparable damage to national security, it's going to jeopardize our relations with allies," Nunes recalls. "But the fact that they used the Steele Dossier for the FISA is not some closely guarded national secret. Wray and Rosenstein were trying to short-circuit the whole process and get the speaker to have us stand down."

Ryan backed Nunes. "He told Rosenstein and Wray, 'No, you're going to give this to Congress,'" says Nunes.

Nonetheless, the struggle between DOJ and HPSCI continued. In January, Rosenstein clashed with Patel. "He didn't like that we were questioning DOJ," says the former prosecutor. "It's just the mentality over there. It was institutional. It didn't matter that Rosenstein came in as a Trump appointee. He was on the side of the institution. He fought us on all these documents."

As Patel wrestled DOJ for more of the underlying documents, the tension between the two sides grew. It came to a head in the middle of January. "We started questioning him about something, and he flew off his seat and started threatening me," Patel remembers. "He threatened to investigate us and subpoena our materials."

Patel says he was surprised that the Justice Department's second-highest-ranking official had threatened him for performing his oversight duties. "I guess Rosenstein had forgotten about the whole coequal branches of government thing."

"You can't invoke discovery on Congress," says his investigative partner, Jim.

The Objective Medusa team shook off Rosenstein's threats and got down to writing the memo.

"I have been and always will be pro-FISA," says Patel. "I didn't think we should attack the process, and everyone was in agreement. FISA is a very sensitive tool, and it has great value, and 99.99 percent of FISAs are totally fine."

The problem, says Patel, was the mentality at Comey's FBI. "They thought that no one was ever going to see it, so no one would ever challenge it."

Patel and Jim were the two primary authors of the Nunes Memo, along with Gowdy. Nunes says that given the amount of work his former colleague put into the document, "it's probably more fair to call it the Gowdy Memo." In one TV interview, Gowdy actually referred to the document as "my memo."

The drafting of the memo took about a month, says Patel. "I'd write up a draft and hand it off to one of my colleagues, get corrections, and then we'd go to [HPSCI staff director] Damon [Nelson]. After that, we went to every member of the committee on the GOP side. I think one member had one syntax correction, but substantively they were all on board."

The next step was to show the work to the FBI. Nunes asked Patel to meet with Wray.

"I met with the director and one of his counterintelligence guys, and we showed them the memo," says Patel. "They came over to our space, and we told them we want to make sure we have this right. They were polite. We spent some time together, and they said they'll get back to us. And then the director asked Devin if I could go over to the FBI and sit down with two more people."

Patel and his investigative partner went to FBI headquarters to meet with Bill Priestap, the head of the counterintelligence division, and FBI attorney Sally Moyer. "We showed them the draft," says Patel. "We told them that we're here for as long as they need us to be here. We sat with them for hours. They probably read it twice. We told them, 'We need to know if there's anything in here that's not correct.' And they said, 'No, there's nothing incorrect, but there's a lot of information that's not in there.' We told them, 'Well, you're free to tell us whatever information you want, and we'll put it in. But based on the totality of the information you've given us, is this correct?'"

They said it was—but that didn't stop FBI and DOJ leadership from attacking the memo, frequently as anonymous sources in the press, as a dire threat to national security.

"What people lose sight of," says Patel, "is that the memo was entirely based on the documents that FBI and DOJ produced to us and the sworn testimony of the witnesses."

On January 18, HPSCI Republicans voted it out of committee.

Patel explains that it was ultimately the White House that declassified the information. "We used our committee's rule as a mechanism to get the memo out of the committee and to the White House."

White House lawyers took it under consideration. During the wait, Patel and his colleagues briefed Republican members. "I don't think this ever happened before," says Patel, "but every single Republican member came down to the committee spaces. We had open time slots for them to walk in, and we'd have copies for them to read. Then we briefed them on it."

The members, says Patel, "were shocked. Shocked that a political party had funded research into the opponent's campaign and took it to the secret court and got a warrant with it and used it to record people during the campaign."

It was the first time that other House members had any insight into what HPSCI had known for nearly a year.

"These members trust us because we're the ones that have eyes on these classified programs," says Nunes. "And if one of these program goes awry, we have an absolute obligation to bring this to the rest of the House."

After they read the memo, says Nunes, "a lot more members of Congress became interested."

———————————

The Objective Medusa team knew they were on the verge of a big win.

"Conservatives were very supportive of our efforts to get the memo out," says Langer. "There was a sense that Devin was onto something and it was important."

Grassroots enthusiasm was apparent on social media, where

Twitter users started a hashtag backing the Objective Medusa team's efforts: #ReleaseTheMemo. Its popularity made it another target for operatives defending Deep State corruption.

"Another move to discredit our work," says Langer, "was the idea that #ReleaseTheMemo was the endeavor of Russian bots. It was part of this ridiculous media operation claiming that not only were all the Trump people compromised by Russia, but anyone casting doubt on that was also compromised by Russia."

After the 2016 election, a gathering of anti-Trump activists— including John Podesta, Jake Sullivan, Michael McFaul, David Kramer, and William Kristol—raised money to track Russian cyberefforts against Western democracies. Their organization, Hamilton 68, claimed that the #ReleaseTheMemo hashtag was yet another Russian-backed cyberoperation.

"Predictably, Schiff and Feinstein jumped on that and sent letters to Twitter and Facebook," says Langer. "Yes, senior Democratic officials demanded an investigation of a hashtag. Both social media platforms responded that they didn't find any unusual Russian bot activity."

If Hamilton 68's accusations gave evidence of how absurd and paranoid US politics had become in the postdossier age, a more serious operation to discredit Nunes's work zeroed in on HPSCI members and staffers themselves. It was the culmination of the first campaign in US history waged, funded, and staffed to defend the systematic corruption of rogue law enforcement officials.

Patel was targeted by a number of hit pieces, most prominently a February 2, 2018, *New York Times* article by Katie Rogers and Matthew Rosenberg. It featured a slanted account of his efforts to speak with Christopher Steele's lawyer in London. Articles in the *Washington Post* and on The Daily Beast hit the same talking points.

"For the press to publish a series of hit pieces singling out one staffer was a real low," Langer says. "The point was to make an example of Kash, to single him out and intimidate anyone else who thought of stepping up. The message was 'Don't think you'll be spared, either.'"

The communications director remembers the two-week period while the memo was at the White House.

"Kash was showing it to members, but this was a classified document," says Langer. "No one outside Congress had read it, but it's still being attacked in the media. 'It's going to destroy national security.' 'It's full of lies.' 'HPSCI misrepresented testimony,' et cetera, et cetera. But none of these reporters had seen the memo. None of them knew what was in it. As always, they were just reporting whatever the Democrats told them to say."

The entire Democratic apparatus was on message.

"The Democrats knew it was bad," says Nunes. "DOJ knew it was bad because they were trying to cover it up and they were trying to stop this from getting out publicly—that the bulk of the FISA application was made up of oppo research and fake news stories. Comey and Clapper and Brennan were out selling the same message about how bad this was going to be for national security—when they knew that they're the ones who were responsible."

It was during that period that the anti-Nunes operation took an even more dangerous turn. "They started to target my wife and the rest of my family," says Nunes.

Activists filed a California Public Records Act request for the emails of his wife, an elementary school teacher. She was targeted on social media, and after her contact information was published, they sent her harassing emails. They were doxxing teachers and administrators at the school and said that Mrs. Nunes was teaching racism and bigotry.

"There was a political structure built to bring tremendous pressure on me and my family to stop me from investigating," says Nunes. "It was clearly being run by professionals. They used technology to mimic my phone number so that family members thought that I was calling them. And then they made it sound like I was kidnapped and that I'd better back off or something bad's going happen to me and them."

Nunes and Langer alerted the United States Capitol Police. "They found a few nut jobs, but we get those all the time," says Nunes. "This was a sophisticated operation. Nearly every one of my family members, and I'm talking about extended family members—aunts, uncles, cousins, as many as two dozen family members—got one of those calls. So clearly they had a whole plan where they called to threaten all of those people."

Some of the calls were worse than others, Nunes remembers. "They called my grandmother, who was ninety-eight at the time," he says. "Maybe the worst was to my mother-in-law. It was early in the morning, multiple calls from what appeared to be my number, and someone on the other end is saying her son-in-law is in danger and will be harmed if he doesn't back off."

The attacks on Nunes and his family resembled the experiences of others who'd been in conflict with Fusion GPS. The journalists who'd reported on Fusion GPS's corrupt Venezuelan corporate clients had been harassed. One of the reporters, Alek Boyd, said that his two young daughters had been threatened.

Nunes's wife and daughters were under twenty-four-hour security, and the local sheriff had a deputy on campus at Mrs. Nunes's school.

"They didn't want any of what we'd found to come out," says Nunes. "And they did everything they could to stop it."

———————————

Prior to publication, the media's job was to discredit the Nunes Memo by warning that it represented a threat to national security.

"The FBI is essentially labeling this a partisan document that uses lies to undermine law enforcement," wrote the *Washington Post*'s Aaron Blake on January 31, 2018.

That is, Nunes was pushing falsehoods on behalf of Trump.

Lawfare editor Benjamin Wittes, a reliable Comey mouthpiece, told MSNBC on January 31 that Nunes, "with the active support and involvement of the President of the United States, is committed to releasing to the public a document that the FBI says has grave concerns, contains sufficient omissions of fact as to be effectively a lie, and that the Justice Department describes the release of as an extraordinarily reckless act."

The memo, we were to believe, was based on a conspiracy theory weaponized to destroy the federal law enforcement agencies.

"The question is not whether there was a plot against Trump at the FBI, as the Nunes memo reportedly alleges," Vox's Zack Beauchamp wrote on January 30. "There is no evidence for such a claim, and it doesn't pass the smell test. The real question is this: Will the FBI and Justice Department remain semi-independent agencies that check the president's authority—or will they be brought under President Donald Trump's direct control?"

Time's Elizabeth Goitein agreed. "This is not a matter of dueling conspiracy theories," wrote the former Senate aide on February 2. " . . . The hypothesis that Trump and his congressional allies hope to exercise political control over the Justice Department is more than likely."

On February 2, 2018, the Nunes Memo was released. "It was a defining event," says Langer. "Despite the nonstop media attacks both before and after it came out, it convinced millions of Americans that there were major problems with the way the government and the intelligence agencies investigated Trump."

The memo laid out plainly the facts that Objective Medusa had uncovered during its investigation of the "Department of Justice (DOJ) and Federal Bureau of Investigation (FBI) and their use of the Foreign Intelligence Surveillance Act (FISA) during the 2016 presidential election cycle."

Nunes and his team had shown that the DNC and the Clinton campaign had paid Fusion GPS to "obtain derogatory information on Donald Trump's ties to Russia." The memo showed that the Steele Dossier had formed an "essential part" of the Carter Page FISA application. Furthermore,

- Neither the initial October 2016 application, nor any of the three renewals, had disclosed the role of the DNC or Clinton campaign in funding Steele's efforts, "even though the political origins of the Steele dossier were then known to senior DOJ and FBI officials."
- The FISA application had used circular reporting by citing as evidence Michael Isikoff's September 23, 2016, article. The article was derived from information leaked by Steele himself. The application assessed that Steele had not directly provided information to Yahoo! News. But Steele had admitted in British court filings that he had met with a reporter from Yahoo! News in September 2016.
- Even after the FBI had officially terminated its relationship

with Steele, the Bureau had used his reporting via senior DOJ official Bruce Ohr. Steele had told him two months before the election that he was "desperate that Donald Trump not get elected and was passionate about him not being president."

- Ohr's wife, Nellie, had been employed by Fusion GPS to compile opposition research on Trump. Ohr had later given his wife's work for Fusion GPS to the FBI. The FBI had never disclosed the Ohrs' relationship with Steele and Fusion GPS to the secret court.

Patel's early suspicions had been borne out. The FBI had never disclosed any of those facts to the FISA court, though it was aware of all of them before submitting the application to spy on a US citizen.

Conservatives around the country might as well have waved the memo like a battle flag. Having had to defend a Republican president from a conspiracy theory for a year and a half, now there was evidence that it had been a fraud engineered by Clinton operatives and Obama officials.

In vindicating Trump, the memo had also documented a terrible sequence of events. The FBI's actions had done lasting damage to its reputation and convinced at least half the country that the law could be turned against them—simply for backing the wrong candidate.

Further, the FBI's actions had put national security at risk. Powerful tools designed to keep Americans safe from terrorism had been used to prosecute a political operation against a presidential campaign. The world's most famous law enforcement agency had squandered the confidence of those it was sworn to protect. How, at this point, could the FBI be trusted to tell the truth about anything?

After the memo's release, the media seamlessly shifted tactics. Having spent weeks decrying the reckless threat the memo posed to national security, they collectively announced, "Nothing to see here."

"The Nunes Memo is a dud," Vox's Beauchamp wrote the day it was released. The writer who just days before had feared that the memo would be used to cleanse DOJ now argued, "There is absolutely nothing here."

Where Lawfare's Wittes had once predicted doom, he now approvingly cited his friend James Comey's tweet, dismissing the memo as a waste of time.

"That's it?" Tweeted the former FBI director. "Dishonest and misleading memo wrecked the House intel committee, destroyed trust with Intelligence Community, damaged relationship with FISA court, and inexcusably exposed classified investigation of an American citizen. For what?"

The message rippled through the media with impressive uniformity: it was a nothingburger.

"In modern parlance we'd call it a nothingburger," wrote the *New York Times*' Bret Stephens on February 2, "but the bun is missing, too."

"Devin Nunes and the nothing burger memo," wrote *Washington Monthly*'s Nancy LeTourneau the same day.

"This memo is a Nunes Nothingburger," Massachusetts senator Ed Markey posted on his Facebook page.

"'Nothingburger' doesn't do this memo justice," wrote *Esquire*'s Charles Pierce on February 2. "This is threadbare. This is shabby. This reveals absolutely nothing."

"Worse than a nothing burger," said California congressman Ted Lieu.

"The memo itself is really just a bad joke," wrote the *Washington Post*'s Greg Sargent and Paul Waldman on February 2. A rebuttal memo being prepared by Adam Schiff, they wrote, "will likely make Nunes' effort look even more absurd."

Two weeks later, HPSCI voted to release Schiff's report. It was riddled with falsehoods and errors. To take only a few from the ten-page document:

> *Steele's reporting did not reach the counterintelligence team investigating Russia at FBI headquarters until mid-September 2016.*

That was false. Ohr had briefed McCabe and Lisa Page on Steele's reporting shortly after he saw Steele on July 30, 2016. Later in August, Ohr had again provided law enforcement officials with Fusion GPS–generated research attributed to Steele.

> *FISA was not used to spy on Trump or his campaign. As the Trump campaign and Page have acknowledged, Page ended his formal affiliation with the campaign months before DOJ applied for a warrant.*

That was misleading. The FISA had allowed the FBI to collect backward and monitor any relevant electronic communications that had taken place before the spy warrant was granted.

> *The Majority mischaracterizes Bruce Ohr's role, overstates the significance of his interactions with Steele, and misleads about the timeframe of Ohr's communication with the FBI. In late November 2016, Ohr informed the FBI of his prior*

professional relationship with Steele and information that Steele shared with him (including Steele's concern about Trump being compromised by Russia). He also described his wife's contract work with Fusion GPS, the firm that hired Steele separately. This occurred weeks after the election and more than a month after the Court approved the initial FISA application.

That was false. Ohr had met with the Crossfire Hurricane team before the election to push information paid for by the Clinton campaign to the FBI. After Steele was fired, Ohr had served as his back channel to the FBI.

We would later learn in Papadopoulos's plea that the information the Russians could assist by anonymously releasing were thousands of Hillary Clinton's emails.

That appears to confirm that the emails Mifsud mentioned to Papadopoulos were not the DNC emails but those that Clinton had deleted from her private server.

———————

A useful response to the Nunes Memo came, surprisingly, from the Crossfire Hurricane team. According to the memo's last lines, the Strzok-Page texts describe "a meeting with Deputy Director McCabe to discuss an 'insurance' policy against President Trump's election." A few months after the memo was released, Strzok and Page themselves explained to Congress what they had meant. The "insurance policy," they said, did not refer to actions to be taken in the event of a Trump presidency. Rather, it referred to a specific detail regarding the Russia investigation: a source.

According to Strzok: "We had received information from a very sensitive source alleging collusion between the Government of Russia and members of the Trump campaign."

The Crossfire Hurricane team, according to Strzok, had debated "how aggressively to pursue investigation, given that aggressive pursuit might put that intelligence source at risk."

It seems that some inside McCabe's office that day had argued that since the polls were overwhelmingly in Clinton's favor, there was no need to risk the source. Strzok had contended that the FBI should push on as aggressively as possible.

"So my use of the phrase 'insurance policy,'" said Strzok, "was simply to say, while the polls or people might think it is less likely that then-candidate Trump would be elected, [that] should not get in the way of us doing our job responsibly to protect the national security."

Lisa Page corroborated Strzok's explanation. The "insurance policy," she said, had referred to the debate among members of the Crossfire Hurricane team. The question, she explained, was "Do we burn sources or not burn sources?"

Strzok had apparently won the argument.

As Nunes has said publicly, declassification of the warrant will explain what Strzok meant by "insurance policy." According to Nunes's public statements, it's something as bad as or worse than the Steele Dossier, something else the Crossfire Hurricane group used to obtain the spy warrant.

Chapter 19

THE CAVALRY ARRIVES

AFTER THE MEMO WAS RELEASED, Nunes's colleagues swarmed to congratulate him. The Republican conference gave him a standing ovation. Members came to the HPSCI chairman on the House floor to express their support and urge him on.

"Every time we took another step forward, more people joined us," says Nunes. "It was a bit different from the year before, when I'm under an ethics cloud and it was harder to find friends."

Indeed, two months before the memo's release, the House Committee on Ethics had cleared Nunes after an eight-month investigation of complaints by left-wing groups that he'd divulged classified information while discussing unmaskings by Obama officials.

It was hard for the Objective Medusa team to know just then if it had severed several snakes at the head or just one. But it was a win, and the moment, says Langer, felt different. "Conservatives, Republicans were fully engaged and really started caring about the issues we'd been working on for a year. It was new for us to have what seemed like a whole army of people behind us. The mainstream media universally attacked our memo and championed Schiff's memo, but all these people just didn't believe them anymore."

Representative Mike Turner, a member of the Intelligence Committee, gives Nunes all the credit for driving forward. "If Chairman Nunes had not led HPSCI into the investigation of the roots of how the Russia investigation began," he says, "there are critical pieces of information we'd have never known.

"And once he'd established there was abuse of power at the FBI and DOJ as a result of partisans attempting to harm Trump, it also shaped the Mueller investigation. The chairman uncovered those facts, foundational evidence that undercuts the credibility of the Russia investigation. Mueller couldn't ignore those facts and continue to pursue rumor and innuendo."

The Objective Medusa team's findings cornered the special counsel. The foundational evidence, as Turner puts it, also exposed a network of corruption at the highest levels of the national security bureaucracy.

"Comey, Clapper, and Brennan did an incredible disservice to the agencies they ran," says Turner. "You can see them on TV today, their constant willingness to spin rumor and malign others. They didn't acquire those traits after they left government. That's how they ran those agencies, with willingness to hurt others, contrary to the purpose of those agencies and our rights."

The conservative press also rallied. A number of journalists had staked their names to a story about widespread corruption in the intelligence community that even many Republican-friendly organizations had shied from. The release of the memo vindicated them.

"I'd been on the story since the Democratic National Convention in July," says FOX Business Network's Maria Bartiromo. "There was an announcement on the floor that the Russians had hacked the DNC's emails, and in the next few hours word started getting out that they'd done it to help Trump. This didn't make sense."

She had run into Nunes in the spring, shortly after he'd stepped aside from the Russia investigation. "I invited him to come on the show," says Bartiromo.

With that Nunes began a string of regular appearances on Bartiromo's *Sunday Morning Futures*, during which the two broke important news on the FISA abuse story. "We got lots of pushback from all sorts of corners," says Bartiromo. "I'm proud me and my staff stuck with the story."

The memo was further reinforced by other documents released at the same time. The first was a letter to the Justice Department from Senate Judiciary Committee (SJC) chairman Chuck Grassley.

"After Grassley's letter came out," Nunes remembers, "the press ignored it. They didn't attack the senator for saying the same thing we'd said. We were taking all the fire."

The SJC staff and Nunes's team were pushing in the same direction at the same time, using many of the same underlying documents. The heavily redacted Grassley letter was dated January 4, and the memo went to the White House on January 18.

The release of the Nunes Memo on February 2 automatically declassified much of the classified source material also used to write the Grassley letter. On February 6, the letter was rereleased in much less redacted form. The key findings were nearly identical to those of the memo:

- The bulk of the FISA application consisted of dossier allegations.

- The application failed to disclose that Steele's ultimate clients were the Clinton campaign and the DNC.
- Bruce Ohr, whose wife worked for Fusion GPS on the Trump-Russia project, warned the FBI that Steele was "desperate" that Trump not get elected.

Like HPSCI, Grassley's staff recognized immediately that the dossier was a fraudulent document. However, the manner in which it had been composed—attributing information to anonymous second- and third-hand sources—protected Steele against charges that he'd lied to the FBI. Even if he were caught out in an obvious falsehood, he was protected by attributing it to a source's source, whose identity he was unaware of.

But there was one way to catch Steele out. As the memo also noted, the FBI had claimed that Steele had not spoken with the press before the October 31, 2016, article that had led to his dismissal. But Steele had admitted to a British court that he had spoken with the press in the summer and fall of 2016, including Yahoo! News, which had published the Isikoff article used as evidence to obtain the FISA.

The FBI had said that Steele hadn't spoken with Yahoo! News.

One of them was lying, either the FBI or Steele. Or both. Grassley meant to force the issue by referring Steele to the Justice Department for a criminal investigation.

———————

The second significant document of the postmemo period was ready to go on March 22. But it wasn't until April 27 that DOJ released a heavily redacted version of HPSCI's *Report on Russian Active Measures*, a 253-page document memorializing the Nunes team's work on the Russia investigation.

"For the Russia Report, we separated out our work on FISA abuse and the other issues," says Nunes. "The report focused on Russian election interference—how they did it, how the US government responded—and issues that came out of that particular investigation, like leaks of information from the 2017 intelligence community assessment."

Significantly, the Russia Report found that former Director of National Intelligence James Clapper, "now a CNN national security analyst, provided inconsistent testimony to the Committee about his contacts with the media, including CNN."

Both Clapper and the CNN journalist with whom he was in contact, Jake Tapper, denied it.

Clapper told *Washington Post* fact checker Glenn Kessler that the first time he had "had any interaction with Tapper" was on May 14, 2017, months after he'd resigned as director of national intelligence (DNI). Moreover, Clapper told Kessler that he had not leaked the dossier when he was in government or talked about it with the media.

The former spy chief blamed Republicans for spreading a false story. However, even Adam Schiff's separate Russia investigation report noted that Clapper acknowledged having spoken with Tapper while he was still serving as DNI.

"Our report stands up very well," says Nunes. "The problem is that it's terribly overredacted. It would have been better if people had been able to read more of what was in there."

Because HPSCI's Russia Report cleared Trump of "collusion," media talking heads dismissed it as a whitewash.

News analysis published the day the lengthy report came out showed that pundits had not needed to read it before passing judgment.

"Although [the report] is meant to exonerate President Trump and everyone around him," wrote the *Washington Post*'s Paul Waldman and Greg Sargent, "what it actually does is bring the utter degradation and disgrace of that committee to its fullest expression."

Some of the reporting on the Russia Report struck a pose of even-handedness. "Though the report," wrote the *Washington Post*'s Matt Zapotosky, Karoun Demirjian, and Greg Miller, "...offers little in the way of new information, the dueling documents give each side of the aisle ammunition to support its long-held arguments about how and why Russia interfered in the 2016 election."

However, it's worth keeping in mind that "one side of the aisle" was pushing a conspiracy theory in partnership with intelligence bureaucrats, political operatives, and a media industry that cloaked its role behind a pretense of objectivity.

In writing about the Russia Report, journalists were covering an investigation of a series of abuses and crimes in which they'd participated. And so, because they themselves were part of the scandal, it wasn't a scandal.

Read alongside the press's hystericized daily coverage of the collusion conspiracy theory, the temperate language used to describe HPSCI's account of two attacks on US institutions (one by the Russians, another by Clinton operatives and Obama officials) is an exercise in gaslighting.

HPSCI Republicans, wrote the *New York Times*' Nicholas Fandos and Sharon LaFraniere on April 27, "faulted aides to Hillary Clinton for secretly paying for opposition research that included information from Russian sources, and castigated federal law enforcement and intelligence agencies for failing to counter Russian interference as well as for purported investigative abuses and allegedly damaging national security leaks."

Nunes was not shocked when Democrats and the press dismissed the report. "But it stands up," he says.

HPSCI produced forty-four findings and twenty-six recommendations that hit all the key parts of Russian actions and the Obama administration's flawed responses.

"The sign of a BS report is that it has no recommendations," says Jim. "We had them. We got it right."

Eight staffers had worked on the report every day, and committee members had been closely consulted. Damon Nelson had written a lot of the report, including the introduction. "He was an excellent writer," says Patel, "always drafting and redrafting."

But Nelson's primary responsibility, says Jim, "was to take care of the team, especially as it got to the end of the year in 2017 and we were in here every weekend. We took Christmas Eve and Christmas off, and that was it. We had a responsibility to get it done. It was clear to us early on that it was an important moment, an epochal moment."

The Russia Report, say HPSCI staffers, is part of Nelson's professional and political legacy. "We're all extremely proud of that work," says Langer. "And Damon was responsible for it."

Nelson had insisted that the report avoid anything that could be construed as partisan. "Damon believed that since we were uniquely positioned to get this information to the public," says Patel's investigative partner, "it was his responsibility to history to get out a report that was as clinical as possible."

The paradox, says Patel, is that "half of it is still redacted."

One of the significant redactions is the finding regarding the Russian troll farms. "We showed how the Russian troll farms work," says Nunes. "We identified the Internet Research Agency a year before the Mueller report came out. But the DOJ and FBI kept Americans from being able to read that information. We lost a

year in educating the American public about what happened in
the 2016 elections."

HPSCI fought against the extensive redactions. "But for a long
time, the only thing they agreed to unredact," says Langer, "were two
pages where Comey and McCabe said the agents who interviewed
Flynn about his conversation with the Russian ambassador didn't
think he was lying."

Comey was promoting his book at the time, says Langer,
"claiming he didn't know anything about the agents saying they
didn't think Flynn lied, so we pressed hard to get it unredacted."

Although the report did not focus on FBI and DOJ investigation
abuses, key findings still reinforced the memo and showed the wide
scope of the anti-Trump operation. For instance:

- Executive branch officials did not notify the Trump campaign that members of the campaign were assessed to be
  potential counterintelligence concerns.
- When asked directly, none of the interviewed witnesses
  provided evidence of collusion, coordination, or conspiracy between the Trump campaign and the Russian government.
- The judgments made by the Intelligence Community
  Assessment regarding Putin's strategic intentions did not
  employ proper analytic tradecraft.
- Leaks of classified information alleging Russian intentions
  to help elect candidate Trump increased dramatically after
  election day, November 8, 2016.

Producing the memo had overextended the resources of the
committee's small team. "We have oversight on seventeen agencies,"

says Nunes. "We had other important issues we needed to get back to."

Further, the fight to get the memo out had drained both Nunes and his staff. They'd taken fire from the national security bureaucracy, the press corps, and other political operatives, but even in the glow of the memo's release they realized they couldn't go through the same process again.

"We were not going to do another memo," says Patel. "So there were two more steps—first was the task force. And for our closing move, we'd ask the president to declassify information that we'd identified."

Nunes brought in the Judiciary and Oversight Committees to share responsibilities. The task force tapped the energies of GOP legislators increasingly angry with executive branch officials who were slow-rolling or outright ignoring their requests for documents and information.

Rod Rosenstein in particular had identified himself as a hostile. Representatives Jim Jordan of Ohio and Mark Meadows of North Carolina wanted to impeach him. Ironically, it was the HPSCI chairman Rosenstein had openly opposed who kept the deputy attorney general from being impeached. "They had the votes," says Nunes.

During a vote on the House floor, Nunes convened a meeting with Jordan and Meadows, as well as House speaker Paul Ryan, Trey Gowdy, and Virginia's Bob Goodlatte. "I said that if we impeach Rosenstein, they're going to shut everything down," he told his colleagues. "They won't give us anything. So let's set up this task force and keep the investigation going."

The next week, Ryan introduced the task force, comprising members of the Oversight, Judiciary, and Intelligence Committees, to the House Republican Conference. The members were enthusiastic. Texas's John Ratcliffe of Texas joined, bringing more prosecutorial experience to the initiative.

Patel walked members through the essential material the Objective Medusa team had uncovered. "I discussed some of the stuff we'd seen, the documents they might want to look at, and who they might want to interview," he says.

The task force wound up interviewing all of the major FBI figures involved in the conspiracy—Comey, McCabe, Strzok, Page, lawyers James Baker and Sally Moyer, as well as DOJ senior official Bruce Ohr and his wife, Nellie.

The other issue handled by task force colleagues was the Strzok-Page texts. The DOJ's inspector general had found the texts in July 2017, and Mueller had removed Strzok from the special counsel.

"Kash had noticed he was reassigned from the special counsel and said, 'Someone doesn't just get moved from one of those jobs unless he's done something bad,'" says Nunes.

HPSCI requested the documents pertaining to why Strzok had been moved to a notably less prestigious posting. In the early fall of 2017, Nunes's team received what they were told was the entirety of the Strzok-Page texts.

"We asked Rosenstein and Wray point-blank if this was everything, and they said, yes, they gave us everything that's relevant," says Nunes. "I think they were being honest. But someone behind them wasn't giving us everything. Someone at the FBI was obstructing our investigation. But these guys think it's a game."

The FBI handed the Objective Medusa team puzzle pieces.

"When we started getting the texts, the FBI gave them to other bodies that demanded them, too," says Nunes. "The Senate, House Judiciary Committee, House Oversight, and us. We were all given different text messages. It was like they were dumping a bunch of different puzzle pieces on different committees—and good luck figuring it out."

It was impossible to piece the story together. "For instance, we'd get piece A and B of a certain text exchange," says Nunes. "Another committee got C and D. Someone else got G and H. No one got E and F—and the missing pieces always turned out to be the worst stuff."

Nunes credits Mark Meadows for putting it together. "He wouldn't stop until he got all the texts. He's the repository for the text message puzzle," says Nunes. "He's been building it."

The four-term congressman credits his staff. "I'll give you an analogy," says the fifty-nine-year-old Meadows. "The FBI threw everything in a big garbage bag and said, 'There it is.' So starting in November 2017, our staff dug through the garbage to find what was hidden to keep the truth from the American people. Most of what people understand about the text messages came from the work of our great staff."

The FBI tried to get ahead of the Strzok-Page texts story and spin it. A December 2, 2017, *Washington Post* article by Karoun Demirjian and Devlin Barrett contended that Strzok had been wronged. "I had the occasion to work closely with Special Agent Peter Strzok and never experienced even a hint of political bias," an anonymous former official told the *Post*. Strzok wasn't just a "competent counterintelligence official," the source continued, but also "a role model." The country, the source concluded, "is tearing itself apart, and men like Pete Strzok are victims."

Nunes's communications director had become accustomed to the press's role in protecting Crossfire Hurricane. "Publishing preemptive leaks was a regular service the *Post* and *Times* offered to its leakers and allies," says Langer.

The text messages did not paint the same heroic portrait of Strzok as the *Post*'s sources, which was why FBI tried to cloak them with extensive redactions.

"The redactions on the texts would not allow for the true story to come out," says Meadows. "That true story is obviously one of bias, but it's also one of a coordinated effort with others in the intel community to make sure that the 'collusion' narrative was not disposed of quickly."

Meadows explains that what he learned came from unclassified text messages. The text messages sent to Nunes were classified. "We never gave Meadows the texts we got," says Nunes. "They were supposedly classified. But they shouldn't have been. It didn't deal with national security issues. They just hid everything under a classified counterintelligence investigation."

The redactions obscured the role of the previous White House. "There were key meetings with Obama officials," says Meadows. "For instance, there's a meeting with White House chief of staff McDonough in which the FBI/DOJ is briefing him on what appeared to be the Russian investigation on August 10, 2016. There's no doubt that Obama officials were involved. But to opine on their motives would be something that I can't do. I think if you were to ask them they would say they were trying to make sure that they were protecting the integrity of our election system from the Russians."

It's not easy to make that case for some Obama officials. The name of the former CIA director, Meadows says, was redacted and kept out of text messages given to Congress. "Brennan knows that there was no coordination, collusion, or conspiracy. He knew that when he left. If he were honest, he would acknowledge the type of work that he not only knew of but also was involved with that would indicate there was no coordination at all with the Russians."

Chapter 20

THE FORGERS

THERE WAS ANOTHER THING the Objective Medusa team wanted. The subject matter was delicate, but even at that stage Nunes and his team couldn't have imagined the response.

"FBI and DOJ went nuts," says Langer. "They started leaking to reporters that Nunes is going to get people killed."

On April 24, 2018, HPSCI sent a classified letter to Attorney General Jeff Sessions, asking for documents regarding sensitive matters. "We didn't want to subpoena them right off," says Patel. "The way things worked with the DOJ was that they said if you want something, just call us or write us. But they would never come through. So in this instance we wanted some specific information. We didn't get it. A week later we issued a subpoena stating that we wanted the stuff that we asked for in the classified letter."

A May 8 *Washington Post* article by Robert Costa, Carol D. Leonnig, Devlin Barrett, and Shane Harris reported that "Information being sought by House Intelligence Committee Chairman Devin Nunes could endanger a top-secret intelligence source." The article's headline noted that the source had "aided" the special counsel investigation.

That was the first in a handful of May 2018 stories in the *Post* and the *Times* illustrating the press's new role in prosecuting the operation.

The previous month, the staffs of the two papers had been awarded a joint Pulitzer Prize for "deeply sourced, relentlessly reported coverage in the public interest that dramatically furthered the nation's understanding of Russian interference in the 2016 presidential election and its connections to the Trump campaign, the President-elect's transition team and his eventual administration."

Many of the twenty stories cited by the Pulitzer committee were sourced to leaks of classified information. Thus the print press had bestowed its highest honor on rogue FBI and DOJ officials who'd coordinated with media operatives in a plot to topple the president.

It was a crime spree, says Patel. "A select few members of the law enforcement agencies charged with the sublime duty of enforcing the law, were the ones regularly breaking it by disclosing classified information to the media for a preemptive story to defuse their next identified failure. HPSCI could have easily done the same but never did. Instead we chose to follow a path the shameful few in law enforcement felt was beneath them."

The May 2018 stories in the *Post* and the *Times* highlighted how the nature of the operation had changed: the press had gone from offense to defense.

With the lead actors in the Crossfire Hurricane group flushed from the FBI—Andrew McCabe was fired in March 2018, Lisa Page resigned in May, Peter Strzok would be gone by the summer—the media lost inside sources.

More important, Nunes and his team were putting points on the board. Now the job of the media was to stop Nunes and protect dirty cops. The *Times* and the *Post* became the public custodians of the Crossfire Hurricane investigation.

As the media's offensive campaign had depended on leaks of classified information, so did the defensive campaign, relying on leaks regarding a counterintelligence investigation, which is classified by definition.

A May 16 *Times* story by Matt Apuzzo, Adam Goldman, and Nicholas Fandos revealed key details of the investigation, including the pop culture–inspired name of the FBI's probe: Crossfire Hurricane.

DOJ invited Nunes and an HPSCI colleague, Trey Gowdy, to a briefing on Friday, May 18. The night before, they were told that no documents would be forthcoming. The two congressmen pulled out of the meeting.

"We knew they were going to try to set us up," says Nunes. "They wanted to leak details of the investigation to the media and say we were the ones leaking. All they needed in the press reports was a line to the effect that Nunes and Gowdy had been briefed."

Nevertheless, the *Times* and the *Post* both went ahead with their Friday, May 18, articles, revealing further information regarding a confidential human source used in the investigation.

"The informant," reported the *Times*' Adam Goldman, Mark Mazzetti, and Matthew Rosenberg, "is well known in Washington circles, having served in previous Republican administrations and as a source of information for the C.I.A. in past years, according to one person familiar with the source's work."

"In mid-July 2016," wrote the *Post*'s Robert Costa, Carol D. Leonnig, Tom Hamburger, and Devlin Barrett, "a retired American professor approached an adviser to Donald Trump's presidential campaign at a symposium about the White House race held at a British university. . . . But the professor was more than an academic interested in American politics—he was a longtime U.S. intelligence source."

Though neither article disclosed the source's identity, it was easy to discern who it was—thanks to Chuck Ross's important March 25, 2018, article on Daily Caller reporting how an American professor from the University of Cambridge had tried to frame Papadopoulos.

Within days, the *Post* did publish his name—in another story with Robert Costa getting the lead byline: "Who Is Stefan A. Halper, the FBI Source Who Assisted the Russia Investigation?"

Costa, it turned out, had known him for years. "Stefan Halper was my professor at Cambridge," he tweeted on May 21. "Took his course, went to his dinners. Stayed in touch over the years. Last spoke with him in 2015. A China hawk, moderate R, highly-connected and gregarious academic."

Nunes wanted to know how many informants the FBI had used against the Trump campaign and when they had been sent in. Had any informants been used before the date the FBI claimed it had opened Crossfire Hurricane, July 31, 2016?

That date, as Patel had explained, had only served to give the FBI bureaucratic cover. Clearly the FBI had been looking into Trump and his associates before the investigation had opened. The July 31 date was a fault line dividing the issues the FBI was willing to discuss from those it wanted to hide.

A timeline bracketing the July 31 date may better illustrate the nature of the operation, a timeline based on the dates that Halper, or his associates, came into contact with the Trump team.

- **January 2016:** Halper associate Christopher Andrew, a University of Cambridge professor, invites British academic

Svetlana Lokhova to dinner on behalf of Halper. The former Reagan aide used Lokhova to dirty National Security Advisor Michael Flynn in a media campaign that served as the basis of an investigation of Flynn.

- **March 2016:** The George Papadopoulos operation, in which Halper will play a central role, commences when a Maltese professor, Joseph Mifsud, meets Papadopoulos.
- **April 2016:** Mifsud allegedly tells Papadopoulos that the Russians have thousands of Hillary Clinton's emails.
- **May 2016:** Alexander Downer meets Papadopoulos in May and passes information to US authorities, which leads to the opening of Crossfire Hurricane in July. Trump adviser Stephen Miller is invited to participate in a July symposium at the University of Cambridge arranged by Halper's academic department. Miller declines.
- **June 2016:** A Halper associate at Cambridge, Steven Schrage, invites a former Trump adviser, Carter Page, to the July symposium. Page accepts.
- **July 2016:** Halper first meets with Page at the Cambridge symposium on July 11 and tries to draw him into a conversation about Trump campaign chairman Paul Manafort. Downer also speaks with Page, who is sitting next to him during the keynote address delivered by former secretary of state Madeleine Albright.
- **August 2016:** Halper invites Page to visit him in Virginia. Contacts between the two increase as the FISA application is being drafted. Halper emails Trump foreign policy adviser Sam Clovis and arranges to meet with him.
- **September 2016:** Halper writes to Papadopoulos, inviting him to London. Both Halper and a US government undercover investigator, Azra Turk, seek to elicit information

regarding Clinton emails supposedly held by the Russians.

- **Fall 2016:** A Halper associate, the former head of MI6 Sir Richard Dearlove, reportedly meets with former MI6 agent Christopher Steele and encourages him to share his findings with active British officials.
- **December 2016:** Halper begins to brief the US and UK press on allegations regarding Flynn and Lokhova.
- **February 2017:** Christopher Andrew writes an article alleging that Lokhova compromised Flynn.
- **March 2017:** The Halper campaign targeting Flynn and Lokhova continues with articles in the *Wall Street Journal* and *The Guardian*.
- **September 2017:** Halper speaks with Carter Page for the last time; the FISA warrant on Page expires.
- **May 2018:** FBI and DOJ leaks to the *Washington Post* and the *New York Times* partially reveal Halper's role in the Crossfire Hurricane investigation. Halper's allegations regarding Flynn and Lokhova appear in the *Post* and *Times*.

The timeline shows that Halper was more than just a source; his contribution appears to have been even more significant than Steele's.

———————————

Christopher Steele took over MI6's Russia desk in 2006, a trying year for British intelligence's Russia-related operations.

In November, Alexander Litvinenko, a high-profile defector from the FSB (the Russian secret service, successor of the KGB) who had been granted asylum in the United Kingdom in 2000, was murdered in London. Steele, according to British news reports, had been Litvinenko's case officer.

Sources are valuable commodities, to be protected at all costs. Yet how was it possible to protect a man as reckless as Litvinenko? He had used London as a rostrum from which he had regularly denounced Putin, claiming there were tapes of the Russian leader proving that he was a pedophile.

Litvinenko needed money. The £2,000 MI6 was paying him monthly was not enough to keep his family afloat in one of the world's most expensive cities. When an Italian official investigating Moscow's infiltration of Rome's political establishment offered Litvinenko work in 2003, he jumped at the chance.

In 2001, the Italians had set up a commission to study the claims made by former KGB officer Vasili Mitrokhin. He had defected to the United Kingdom in 1992, taking with him notes on the KGB's foreign operations, including reports on Western officials compromised by Russian intelligence.

However, not everything Mitrokhin told Western officials was true, says Svetlana Lokhova. The Cambridge historian who says she was smeared by Halper had worked extensively in the Mitrokhin archives. Her former professor Christopher Andrew had cowritten several books with the Russian defector, including *The Sword and the Shield: The Mitrokhin Archive and the Secret History of the KGB*.

"After the Soviet Union broke apart, you had all these former KGB spies who were broke and with no way to make a living," Lokhova explains.

Like spies from time immemorial, Mitrokhin found he could improve his quality of life by giving the other side information it valued. He talked to Western intelligence agencies and kept talking for as long as he was paid to do so.

Mitrokhin did not have copies of actual KGB files. "He had taken notes on the files that he'd seen," said Lokhova. "Some of those notes were ambiguous or led to different interpretations.

Much of the time Mitrokhin was telling the truth, but other times, he was just saying what Western intelligence services or politicians wanted to hear. He was getting paid to talk."

Mitrokhin pioneered a post–Cold War cottage industry: billing Westerners for stories about how Moscow manipulated other Westerners. Litvinenko picked up where Mitrokhin had left off. At first the Italians wanted to know if the KGB had compromised senior officials in the past, but by the time Litvinenko came on, the commission convened by Italian officials had become a weapon that then prime minister Silvio Berlusconi was using against his current opponents. Litvinenko said that Democratic Party leader Romano Prodi was "the KGB's man in Italy."

Litvinenko's information, according to reports, "was very difficult to verify and cross-check. It was a little bit out on a limb."

Litvinenko was poisoned in a London hotel, and Steele led the inquiry into his death. Steele, according to reports, was among the first to claim that Litvinenko's murder had been a Russian state operation. Within months, Steele left MI6.

In the private sector, the former MI6 Russianist's work often involved Russia-related matters. It's true that he hadn't been to Russia since the early 1990s, but there were plenty of sources at hand, thousands of Russians in London alone, including oligarchs who parked their cash in the British capital. Steele worked for one of them, Oleg Deripaska.

Steele cultivated a reputation as the man to see for Russia-related issues. He frequently coupled his work with similar projects for other clients, sometimes getting paid twice for the same job. The public record suggests that the accuracy of Steele's information on Russia was mixed at best.

For instance, in 2009, when Steele was hired to investigate Russia's bid for the 2018 World Cup, he made inroads with the FBI by introducing its agents to Andrew Jennings. The British journalist had been following FIFA corruption for nearly a decade, and his information helped the FBI's investigation.

As for Steele's own investigation into Russian corruption in the World Cup bid, UK authorities buried his uncorroborated allegations. He nonetheless leaked them to the press.

After Russia's invasion of Ukraine, Steele was hired by a private client to write reports on the situation. He shared those memos, reportedly more than a hundred of them, with State Department official Jonathan Winer. According to a former State Department official, "occasionally, [Steele's] sources appeared to exaggerate their knowledge or influence."

The information Steele gave to US diplomats actually belonged to the client, without whose permission to share it, he would have been giving away proprietary information. What's more likely is that the client was paying Steele at least in part to distribute his reports to the State Department.

Another private client hired Steele for a different Russia-related job. According to *New Yorker* writer Jane Mayer's March 12, 2018, profile of Steele, the former MI6 man called that investigation "Project Charlemagne." It touched on Russian election interference in Europe, the Kremlin's use of social media warfare, its "opaque financial support" for European politicians, and its relationship with former Italian prime minister Silvio Berlusconi and France's right-wing firebrand Marine Le Pen.

In other words, Steele was carrying on Litvinenko's work. Except where the Russian was hired to accuse Berlusconi's rivals of working with the KGB, Steele's job was to turn the tables on the former Italian prime minister and accuse him of cozying up to Putin. He claimed that the Kremlin's goal in supporting right-wing European politicians was to "destroy" the European Union to bring an end to its Ukraine-related sanctions.

But that makes no sense. The European Union is the number one foreign consumer of Russian energy, a sector that accounts for more than half the country's revenues. Why would Putin want to *destroy* Moscow's most important customer and send the Russian economy into a tailspin?

Most famously, there was the Trump-Russia research, which Steele gave to the FBI and the press as well as his employee, the Clinton campaign. Steele admitted in a British court that his reports on Trump had not been verified.

Despite the media testimonies regarding Steele's talent for uncovering Russian intrigue, the public evidence shows that Steele was bad at his job—unless his job was to use his spy credentials to fool people into believing all the things he said about Russia, as Mitrokhin and Litvinenko had.

Glenn Simpson usually accompanied Steele when he briefed the press because the former MI6 agent didn't know the details of the reports he was supposed to have written.

On October 11, 2016, Jonathan Winer introduced Steele to a State Department colleague. It was a week before the first FISA and a little less than a month before the election. Steele downloaded everything Fusion GPS had on Trump and Russia.

Foreign service officers take good notes. Learning to report meetings and interviews with foreigners quickly and accurately is one of the most important parts of a US foreign service officer's training. The notes of career foreign service officer Kathleen Kavalec are evidence that Steele was not the author of the dossier.

Steele told her that the Russians were running operations through their consulate in Miami. Kavalec remarked in her notes that there is no Russian Consulate in Miami. Steele had flubbed his line. The dossier never mentions a Miami consulate. Rather, Dossier Report 95 claims that the Russians were using *consular officials* to run operations in Miami, as well as in New York and Washington.

The former spy told Kavalec that "Manafort has been the go-between with the campaign." But Manafort had left the campaign nearly two months previously.

Steele told the State Department official that Carter Page had had two secret meetings with Rosneft chairman Igor Sechin earlier in 2016.

According to the dossier, however, Page had had only one meeting with Sechin, during his July 2016 trip to Moscow. But there are two separate *reports* of the same meeting. The first is dated July 19. The second, dated October 18, revises the account of the meeting to allege that the Trump aide is part of a bribery scheme.

As Kash Patel said of the actions described in that second report, "a US person, who is believed to be acting as a foreign agent, and commits a crime" is what you get a FISA for.

Steele's October 11 meeting with Kavalec was one week before the date of the second report; the former spy appears to have inadvertently revealed that his employers were cooking up a memo tailored to obtain the spy warrant.

Steele told Kavalec that "Presidential Advisor Vladislov Surkov and Vyacheslov Trubnikov (former head of Russian External Intelligence Service—SVR) are also involved."

But according to Kavalec's handwritten notes, Steele told her that Surkov and Trubnikov had also been *sources* for his reports. So were the two Russians plotting to undo US democracy, or were they warning Steele about Putin's plans to use Trump to undermine NATO?

Surkov was a well-known figure in State Department Russianist circles during the latter years of the Obama administration. He was Moscow's point man for a bilateral channel to discuss Ukraine. Representing the United States was Assistant Secretary of State for European and Eurasian Affairs Victoria Nuland—Kavalec's boss.

Maybe when Steele's employer Glenn Simpson was meeting with Nuland he talked about Surkov. But if the Russian really wanted to convey information about Putin's plot against the United States, why didn't he just tell US officials directly about Trump's Kremlin ties? He had several chances during his several meetings with Nuland. She was a Clinton ally, a possible candidate for secretary of state in a Clinton administration. She might have welcomed information damaging to Trump.

As for Trubnikov, Bruce Ohr seems to have confirmed that Steele had claimed him as a source. "One of the items of information that Chris Steele gave to me," Ohr told Congress, "was that he had information that a former head of the Russian Foreign Intelligence Service, the SVR, had stated to someone—I didn't know who—that they had Donald Trump over a barrel."

Stefan Halper knew Trubnikov.

———————

Halper brought the ex–intelligence chief to the University of Cambridge twice, in May 2012 and again in May 2015. Halper claimed that Trubnikov had been one of his sources.

Naming sources for his 2015–2016 Pentagon-funded study, "The Russia-China Relationship: The Impact on the United States' Security Interests"—Halper listed V. I. Trubnikov. He described him as a member of the Russian Academy of Sciences. Halper also listed a second Trubnikov as a source: V. S. Trubnikov, described as the "Former Russian Deputy Foreign Minister and Russian ambassador to India."

The two are the same person. Vyacheslav Ivanovich (i.e., "V. I.") Trubnikov is a member of the Russian Academy of Sciences— as well as former ambassador to India and onetime deputy foreign minister. He was also once the head of Russia's foreign intelligence service. There is no V. S. Trubnikov on record who served in any of these posts.

Halper was employing a variation of a well-known journalistic trick: reporters use several descriptions of the same person to suggest that their stories are attributed to several anonymous persons rather than to only one unnamed source. For instance, in an article anonymously sourced only to Adam Schiff, a journalist might describe him as "a member of the Democrat leadership," "a senior intelligence official," "a veteran California legislator," and so on.

Many of the descriptions of sources used in the dossier could apply to Trubnikov, including the first two sources named in the very first memo. They assert the dossier's central claim: that Trump had been compromised by the Russians.

The June 20 report introduces "sources A and B, a senior Russian Foreign Ministry figure and a former top level Russian intelligence officer still active inside the Kremlin respectively." According to the two sources, "the Russian authorities had been cultivating and supporting US Republican presidential candidate, Donald TRUMP for at least 5 years."

It looks as though the dossier author is doubling up on Trubnikov, just as Halper did in his Pentagon report. A former

deputy foreign minister and ambassador to India would certainly
qualify as a senior Russian Foreign Ministry figure, like source A.
Source B is almost surely supposed to be Trubnikov.

> *Speaking separately in June 2016, Source B [the former top
> level Russian intelligence officer] asserted that TRUMP's
> unorthodox behavior in Russia over the years had provided
> the authorities there with enough embarrassing material
> on the now Republican presidential candidate to be able to
> blackmail him if they so wished.*

To put it another way, as Steele told Ohr—the Russians had
Trump over a barrel. Could it be true?

Sure, Trubnikov might have said such things to Steele—or his
"subsources." And they might have been true. Maybe the Russians
really had been cultivating Trump for more than five years—or since
shortly before Halper first spoke with Trubnikov at Cambridge in
2012. Trubnikov might have told them true things, or he might
have been seeding the Fusion GPS reports with disinformation to
deceive US and UK intelligence services.

But the evidence points to something else.

If Steele really believed that the future of the "Western alliance,"
as the dossier put it, was under attack, a former MI6 officer would be
expected, at the very least, to remember details from the intelligence
reports he'd supposedly written to document the subterfuge.

But the dossier is not an "intelligence" product. It's a fiction, a
literary forgery, populated with real characters, but who did not do
or say the things attributed to them. And the dossier's authors are
not intelligence officers but journalists and academics accustomed
to running smear campaigns and dirty tricks operations and lying.

Halper misled the United States government regarding the sources of his 2015 China Russia report to the Pentagon. He even invented a source, claiming he had two different men named Trubnikov as sources.

Washington Times reporter Rowan Scarborough proved that Halper was lying by phoning former CIA chief Michael Hayden and others, who denied having been Halper's sources for his Pentagon research.

It would have been nearly impossible for anyone to corroborate whether a former Russian spymaster had truly told Halper anything about Trump or anything else.

Halper wasn't a spy; he was a dirty tricks operative with four decades of experience. He was a con man the FBI was determined to protect.

Chapter 21

THE HARVEST

ROWS OF WALNUT TREES line the road to Tulare, California, casting jagged shadows in the morning light. Many have already been harvested, electric shakers tethered to the tree trunks shocking the green nuts from their branches. The weather is still warm in the valley during the day, but within a month the skies will turn gray and the snow will start to fall in the Sierra Nevada.

It's election time, and Nunes is driving through his home district, California's Twenty-second. His daughters Julia and Margaret are in the back seat chatting quietly, accustomed to making the Saturday-morning rounds with their father. Their route encompasses the entire district, Tulare and most of eastern Fresno, as well as Visalia and Clovis.

On the highway into Visalia, it's plain that Russiagate madness has migrated like pollution from Washington, DC, fouling the warm Central Valley air. Billboards in Russian with Nunes's picture portray him as a Putin stooge.

This is the new local landscape that the national media has shaped. Days before the Nunes Memo was released, MSNBC analyst

John Heilemann asked Connecticut senator Chris Murphy if "we actually have a *Russian* agent running the House Intel Committee on the Republican side?"

Many of Nunes's constituents have been poisoned by the propaganda campaign aimed at him. Outside activists have flooded the district, calling the congressman a traitor.

At a Starbucks in Visalia, a middle-aged woman in dark glasses corners Nunes and his two girls. "This is not why we sent you to Washington," she says. "Not to support Trump. We're very disappointed in you. We need to have a town hall for you to answer questions."

"I'm here for you right now," says Nunes, putting himself between the woman and his daughters. "What did you want to talk about? Have you contacted my office to set up a meeting?"

"Actually," she admits, "I'm not in your district."

The self-styled anti-Trump "resistance" that has zeroed in on Nunes is anything but a progressive grass-roots movement. Rather, it's a function of Democratic Party donors underwriting tactics designed to protect the privileges and prerogatives of the coastal elite, from the Beltway to Hollywood. The "resistance" is how college-educated leftist masses have been mobilized to march on behalf of political corruption.

"They're trying to teach me a lesson," says Nunes during the drive. "'If you go after the bad things we do in Washington, we'll come after you at home.'"

Home is partly the sequence of routines determined by the people who inhabit a place. "I've had the same friends, known all the same people, since I was a kid," says Nunes.

For him, Saturdays typically begin with coffee brewed by Basil Perch, the seventy-seven-year-old former mayor of Visalia. Perch holds court every Saturday morning in the offices of his construction firm housed in a local industrial park.

Posters of Perch's granddaughter's high school soccer team and photographs of his grandfather as a young man just escaped from the Armenian genocide fill the walls.

Perch sits at the head of a large table surrounded by other local businessmen—such as Mike Fistolera, another builder—who like talking about politics, national and local. "I have people on the inside who talk to me," he says with a smile. He's chewing on an unlit cigar and asks Nunes about Washington. Perch likes Trump. "He knows what real leadership is all about," says Perch. "So does he," he continues, pointing his cigar at the congressman.

Nunes mostly listens. With Perch and the others, the GOP maverick who's energized half the nation by taking on virtually every authority and entrenched institution in the national capital is a younger man among the elders, men of his father's generation.

Nunes's circle is bound by old-world values drawn from the various immigrant blocs that make up his constituency—among others, Portuguese, like his family, Armenians like Perch's, and Mexicans, the latest arrivals.

Later we head to a parade ground to watch Nunes's eldest daughter, Evelyn, drill for her middle school marching band, and it appears at least half of the kids from the dozen or so bands are from Latino families. English is their first language. They don't speak Spanish because their parents want them to grow up as Americans.

Nunes says he doesn't have much trouble identifying his supporters from a distance. "Boots, jeans, pocket T-shirts, it doesn't matter if it's a white guy or a Mexican guy," he Nunes. "They're dressed like normal Valley people, own trucks and the like. When you see older retired white bureaucrats or professors in expensive hybrid cars, chances are good they're not my supporters."

Before the Russia investigations, Nunes had enjoyed the support of independents and moderate Democrats. He was first elected in 2002 when he promised to take on environmentalists who wanted to divert water into the ocean and choke the land.

"Devin was originally elected because he promised to fight the water wars," says Ray Appleton, central California's top-rated radio talk show host.

Appleton started in radio nearly fifty years ago on the music side. The long-haired, gray-bearded, thick-chested sixty-six-year-old in a leather jacket looks less like a conservative pundit than a rocker who is surprised by nothing that humans do. He first met Nunes during his initial congressional race. "Oddly, I supported the other guy," Appleton tells me. "But Devin was the best man for the job. Even his opponent said so. Now we're all close friends."

The 2018 race was hardly as cordial. The Democrats spent more than $9 million on his opponent's race. Local political analysts estimate that they spent another $2 million in dark money. That made his opponent, who had no prior political experience, one of the biggest fund-raisers in the entire congressional election cycle. Money on that scale buys a lot of mail pieces and TV ads in a small media market like the Central Valley. Nunes's opponents inundated the safely Republican district with attack ads. They weren't trying to unseat Nunes but to punish him—and his family.

After the attacks on his family and the death threats in the run-up to the release of the memo, the anti-Nunes operation gathered steam, with operatives and the press looking for any dirt with which to smear him.

Esquire magazine sent reporter Ryan Lizza to Iowa for a story purporting to blow the lid off a "secret" farm owned by Nunes's father.

It was hardly any secret; Nunes senior had moved to Iowa more than a dozen years before to help his younger son. Lizza tracked Nunes family members who had become concerned after they'd discovered the reporter had been fired from a job for sexual misconduct.

They went after Nunes's family in California, too. In September, a film crew trespassed on Tulare land farmed by his Uncle Gerald to generate a story out of his outrage and put it on film.

"The point was to use me as another thing to go after Devin," says Gerald, a broad-chested man with the forearms and permanent tan of a professional baseball coach. He drives me on a tour of the dairy farm, first bought by his grandparents. He points to the wooden house where he grew up, a little more than a decade before his nephew was born. Hundreds of light brown cows are grazing in the afternoon sun.

"Cows are great animals," says Devin Nunes. "But it was always my goal to be in the wine business. My mother's father owned a vineyard and grew grapes."

Nunes's agricultural background is a frequent point of attack for his Deep State adversaries and the press. "When I'm home in California, I do a lot of interviews from the World Ag Expo in Tulare because it's closer to my home than the TV studios. An extra benefit is that the tractors in the background drive the Left crazy. One thing I've learned is that it's really easy to troll these people."

Clovis is a small, bright California town that looks like a set out of a western produced by conservatives: clean, polite, and devout.

Nunes steps into a coffee shop owned by a former NFL linebacker, Zack Follett, an evangelical Christian who starred at Clovis High School before going on to the University of California at Berkeley. After a neck injury brought his career to an end, he opened a chain of Christian coffee shops. A few college students are scattered around the shop, sipping caffelattes with their laptops open, writing term papers on the Bible.

Nunes waits in line for coffee, shaking hands with supporters and deflecting praise with a short laugh. A man in operating room scrubs wants to speak with him about the investigations.

Josh LeRoy, a thirty-seven-year-old medical device salesman, tells Nunes that many of his friends and family follow his efforts to hold the conspirators accountable.

"I'm not starstruck or anything," LeRoy tells me later. "If it was Michael Jordan, I wouldn't care. But I felt I needed to thank Devin for what he is doing for our country because I truly feel he is risking his life fighting for us."

LeRoy didn't know about the death threats against Nunes. "It takes real courage," he says. He notes one of the most interesting aspects of the Nunes phenomenon: "The only guy to take a stand is from California," says LeRoy, "the most liberal state of the union."

It's not easy to become a national figure from a state dominated by left-wing politics. Nunes became a national figure not by adjusting his message to gain admirers around the country but by projecting the values of the local community that raised him.

LeRoy asks when the documents the HPSCI chair asked for will be declassified.

It's a year and a half into the investigation, and Nunes is still surprised that so many people who come up to him know all the details of the plot against Trump, the figures involved—Comey, Brennan, Steele, Simpson, McCabe, Strzok and Page, the Ohrs—and the status of HPSCI's investigation. The first rallying cry was to release the memo. Now it's to declassify the documents.

———————

After the Objective Medusa team had pushed out the memo, Patel argued that the best thing would be if Americans could see for themselves what the Crossfire Hurricane team had done. "We assembled a number of buckets of information provided to us by the FBI and DOJ that would best tell the story without jeopardizing national security interests," he says.

During the summer, Nunes had asked the White House to declassify the information. "It was pages ten to twelve and seventeen to thirty-four of the third and final FISA renewal," says Patel. "There was also the twelve Bruce Ohr 302s—which is just a loose description because they're not just about Bruce Ohr. And finally exculpatory information that was withheld from the FISA court."

Patel says that he considers the last item the most significant. "For me as a prosecutor," says the former DOJ lawyer, "the biggest thing in the world is Brady."

The "Brady rule," established by the Supreme Court in *Brady v. Maryland* (1963), requires the prosecution to turn over exculpatory evidence.

"It is the duty and the ethical responsibility of the DOJ to provide that to the court," says Patel. "It would be one thing if DOJ went in there and said, 'We didn't have this in our system. There was no way for us to know this.' And sometimes that happens. But in this instance we found the documents that showed they knew the exculpatory evidence existed. They created it, they could have presented it and chose not to. They withheld it from the court."

On September 17, Trump had ordered the material to be declassified. A few days later, Andrew McCabe had appeared to send a warning to the DOJ official who could convince Trump not to declassify.

A *New York Times* story by Adam Goldman and Michael Schmidt sourced in part to McCabe's memos reported how in May

2017, Rod Rosenstein had talked about recording the president and invoking the Twenty-fifth Amendment to remove him from office.

Rosenstein denied it in a comment to the *Times*. In a *Washington Post* article intended to douse the fire the *Times* piece had started, an unnamed Rosenstein ally claimed that the DOJ official had been joking. The comment had been meant sarcastically, "along the lines of: 'What do you want to do, Andy, wire the president?'"

The light McCabe had shone on Rosenstein's zeal to topple the president just a year before might have helped remind the deputy attorney general that there were plenty of documents memorializing the misdeeds of many, including Rosenstein. In any event, Rosenstein dissuaded Trump from declassifying documents that would have spelled trouble for the Crossfire Hurricane team. On September 21, the president tweeted:

> *I met with the DOJ concerning the declassification of various UNREDACTED documents. They agreed to release them but stated that so doing may have a perceived negative impact on the Russia probe. Also, key Allies called to ask not to release.*
>
> *Therefore, the Inspector General has been asked to review these documents on an expedited basis. I believe he will move quickly on this (and hopefully other things which he is looking at). In the end I can always declassify if it proves necessary. Speed is very important to me—and everyone!*

Nunes and his team recognized Rosenstein's hand immediately. Using the "allies" as an excuse, says Patel, was the same thing DOJ had done when it had resisted providing the information HPSCI had requested for the memo.

"I imagine something like: Rosenstein called his counterparts in the UK to say, 'Hey, this is a really sensitive investigation. I'd appreciate if you agreed with me that the disclosure of any information would jeopardize our relationship.' And the guy over there says, 'Yeah, that sounds good. Tell the president we agree with you.' So Rosenstein goes to Trump and says, 'I talked to England. They said they don't want to jeopardize our relationship.'"

Patel says he can't help but be impressed by Rosenstein's ability to maneuver in tight places. "He's a very good bureaucrat. That's how they operate. I've been in those meetings. It's very easy for them to gloss over embarrassing details and use the institution as a shield."

Rumors circulated that the Australians and British were worried about having their role in Crossfire Hurricane exposed. Nunes and Patel discount the likelihood that foreign governments had participated in the operation.

Australia wasn't involved, says Nunes. "It was not official Five Eyes intelligence that opened the investigation." It was a rumor that Downer had passed to the State Department, which had relayed it to the FBI.

Patel speculates on what the UK intelligence services might or might not have known about the operation. "My hunch is that England doesn't know the depth of what the FBI did over there and how they did it," he says.

He explains the steps the FBI must take to investigate crimes on foreign soil: "The FBI cannot just go and run an investigation in a foreign country." They must be invited by that country. That is a mandatory requirement. So they contact our embassy there and say we need help. And sometimes there's an FBI representative in the embassy, the legal attaché. We get the invitation, tell them who will come, and what we intend to do. You can't just unilaterally go in, especially in a place like England. No way."

Patel thinks the DOJ and FBI were not forthright with London. "I suspect Rosenstein was worried about that coming out," he says. "That's one reason why he scared off the president on declassification. That's why he fought us on the FISA and the memo, on declass, and why he fought us on these documents every step of the way."

Objective Medusa didn't get the documents declassified in September. But there was an upside. "I always said that when DOJ and the FBI started shooting at each other like McCabe and Rosenstein did, it means we won," says Patel.

Conservatives argued that declassification would have helped at the polls. Making public more details of the coup might have turned voters against a Democratic Party that had paid a foreign spy to undermine a US presidential campaign.

Nunes isn't sure. "If those same voters weren't already moved to anger by what we'd shown in the memo, they were never going to wake up. But of course, had the same thing been done to Hillary, they'd have been burning tires in the streets."

Nothing will happen, says Nunes, until there's a new attorney general. "Trump couldn't fire Sessions before the elections, or that would definitely hurt at the polls," he says. "But no matter what happens on Tuesday, Sessions is gone after the election."

It's election day 2018. Nunes is far up in the polls but isn't optimistic about the Republicans' chances in the House. And he's distracted. HPSCI staff director Damon Nelson has been diagnosed with a serious illness that struck suddenly. He's dying. Nelson kept the committee, the congressman, and the staff focused, sharp, and optimistic during their hardest days of the last eighteen months.

"All of my friends and family know Damon, too," Nunes of his old high school friend.

Robert Quinn is another old friend, Nunes's roommate at Cal Poly and a pistachio farmer. Quinn's father, Ron, pulls me outside for a smoke. He's a Marine Corps veteran who fought in Vietnam and went back to the farm when he returned. "I learned the most important thing in my life in the Marines: don't quit, don't surrender," says the elder Quinn. "I like to think Devin got some of that from me. I'm really proud of him. I've known him since he and Robert were kids. When he first got into politics, I encouraged him to do it and told him he'd win."

Most of Nunes's circle are at the election-night gathering in a large Portuguese American meeting hall in a rural area outside Tulare: Nunes's wife and children, his Uncle Gerald, and Basil Perch.

Supporters, some of them in Team Nunes baseball caps, fleeces, and T-shirts, wait in line for tacos and beer. The mood is festive, and with Nunes up by thirteen points, most are watching the national results. Weeks after the election, Nunes's winning margin will close to six points. Part of that is because of ballot harvesting.

"The Democrats are out registering everyone," the congressman explains. "Then they go pick up the ballots from people's houses."

With the Democrats' victory in the House, Nunes lost the gavel and Adam Schiff took control of HPSCI. The Objective Medusa team had always known they were running against the clock. But they finished their work on time.

They showed that law enforcement had used a politically funded document to spy on a presidential campaign. They showed that after the election, the sting operation had turned into a coup. They showed that the press had partnered with dirty cops and political operatives to topple Trump and undo the laws, principles, and institutions that sustain the country. Nunes and his team uncovered the biggest political scandal in US history: a governmentwide plot targeting not only the commander in chief but also the American public as a whole.

In retrospect, it's not surprising that in this instance, the defense of the United States started in the Central Valley. Nunes's constituents are the descendants of the people who populated John Steinbeck's novels, his most famous—*The Grapes of Wrath*—set only miles from the Portuguese American meeting hall.

The immigrants, from the Azores and Armenia and Mexico and elsewhere, together with the internal refugees who fled the Dust Bowl, turned this area into the world's most fertile region. The farmers, small-business owners, and others celebrating Nunes's victory together tonight inherited the instinctive generosity and native shrewdness of the men and women who settled the district.

Yet their success, often their survival, required a certain hardness. It demanded that they have not only a feel for the land but also the ability to read human nature. Not being able to discern character, to spot at first glance a predator, no matter how well he spoke or what he promised, left those they were supposed to protect vulnerable.

That's why the establishment, the press, the permanent bureaucracy, the tech oligarchs, the urban aristocrats, the Deep State, and all the rest of the ugly beautiful people, will never forgive Devin Nunes. It belittled them that he didn't care he wasn't their sort but was proud to be a farm kid, a townie with dirt under his fingernails. What truly drove them mad was that for all their trappings of power, their genuine ability to bend outcomes to their own will, their claims to expertise, their false prophesies, and above all their threats, he saw through them.

Chapter 22

THE POSSESSED

NUNES WAS RIGHT. Jeff Sessions was fired on November 7, one day after the midterm elections. He was, as Nunes had said, an honorable man.

Yet he had not been prepared to do what the job of attorney general required at the time: put down a coup rooted in the institution he led, the Department of Justice.

The president who had hired him was angry. By recusing himself, Sessions had given the conspirators an open shot to topple the commander in chief. Trump was also right: the special counsel investigation was a witch hunt, with dire consequences for the republic.

The investigation was based on a conspiracy theory. The media rationalized the paranoid fictions attributed to Christopher Steele by arguing that none of them had been disproven. Thus the burden was on Trump and his associates to prove they were innocent.

The charges didn't have to be tested in a court of law; lives could be destroyed by allegations drawn from a dark dream world. It was up to the accused to demonstrate that they weren't witches.

That reversal perverted the founding principle of the US legal system—the presumption of innocence—while opening the door to superstition and fanaticism. What gruesome myths and imaginary horrors would the public not believe now that the media had legitimized the Steele Dossier, now that a special counsel had been named to investigate a fantasy produced by a corrupt elite to defend its privileges?

Despite the pandemonium that filled the vacuum left by Sessions's recusal, Nunes sees an upside. "If he hadn't been the AG, we might not have known how bad it was," he says.

That is, it wasn't just Sessions who was taken by surprise. No one outside the circle of conspirators had known how deep the rot ran. Not even the chairman of the congressional committee tasked to oversee the intelligence community had known how bad it was—until senior US intelligence officials went to war against the United States.

It's several months after the midterms, and Nunes is sitting with friends in the backyard of his Tulare home. Ray Appleton, the radio talk show host, is here; so are the Kapetan brothers, a handful of other constituents, and a few writers. Nunes is grilling beef and pouring his Alpha Omega wine.

"If an attorney general had come in who knew what he was doing, they wouldn't have tried any of the stuff they pulled," says Nunes. "Or after the Flynn leak, another AG would've sent a hundred FBI agents to find the leakers and that's the end of it. But these guys thought they had free rein to do whatever they wanted. And so they were actually drawing a map for us of all the bad things they'd done and were capable of doing."

Nunes's assessment of the last two years is blunt. "The whole special counsel investigation was a fraud," he says. "They knew from the beginning that there was no collusion, but they moved it forward to set an obstruction of justice trap."

Like the FBI's investigation and the FISA on Page, the special counsel was based on the Steele Dossier.

"Remember that at the beginning we thought Mueller was going to do a good job," says Nunes. "Then Rosenstein goes and writes a memo in August about the scope of the investigation. They wouldn't show it to us or any of the other oversight committees. Kash and Gowdy started asking questions about it. *But* it was a big black hole."

The first evidence of what was in the scope memo came from Paul Manafort's trial in a Virginia court. The judge asked to see it, and a heavily redacted version of the scope memo was published. According to the few lines not redacted, the memo includes allegations that Paul Manafort:

Committed a crime or crimes by colluding with Russian government officials with respect to the Russian government's efforts to interfere with the 2016 election for President of the United States, in violation of US law.

Manafort was convicted of offenses ranging from bank fraud to tax fraud—but nothing remotely connected to Russian election hacking, the charge Mueller had been tasked to investigate.

"The only place those Russia allegations are made is in the dossier," says Nunes. "So our belief is that the dossier is part of the scope memo, and that there's more dossier stuff that was given to Mueller."

Nunes shakes his head. "The dossier is part of the special counsel's scope memo. Absolutely incredible."

The Objective Medusa team had taken the dossier apart—showed who had paid for it and how the FBI had used it to get a warrant to spy on Trump. Nunes and his team had forced the conspirators to switch horses. The FBI claimed it hadn't started investigating until it had found out what the mysterious Maltese professor Joseph Mifsud had told George Papadopoulos about Clinton's emails.

"Mifsud," says Nunes, "is their Achilles' heel. If we get that, the entire operation is exposed."

Even though HPSCI came under control of the Democrats with their election victory, Nunes has no intention of stopping. Rather, he seems energized. Trump has a new attorney general who looks like he's serious about holding accountable the men and women who plotted against the president. And, says Nunes, Mueller's due to file his report any day.

A guest asks Nunes how he's so sure. For months the report has been rumored to be on the way. But that was a rumor planted to keep Trump off balance and Republicans quiet.

Mueller had to sustain the possibility of "collusion" at least through the election. Any lingering doubts or suspicions about Trump in voters' minds might help the Democrats take the House, an essential step in bringing down the president. If the Republicans held the majority, to whom would Mueller hand off obstruction charges? Devin Nunes?

The HPSCI ranking member explains how he knows the special counsel is wrapping up. "On March 4, the DOJ said the new attorney general doesn't have to recuse himself from the Russia investigation," says Nunes. He pauses to emphasize the absurdity of the idea: "The top lawman in the country is cleared to do his job."

He continues, "On March 14, Andrew Weissmann announces he's leaving the special counsel. That's Mueller's 'pit bull.' If he's leaving, they're done. The report will drop on a Friday because these guys have been dropping stuff on Fridays since after the 2016 election."

Nunes settles on two Fridays down the road, March 22. He is reminded that that's the one-year anniversary of the date HPSCI released the Russia Report and the two-year anniversary of his walk into the valley of death.

The year before that, Trump had given his March 21 interview to the *Washington Post*, after which Clinton operatives and the FBI had begun to target Page and Papadopoulos.

As it happened, much of the struggle between the Objective Medusa team and the Deep State the last several years, the contest between light and darkness, turned on the vernal equinox.

———————————

Evidence of a flanking movement to encircle Mueller began to appear more than six months before Trump appointed the new attorney general. What checked the momentum of the Paper Coup was more paper.

On June 2, 2018, the *New York Times* published a letter that Trump's legal team had sent to the special counsel. It's unlikely that the White House leaked a letter showing that the president's legal team was overmatched.

However, if it was the special counsel that leaked the correspondence, it was a blunder. The *Times'* accompanying commentary noted that the Mueller team was up to no good.

In the letter, the president's lawyers argued that he could not have obstructed the FBI's investigation of Flynn by expressing to Comey his hope that the FBI director "could let it go." The lawyers cited what they believed to be the relevant statute, which forbids "anyone from corruptly, or by threats of force or by any threatening communication, influencing, obstructing, or impeding any *pending proceeding before a department or agency of the United States,* or Congress [author's italics]."

Since there was no precedent holding that an FBI investigation is a "proceeding," the president was in the clear.

Alongside this passage from the letter, the *Times* published an annotation written by reporter Charlie Savage, guided by "legal experts" who had been briefed on the Mueller team's strategy—or had crafted it themselves. They argued that Trump's lawyers were operating according to an "outdated understanding of the law." The *Times* reporter cited a different statute, which "criminalizes the corrupt impeding of proceedings even if they have not yet started—like the potential grand jury investigation an F.B.I. case can prompt."

The special counsel was rolling out a novel theory. It didn't matter if there was no proceeding pending; Trump could be charged with obstruction if the intent behind his actions was deemed corrupt.

The *Times* article caught the attention of seasoned legal minds. Less than a week later, a former attorney general in the George H. W. Bush administration wrote a letter to deputy attorney general Rod Rosenstein sharply critical of the special counsel's apparent approach. Under Mueller's theory, wrote William Barr,

> *simply by exercising his Constitutional discretion in a facially-lawful way—for example, by removing or appointing an official; using his prosecutorial discretion to give direction on a case; or using his pardoning power—a President can be accused of committing a crime based solely on his subjective state of mind.*

Barr noted that "this theory would have potentially disastrous implications." If the Justice Department accepted Mueller's theory, it would legitimize political prosecutions. Any president or his appointees could be targeted for political differences—i.e., the "corrupt" intention behind their lawful actions. He argued that "the President's motive in removing Comey and commenting on Flynn could not have been 'corrupt' unless the President and his campaign were actually guilty of illegal collusion."

But if they had "colluded," why was the special counsel formulating a case for obstruction?

"Either the President and his campaign engaged in illegal collusion or they did not," wrote Barr. "If they did, then the issue of 'obstruction' is a side show. However, if they did not, then the cover up theory is untenable."

The special counsel was building not a case but a gallows to string up the president. Barr recognized the play; he'd seen it more than a decade before. Mueller's tactics bore a remarkable similarity to those employed in the DOJ's 2003 investigation of an unauthorized disclosure of the identity of a CIA official. Both cases even featured James Comey as a central character.

———————

In 2002, Valerie Plame's CIA affiliation was published in the press after her husband, Joseph Wilson, cast doubt on the Bush administration's justification for going to war in Iraq. The leak was seen as retaliation from a vengeful Bush White House.

When the FBI first opened its investigation in early October 2003, it learned from Deputy Secretary of State Richard Armitage that he had been the source of the leak.

Comey, then deputy attorney general, persuaded Attorney General John Ashcroft to recuse himself from the investigation and appointed his friend Patrick Fitzgerald, godfather to one of his children, as special counsel.

Both Fitzgerald and Comey already knew that Armitage had disclosed Plame's identity to the press. But they saw the investigation as an opportunity to hunt big game—in particular Vice President Dick Cheney. To position himself for a shot at Cheney, Fitzgerald targeted his chief of staff, I. Lewis "Scooter" Libby.

Fitzgerald put Libby through roughly twenty hours of FBI interviews and grand jury testimony. He threatened to indict Libby for obstruction of justice, making a false statement, and perjury. He told Libby's lawyers he'd drop the indictment on all counts if Libby gave up the vice president.

So what if Cheney hadn't broken any laws? Libby was a lawyer; he could make something up that would stick to Cheney, something good enough to save his own skin. But he refused to perjure himself.

Libby was found guilty in 2007, and Bush commuted his sentence in 2008. After a key witness admitted that she had testified falsely at trial because Fitzgerald had withheld key evidence from her, Libby was reinstated as a lawyer. In 2018, he was finally pardoned by Trump.

Barr and other leading members of the DC legal community had concluded that the Libby case had been a baseless media-driven scandal, a press frenzy that had resulted in a miscarriage of justice.

Mueller 2017 was a replay of Fitzgerald 2003. The latter went after Cheney, the former Trump.

"If a DOJ investigation is going to take down a democratically-elected President," Barr wrote in his June 2018 memo, "it is imperative to the health of our system and to our national cohesion that any claim of wrongdoing is solidly based on evidence of a real crime."

When Trump nominated Barr for attorney general on December 7, the Mueller team saw their window of opportunity closing. After the new attorney general was cleared to oversee the special counsel in March, they knew the only option was to use the report to hang a dark cloud over Trump and increase the rift dividing the country.

On March 22, Mueller filed his report with the Justice Department, and two days later Barr summarized its findings in a letter.

Part one established that the Russians had interfered in the US election. There were two components: the Internet Research Agency, a Russian troll farm, had waged a disinformation campaign through social media, and further, the Russian government had been involved in computer-hacking operations to influence the election.

Mueller charged Russian nationals and entities in connection with those activities and found that there had been no coordination with any Americans, including the Trump campaign.

In part two, the special counsel considered a number of Trump's actions that had raised "obstruction-of-justice concerns."

However, rather than deciding whether to prosecute or decline to do so, Mueller punted. He left it to Barr, who determined that the evidence did not establish that Trump had committed an obstruction of justice offense.

At the same time that Mueller, a career prosecutor, abdicated the special counsel's traditional prosecutorial role, he dirtied Trump's presidency. "While this report does not conclude that the President committed a crime," stated the special counsel, "it also does not exonerate him."

For Patel, it was another instance of an unaccountable DOJ acting recklessly. "Exoneration," he says, "is not the job of the prosecutor in a system that presumes innocence. Your only job is to make a charging decision. If you decline, then it's on to the next case."

Patel had seen it before with the Clinton email case. Comey had overstepped his bounds when he had announced that Clinton would not be charged in the email case. That was not the investigator's role; rather, it was the job of the prosecutor to decide whether or not to charge.

"Not only did Mueller fail to do his job as special counsel by refusing to make the call," says Patel, "he went so far past the rules and ethics with his 'exoneration' charade. It was a complete bastardization of prosecution and due process. It was the epitome of a prosecutor gone rogue."

Further, by leaving it to Trump's attorney general to conclude that Trump's conduct did not constitute obstruction, Mueller meant to paint Barr as a political lackey. Rather than resolving the investigation in order to edge the country back to national cohesion, the special counsel chose to institutionalize the political divide.

Barr countered, using an instrument close to hand: the deputy attorney general.

In January, after Barr's confirmation, Rod Rosenstein had announced that he was retiring, but the new AG had insisted he stick around to help clean up the mess he'd helped make.

"It's clear that Rosenstein flipped at some point," says Nunes. "Whether Barr initiated it or Rosenstein offered himself up, he started becoming very helpful."

On April 18, Barr announced the release of the full Mueller Report. At the press conference, the attorney general stationed the wooden-looking Rosenstein directly behind him, like a prop. It was a masterful piece of stagecraft, dramatizing the point Barr wanted to make: that it wasn't just he, a recent Trump appointee, who had concluded that the evidence of obstruction of justice was insufficient. No, he *and* Rosenstein—the man whose antipathy to the president was so profound that he had suggested recording him for the purpose of removing him from office—agreed there was no evidence of obstruction.

"Barr didn't say anything we didn't already know about there being no collusion," says Nunes. "Everyone knew there was nothing there and the dossier was a fraud. The special counsel used smoke and mirrors to set the obstruction traps for Trump. Barr called them out."

Nunes took to calling the special counsel's report the "Mueller Dossier." Like Steele's reports and the January 2017 intelligence community assessment, it was a political document collating the efforts of anti-Trump operatives, compromised intelligence officials, and the press to undermine Trump. As an account of reality, it was worthless.

"If Americans really want to know what happened in the 2016 election cycle," says Nunes, "they should read our Russia Report. It's got all the facts, and we didn't bill the US taxpayer thirty million dollars for a document that reads like a bad Russian spy novel."

"The sign the Mueller Report was a BS report," says Jim, Patel's investigative partner, "is that there are no recommendations."

Excepting, of course, the special counsel's barely veiled recommendation to impeach the president.

The more than four hundred pages constituting Mueller's *Report on the Investigation into Russian Interference in the 2016 Presidential Election* are riddled with countless errors and misstatements of fact woven into a tapestry of innuendo and invective further smearing Trump and his associates.

But the character of the Mueller Dossier is most clearly conveyed by three key omissions.

First, the report made no mention of Fusion GPS or its principals, such as Glenn Simpson. It refers, once, to "the firm that produced the Steele reporting." Mueller frequently cited Steele. But the former British spy was just a front man. By omitting Fusion GPS's role, Mueller buried the central facts of the Russia investigation that Nunes and his team had uncovered: that Fusion GPS had been paid by the Clinton campaign to smear Trump in the media and federal agents had used the politically funded dirt as evidence to spy on the opposing presidential campaign.

The second omission deals with the origins of the FBI's Russia investigation—the information about Clinton emails that Mifsud passed to Papadopoulos. The Mueller Report mentions Mifsud dozens of times but does not explain who the mysterious Maltese professor is. Surely he must be a Russian spy or at least an asset that would make the information "Kremlin sourced." If not, then the FBI had no basis on which to open its Trump-Russia investigation. Yet after spending nearly two years and tens of millions of taxpayer dollars, the special counsel produced no evidence that Mifsud is in any way connected to Russia.

Finally, there is no mention of Stefan Halper. The dirty tricks operative and "October surprise" specialist whose fingerprints were on nearly every part of the investigation—Flynn, Page, Papadopoulos, and the dossier, too—was nowhere to be found.

Mueller was hired as a fixer, to ensure the success of the coup. After Barr stopped it, the special counsel became a cleaner, who erased any evidence of it.

Across the country, scores of Americans who had enlisted in the collective madness inspired by a fake text felt let down by the special counsel; Trump was still there.

But they continued to believe in Mueller. The furies of the new dynamism he had brought with him required breaking with the old ways—especially the things that shape how Americans live with one another, such as law and politics. So the collusion faithful had nothing else to believe in.

At the end of May, Mueller made a brief TV appearance. His ashen complexion and unsteady demeanor fed rumors that he was ill. Nevertheless, he once more pushed against the pillars of the US justice system. "If we had had confidence that the president clearly did not commit a crime," he said, "we would have said so." In other words, the enemies of the political establishment do not merit the presumption of innocence.

Having failed to bring down Trump, the lesson of the special counsel was that terror tactics would be directed against anyone who threatened the power held by the top echelon of unelected bureaucrats. Not only had the dossier outlined the scope of the special counsel, it had also become the means through which reason had been replaced with the ethos of the witch trial.

In June, Schiff conducted a public hearing on the Mueller Report and invited two retired FBI counterintelligence officials to testify. The ranking Republican member made opening remarks.

"For two years," said Nunes,

the American people were subjected to endless hysteria by the media, Democrats, and anonymous intelligence leakers. Seemingly every day the media triumphantly published a supposed bombshell story, often based on classified documents the reporters had not actually seen, which purportedly proved that President Trump or some Trump associate was a treacherous Russian agent. Democrats on this committee regularly joined cable news pundits in denouncing the traitors.

Committee Democrats whispered to each other as congressional aides conferred with members of the press. They ignored what Nunes was saying.

The entire scheme has now imploded and the collusion accusation has been exposed as a hoax. One would think the Democrats would simply apologize and get back to lawmaking and oversight. But it's clear they couldn't stop this grotesque spectacle even if they wanted to. After years of false accusations and McCarthyite smears, the collusion hoax now defines the Democratic Party. The hoax is what they have in place of a governing philosophy or a constructive vision for our country. . . .

I'd like to remind the Democrats that this committee was created to do important oversight of our intelligence agencies. This work is even more crucial now that the media have abandoned their traditional watchdog role and instead have become the mouthpiece of a cabal of intelligence leakers.

Reporters sat in the back row. A young woman next to me slid out of her shoes and massaged the thick carpet with her toes. The reporters ignored Nunes. They came to attention when Schiff's two witnesses spoke.

Stephanie Douglas and Robert Anderson were former executive assistant directors in the FBI's National Security Branch. One of them had been Strzok's supervisor. They said they had been surprised by the evidence of his bias.

Nunes said he was shocked that "there's not more former DOJ and FBI officials who aren't out there saying 'Look, this is wrong.'"

Anderson and Douglas said they hadn't prepared to discuss Fusion GPS's role in the investigation. They'd prepared only to talk about the report filed by their former boss. Mueller's report didn't mention Fusion GPS.

"This counterintelligence department over at the FBI," Nunes said, "is in big trouble."

Both former agents testified that they had not read the dossier. Their former colleagues had used the dossier to obtain a spy warrant on the Trump campaign. It was the centerpiece of the biggest scandal in FBI history. Or, for those among the legions of the possessed, the dossier was proof of collusion, for which there was no other evidence.

Schiff, who'd invited the former agents to testify, had read large parts of the dossier into the *Congressional Record* when another former FBI colleague, James Comey, had testified in March 2017. But the ex-spies said they hadn't read it.

Schiff didn't push them. He'd invited them in order to keep the wheel turning: spies, political operatives, journalists. They were enacting the scene that Nunes had described in his opening statement:

Mueller produced a perfect feedback loop: intelligence leakers spin a false story to the media, the media publishes the story, Mueller cites the story, and the media and the Democrats then fake outrage at Mueller's findings.

It was as if Nunes were guiding a tour of the underworld, describing to the living the proceedings of the dead. The dead could no longer hear him.

Chapter 23

A RECKONING

WITH THE MUELLER REPORT FILED, the hunted became the hunter. Nunes warned, "I'm coming to clean up the mess." He pushed the advantage and began moving on new fronts. He put his faith in the law.

He announced that he was sending eight criminal referrals to the new attorney general. He also brought two suits against social media and media organizations and said it was just the beginning. "I think people are beginning to wake up now," he said. "I'm serious."

In March 2019, he filed a defamation suit seeking $250 million in compensatory and punitive damages against Twitter and several of its users, including political operative Liz Mair. The complaint accused the platform of secretly hiding Nunes's content by "shadow-banning" him, while hosting and monetizing content defaming Nunes, such as Mair's.

A second suit in April again named Mair along with the US media conglomerate the McClatchy Company. Nunes asked for

$150 million in compensatory and punitive damages. A McClatchy publication, the *Fresno Bee*, had published a defamatory piece falsely implicating Nunes in a sleazy yacht trip.

The press ridiculed Nunes for bringing the suits. They said he had thin skin. But it wasn't personal. If he didn't take action, what was already happening—conservatives being thrown off social media platforms and defamed in the press—would only get worse.

In fact, it was already worse. Americans had been spied on because they had backed a candidate that intelligence bureaucrats and the press didn't like. The legal system had been used to drain them of their homes and savings, sometimes their liberty, while their names were savaged in the media.

Their punishment had been a warning to others tempted to enjoy the right to participate in political campaigns or even express their opinions: Don't step outside the political consensus, or you'll be silenced or smeared or fired or deplatformed or arrested. The suit was to defend Americans in danger of being "disappeared."

Another purpose of the legal action was to hold accountable the various institutions and individuals who'd sought to hinder HPSCI's investigation. The last two years of the Russia investigations had shown Nunes that the problem was larger than just the Russia investigations. What those institutions and individuals had done to a president and a political campaign could be done to the entire country and any American. The last two years had hardened him.

Though many would find it hard to believe, another of Nunes's aims in targeting the media and social media was to try to restore the integrity of one of the institutions that had been waging war on him for two years running: the free press.

———————————

The current state of the US press is partly a function of social media and their unique financial model.

With the rise of the Internet in the mid-1990s, publishers assumed that digital advertising would eventually make up for the enormous losses in print advertising. While they waited, publications around the country shut down for good, others hemorrhaged cash, and thousands of media professionals were laid off.

With much of the infrastructure damaged or destroyed, the press's ability to produce reliable information was severely impaired. The tragedy was compounded when the bulk of the digital advertising that was supposed to rescue the press went instead to Silicon Valley's new hybrid models: social media.

Today, social media platforms—Facebook, Google, Twitter, and so on—own nearly the entire advertising market. Facebook is worth $350 billion—more than one hundred times the value of the *New York Times*.

The hybrids have two enormous advantages. One, they don't have to pay to create content. Since it comes free, they're spared having to invest in the infrastructure that sustains other content producers, such as news organizations. Traditional media companies have to pay reporters, photographers, illustrators, and other professionals to produce content. Two, social media have no legal responsibility to provide reliable information. Therefore, they have no need to pay for people to ensure that content is accurate, such as editors and fact checkers, as well as legal teams, who also fight First Amendment challenges.

For social media companies, all those costs are borne by regular media companies. News organizations give their content away for free because they have little choice. Rather than bite the hand that feeds them, they trust that the social media giants will continue to send traffic their way—even as they know the overlords can redirect or close down that traffic through proprietary algorithms.

How did this happen?

In the 1990s, tech visionaries and forward-thinking legislators were eager to protect America's great internet adventure. One concern was that if service providers—websites and so on—were constantly sued for posting objectionable content or filtering or blocking content providers (porn sites, for instance), digital innovation would grind to a halt.

Congress wrote a law, Section 230 of the 1996 Communications Decency Act, that distinguished between interactive computer services, which Google and Twitter would eventually become, and information content providers, which created or developed information.

The law absolved interactive computer service providers of liability. According to the CDA, "No provider or user of an interactive computer service shall be treated as the publisher or speaker of any information provided by another information content provider."

Nunes's suit argued that Twitter is in fact an information content provider or developer in itself.

Twitter is not a bulletin board like Yelp, for instance, that allows anyone to post a review of Restaurant X or Handbag Store Y. By shadow banning and deplatforming some users—conservatives— while promoting others, even monetizing their feeds with advertising, Twitter shapes a particular political narrative. Because Twitter tells a story, it is an information content provider. Nunes and his lawyer Steven Biss challenged Twitter's immunity from defamation suits.

The direct effect of the suit would be to make social media platforms such as Twitter decide: Are they, as the CDA described the internet, forums "for a true diversity of political discourse, unique opportunities for cultural development, and myriad avenues for intellectual activity"? Or are they platforms pushing particular politicized narratives while excluding others? If the latter, they must be held liable, like any other content provider or content developer.

A possible, and indirect, effect of Nunes's action might be to strip the social media giants of their twofold advantage over traditional media organizations: not paying for content and not being held liable. Maybe leveling the playing field will encourage entrepreneurs to compete in a fairer media market for audience and advertising.

"We need a real press corps," says Nunes says. "Policy makers and especially the US public."

―――――――――

The suit against McClatchy underscored the character of a media organization unmoored from its obligations to deliver reliable information to its readers. The complaint cited a May 23, 2018, article published by the McClatchy-owned *Fresno Bee*: "A Yacht, Cocaine, Prostitutes: Winery Partly Owned by Nunes Sued After Fundraiser Event." The article, which insinuated that Nunes might have been involved in a sordid yacht party, was quickly debunked when it emerged that had Nunes had no connection to the event at all and was not even mentioned in the lawsuit on which the story was based.

The *Fresno Bee* article, published weeks before Nunes's June 5 primary race, was, according to the suit, "part of a scheme to defame Nunes."

Journalists, said Nunes, had "abandoned the role of journalist and chose to leverage their considerable power to spread falsehoods and to defame" for "political and financial gain."

McClatchy was notorious in that respect. Its Washington, DC, news bureau had taken a strong position on the Trump-Russia conspiracy theory, moving it wholesale on behalf of its original producers, Fusion GPS.

Unlike the Pulitzer Prize–winning *Time/Post* crew, elite media operatives who processed leaks of classified information from current and former senior government officials, the McClatchy group consisted of bottom feeders. They published stories that no one at the top of the media food chain would touch.

"Among the many media stooges for Fusion GPS, McClatchy was the most shameless," says Jack Langer. "They had a template for stories spoon-fed to them by Fusion GPS, and they just filled in the blanks: 'A is investigating Trump associate B for the terrible crime of C, according to two sources familiar with the matter.'"

Between January 2017 and January 2019, a small McClatchy team—including most notoriously Peter Stone and Greg Gordon—distinguished itself with a series of Trump-Russia stories employing a pattern that proudly broke with journalistic standards in order to prosecute a political operation.

"The McClatchy template was absurd," says Langer. "They simply claimed, in an extremely vague way, that Mueller or the FBI was investigating some Steele Dossier allegation or some other outlandish Fusion GPS conspiracy theory."

Note, for example, McClatchy's April 13, 2018, story, "Sources: Mueller Has Evidence Cohen Was in Prague in 2016, Confirming Part of Dossier."

Much of the story confirming the dossier is largely a retelling of the dossier itself. Further, the article offers no evidence of Cohen's trip to Prague independent of the account given in the dossier. The report may simply be Fusion GPS repackaging the dossier—the "evidence" in Mueller's possession—as a news article more than a year after it was first published.

Langer notes that McClatchy's stories were also marred by weak sourcing. "It's not FBI sources or, even more vaguely, law enforcement sources," he says. "It's just 'people familiar with the matter,' and that could be people who have simply been told something second- or thirdhand. Or it's just Glenn Simpson and one of his Fusion GPS confederates—they themselves are obviously the 'people familiar with the matter' in a lot of these stories."

In a March 15, 2018, story, McClatchy journalists Peter Stone and Greg Gordon broke ground on another Fusion GPS conspiracy theory. According to the report:

> Congressional investigators are examining information that an ex–National Rifle Association board member who had done legal work for the group had concerns about its ties to Russia and its possible involvement in channeling Russian funds into the 2016 elections to help Donald Trump, two sources familiar with the matter say.

The board member was Cleta Mitchell, a campaign finance lawyer in Washington, DC. In a lengthy correspondence with the McClatchy reporters, she denied their account, explaining that she had had no involvement with the NRA since her board term had expired in 2012. She told the reporters repeatedly that the story was false, and they published it nonetheless.

Bruce Ohr told Congress that Simpson had been the source of the story about Mitchell and the NRA. Ohr had apparently relayed Simpson's account to the FBI and other government bodies. Schiff said the Mitchell-NRA story had been a further reason to continue investigating Russian interference in the 2016 election.

In an email message to the lawyer and journalist Scott Johnson, Mitchell claimed that Simpson lied and that Gordon and Stone acted as willing conduits for his and others' false statements:

> *They were the mouthpiece for the leaks from the FBI about the NRA and the Glenn Simpson lies about me, the NRA, etc.—plus, they were the shills for the Adam Schiff lies from the House Democrats on Intelligence committee. It is a sordid situation—the FBI takes lies from Glenn Simpson, and instead of prosecuting him, they do his bidding and the whole cabal leaks to McClatchy—it is despicable.*

"McClatchy stood by these conspiracy theories, long after they were debunked." says Langer, "yet the media hailed this dreck as legitimate, bombshell stories. They ignored the weak sourcing, the lack of detail, the objective unlikelihood that these things actually happened, and the fact that McClatchy's previous 'bombshell' stories were untrue. The media simply didn't care if the reporting was transparently false so long as it furthered the preposterous narrative that Trump and his associates were Russian agents."

––––––––––––

Even as Nunes put the press on notice, there were still efforts to go after him. In the winter, *The New Yorker* sent Adam Entous, recently hired away from the *Washington Post*, and Ronan Farrow to poke around in Nunes's hometown, Tulare. "Everyone in the Valley knew that they were there to do a hit job on me," Nunes says. Entous denies he was there to do a story on Nunes.

The February 18, 2019, story they published about a private

Israeli spy firm hired to follow a candidate in a hospital board election had a big hole in it. Like Ryan Lizza's article about Nunes's "secret" Iowa farm, it was missing the sensational scoop implicating Nunes that was to hold it all together. Instead, Entous and Farrow came away with a story that read like an oppo research file: names, places, facts, and the outline of a story.

That was typical of *The New Yorker*'s signature Trump-Russia reporting, much of which sprang from Fusion GPS research. The magazine's editor in chief, David Remnick, had been an early adopter of Russiagate. His pre-2016 election article "Trump and Putin: A Love Story," had used Page and Manafort talking points from the protodossiers.

Unsurprisingly, *The New Yorker* was one of the publications that Fusion GPS arranged for Steele to brief prior to the 2016 election. Staff writer Jane Mayer acknowledged in her March 2018 profile that she had been among the "handful of national-security reporters" who had met with the former British spy.

"Despite Steele's generally cool manner, he seemed distraught about the Russians' role in the election," wrote Mayer. "He did not distribute his dossier, provided no documentary evidence, and was so careful about guarding his sources that there was virtually no way to follow up."

But she did follow up, with a profile of Steele as a hero, for which the former British spy, though unnamed, is clearly a source.

New Yorker writer Adam Davidson published two articles drawing on themes outlined in the undated Fusion GPS protodossier on Trump's alleged ties to post-Soviet states. His March 13, 2017, article, "Donald Trump's Worst Deal," syncs with Fusion GPS's "Trump in Azerbaijan" report. Davidson's August 14, 2017, story, "Trump's Business of Corruption," runs parallel with Fusion GPS's "Trump in Georgia" report.

The article on Azerbaijan reworked the same material gone over in previous "Trump in Azerbaijan" articles published in the *Washington Post* and by the Associated Press with *The New Yorker*'s customary flair.

Davidson followed up with a report a few weeks later after Democrats called for an investigation of the allegations made in his previous article. It was a trademark Fusion GPS operation: credential a story through the press for friendly government officials to open an investigation for the press to then report. Davidson refashioned the Azerbaijan story many times over the next several years, sometimes pushing it in tandem with the Georgia article.

An October 8, 2018, article by *New Yorker* writer Dexter Filkins revived the false story holding that Trump Organization computer servers were in secret communications with those of a Russian financial institution, Alfa Bank.

Fusion GPS had given the story to Franklin Foer for his October 2016 Slate article, which had quickly been debunked. Apparently it was worth recycling now that Fusion GPS had a different funding stream, the Democracy Integrity Project, run by Daniel Jones. The former aide to Senator Dianne Feinstein was a source of the Filkins story, which does not mention Fusion GPS, never mind its role in pushing the Alfa Bank story.

After the Mueller Report came out, Susan Glasser interviewed Adam Schiff for an April 4, 2019, *New Yorker* article. "Will history remember the Russia investigation as a hoax," she asked him, "or as a genuine scandal?" Her question betrayed a discomfort rarely recorded among journalists on the Trump-Russia beat. There was no going back and changing the fact that the media had pushed a conspiracy theory for the past three years.

Nor would an industrywide apology solve the problem. To admit that the whole thing had been a lie, to acknowledge that the press had waged a political campaign based on a series of criminal leaks of classified information, would still devastate the media's credibility.

The larger problem was that the Steele Dossier had become a part of the press. It was no longer just the centerpiece of a conspiracy theory that the press had turned into the biggest story in a generation; rather, the industry had taken the form of the dossier.

The postdossier era saw a surge of fabricated news stories, all zeroing in on Trump policies.

After nominated in summer 2018 to the Supreme Court, justice Brett Kavanaugh was targeted by a joint media–Democratic operative smear campaign labeling him a rapist. His accuser, who could not remember the date or place of the alleged assault, was said to be a "credible" witness.

Schoolboys from a Catholic school in Kentucky visiting Washington, DC, in January 2019 were demonized for wearing MAGA hats. The press reported that they'd harassed an elderly tribal leader, a Vietnam veteran, at the Lincoln Memorial. Social media erupted on cue, with well-known media figures threatening violence. The story was false. The point was to intimidate anyone outside the establishment consensus: this could happen to you, too, even your children.

After the rogue Saudi Arabian intelligence officer Jamal Khashoggi was murdered by Saudi intelligence officers in October 2018, the press used the story to target Trump foreign policy. Khashoggi was misrepresented as a journalist and US green card holder. The point was to pressure Trump to break with the United States' ally and major oil producer Saudi Arabia—thereby crashing the world economy and sacrificing hundreds of thousands of American jobs—and restore Obama's anti-Saudi and pro-Iran policy.

In August 2019, *New York Times* executive editor Dean Baquet
made clear that the press now believes its central purpose is to
run political operations. In a meeting with the entire *Times* staff,
Baquet praised the paper's Trump-Russia coverage. "That was a
really hard story, by the way, let's not forget that. We set ourselves
up to cover that story. I'm going to say it. We won two Pulitzer
Prizes covering that story."

Those Pulitzers rightly belonged to the DOJ and FBI, which
used the *Times* and the *Post* as platforms for a criminal campaign
of leaks of classified information to prosecute an operation against
a sitting president. In spite of the press's contributions, the coup
failed.

"Our readers who want Donald Trump to go away suddenly
thought, 'Holy shit, Bob Mueller is not going to do it,'" said
Baquet. Thus it was the job of the paper's top editor to prepare
the staff for the next anti-Trump campaign. Maybe, as Baquet
suggested, describing the president a white supremacist the next
two years would drive him from office. If not, there would be other
opportunities for further operations.

There was still real news, and the media often covered it, but
that was irrelevant. The shape of the press itself was different,
twisted into something like a credibility curve diagramming the
escalating cost of self-induced delusion and the increasingly steep
rise in conspiracism as a worldview.

And that was the point. If people can be persuaded to believe
the perverted dreamworld of the dossier simply because it reflected
the thwarted hopes of the ruling class, there is nothing they won't
believe.

Taking Russiagate as a ground truth was evidence that the
collective psyche of the political and cultural elite, as expressed
in the media, was broken. No responsible adult could continue to

jeopardize the future of his or her family or community by assuming that the press's representation of the world matched reality. For the US media, the collusion narrative was an extinction-level event.

In his response to Glasser, Schiff hedged his bet. "The bar is not only what's criminal," he told her; "it should also be what's ethical and what's right."

It's difficult to lie for as long as Schiff did about Trump and collusion—nearly three years—without believing that lie serves a higher cause. The reason can't be just partisan politics or power or money. People lie for what seems to them to be ethical reasons until the lie itself becomes their evidence that they are ethical people.

Russiagate was a lie like that, a collective lie that divided the country, leaving American institutions in ruins while damaging our founding principles, including presumption of innocence. Those responsible needed to be held accountable.

"They have to admit what they did was wrong," says Nunes. "And they have to be prosecuted."

Of the eight criminal referrals Nunes sent to the attorney general, five were what he called "straight-up referrals." They named specific people and their specific crimes: lying to Congress, misleading Congress, and leaking classified information. The other three, Nunes said publicly, are more complicated, related to conspiracy charges. One regards a conspiracy to lie to the Foreign Intelligence Surveillance Court, which may touch numerous individuals. The second involves manipulation of intelligence, which may also name several US officials. The third and most innovative of the charges references what HPSCI lawyers call a "global leak" referral.

As Nunes said publicly, over the last two-and-a-half-plus years, there have been a dozen or more highly sensitive leaks of classified information—including Flynn's conversation with Kislyak and Trump's talks with the leaders of Mexico and Australia. The leaks of classified information went to a select group of reporters.

Nunes believes he and his team have good leads on some of the current and former senior officials who were involved in an intelligence operation to topple Trump by using leaks to the press. The names of those referred are not public and may never be made public. But it's not difficult to see who may be involved.

Glenn Simpson, Objective Medusa investigators believed, lied to Congress.

Christopher Steele was already the subject of a criminal referral issued by Senator Chuck Grassley in January 2018 for lying to the FBI.

Nellie Ohr, according to Objective Medusa investigators, misled Congress repeatedly.

Bruce Ohr, says Nunes' team, also appears to have misled Congress.

The Crossfire Hurricane team—especially Andrew McCabe, Peter Strzok, and Lisa Page—imagined itself as the next Deep Throat, leaking to the press in order to depose a president.

James Clapper, according to HPSCI's Russia Report, gave inconsistent testimony to Congress.

John Brennan directed the handpicked team of analysts whose flawed tradecraft produced the January 2017 intelligence community assessment.

In order to get a special counsel named, James Comey leaked classified information to the *New York Times*.

Cambridge professor Stefan Halper, who spied on Trump associates, appears to have misled US officials.

With the referrals, Objective Medusa was done. In exposing the truth, Nunes and his team had given the American public a true accounting of the operation to take down the president. It would be someone else's job to make sure those behind the plot were held accountable. Nunes handed the attorney general a loaded gun.

If there is no reckoning, the rift splitting the country will continue to grow. The divide is not between two political parties and their chosen candidates; rather, it is the question that Nunes and the Objective Medusa team's investigation pushed into the light: Will we be governed under one law or according to a set of privileges enjoyed by an elite confederation of the national security bureaucracy, political operatives, tech oligarchs, and their courtiers in the media industry?

"I'd rather be us than them," says Nunes.

Chapter 24

CONVICTIONS

NUNES HAS A NICKNAME for nearly everyone: Baby Cat, Deep State Bill, Deep State Lisa, and Andy Land—that's how he's going to refer to and acknowledge the four Objective Medusa team members who couldn't be named as sources in the investigation of the FBI's Trump-Russia probe.

Nunes thanks them and nearly everyone else he can think of. The two retired senior army intelligence officers who are among his closest advisers, HPSCI Republicans and their staff, task force members and their staff, the entire House Republican Conference, and everyone else who supported their efforts.

He has particularly warm words for his late staff director, Damon Nelson, who died in November. "I have lost one of my oldest friends," he said at the time. "He dedicated nearly his entire adult life to public service."

"Losing Damon was a real blow to us," says Langer. "On the staff level, he was our leader; he kept the whole thing together. Without him, we wouldn't have accomplished what we did. He was thrown into a tornado, but he handled it all with grace and class."

Nunes pours a glass of wine, raises it, and makes sure everyone else's glass is filled, too. Another bottle comes to the table. The Nunes party is seated in the back of the second-floor dining room of the Capitol Hill Club, a Republican social club a few blocks from the congressman's Longworth office.

"This is where Gingrich kicked off the Republican revolution in '94," says Nunes. And it's where the Objective Medusa team walks offstage after nearly two years of fighting unelected bureaucrats who tried to overturn the results of an election and hid their plot behind classified intelligence and a secret court.

"Maybe we'll have a reunion in five years," says Patel.

"I doubt I'll ever do anything as significant," says Jim. "What we uncovered is worth thousands of conservative articles about the dangers of the administrative state. We showed what they actually do." He adds, "I didn't know we'd be the tip of the spear in the battle for the republic."

"I thought it was going to be a pretty high profile investigation, at least in government circles," says Patel. "What I didn't know—"

"—is that it was going to be the main news story," says Langer.

"Right," says Patel. "I didn't know that we would be at the center of the media cycle over the next twenty-four months."

Langer thinks it will be hard for the press to recover. "The last few years showed that America's biggest media outlets can't be trusted," he says. "They discarded ages-old journalistic conventions designed to keep reporting accurate, while they hyped leaks of badly spun or outright false information—all just to damage the Trump presidency."

Nunes had come to see the press's actions as a cue to keep pushing forward. "The easiest way to cover all this up would have been for them to ignore our work," he says. "But the more they hit me, the more I knew we were over the target."

Before Patel joined the committee, he wasn't sure he wanted to work on Capitol Hill. "I didn't even really know what HPSCI was," says the former prosecutor. Two years later, he's proud that the investigation fulfilled the committee's constitutional mandate to provide oversight on behalf of the American public. "I think the investigation was righteous," he says. "I think we crushed it."

But it's still unfinished. "There's no actual accountability yet," he says. "When we have that, then I'll be satisfied."

Nunes agrees that holding the conspirators responsible for what they did is essential. He has faith in the new attorney general, but there's a lot that has to be done to set things right. "It's going to be a long time before the FBI has the confidence of at least half of America—conservatives, including members of Congress," he says. "The fact that Comey was investigating a presidential campaign. They do it behind Congress' back by not briefing us. And then when we started looking at it, they come after people personally to threaten them. In my case, they spent over ten million dollars to try to cover this up."

Taking fire for two years has affected the congressman. He acknowledges that he has become harder—not cynical, exactly, but better prepared to see things he missed before, darker things. It's still hard for him to believe that Americans did this to other Americans.

Patel is less surprised. He already knew there were some FBI agents who lied and that a select few filling the senior levels at DOJ hold themselves above the law they're sworn to uphold. He was prepared not only to see it but to explain it as well. "When they interview you for a job as a public defender," he says, "one of the first things they ask is, 'Are you prepared to call federal law enforcement officials liars in court?' I said, 'Yes. If that's what the evidence shows, I'm ready to call them liars.'"

Someone talks about reforming the FISA court, and Nunes agrees that that's the very least DOJ has to do. "They're going to have to admit that the FISA process was abused," he says. "And there are going to have to be new laws. The easiest call is that there has to be a representative at the secret court for any American they're thinking of getting a FISA warrant on. If not, they'll do this again."

But it's unlikely that Republican loyalists will be in a position to punish the next Democratic White House in retaliation for what Obama officials and Clinton operatives did to Trump and his team.

"These bureaucracies are basically all run by Democrats," says Nunes.

"They're institutionalists," says Jim.

And the institutions they serve and protect are appendages of a larger organism. Trump calls it the Swamp, but it's more like a living thing. Evidence is that it rose to defend itself when Michael Flynn threatened to starve it. The Crossfire Hurricane group was part of a whole, the particular instrument used against Trump.

"They had the whole system wired," says Nunes of the small FBI group at the center of the coup. "That's why they wanted this to be a counterintelligence investigation—because there's no checks and balances to it. They all knew what they had to do to get this rolling."

"Deep State" is another way to describe what classical philosophers meant by the word "regime." It refers not only to a form of government but also to the values and virtues that form of government prizes and the leading persons who embody them. Thus, many of the leading persons of the United States' political bureaucracy had starring roles in the coup.

There was CIA director John Brennan, a Beltway careerist who used his agency's authority to credential a conspiracy theory.

And James Comey, the former prosecutor who kicked off the series of obstruction traps set to bring down the president.

His predecessor at the FBI, Robert Mueller, managed the coup until he was stopped.

But no one represented this establishment, its arrogance and corruption, more perfectly than Hillary Clinton. That's why her loss made the regime even fiercer. If she didn't get what she believed she was entitled to, all of their privileges and prerogatives were vulnerable.

Clinton was the operation's center of gravity. Not only was it first conducted on her behalf, but her fears gave it form: fear that she wouldn't get into the White House, fear that the dirt on her would go public.

Had Clinton won, the operation would have been buried and no one would ever have known what had happened. But there were additional factors that had to fall into place for the plot against Trump to be uncovered. The Objective Medusa team had to be there.

Nunes, a California farm kid who didn't know better than to speak his mind and tell the truth, had to be head of the House Intelligence Committee. And there had to be that staff—Nelson and Langer and Jim and the rest—and Nunes had to know how to keep them inspired to manage the kind of crisis that no one had ever seen before. And that team needed Patel, a fast-talking outer-borough New Yorker who knew where to find things and liked kicking in doors.

Take away any of those factors, and the United States would have been one step closer to becoming a third-world, one-party security state.

"There was no one coming in behind us," says Patel.

And next time there may not be anyone taking the lead. The struggle for America will outlast what eight people accomplished in helping to put down a coup. Even now, some of their victory is still buried under the same classifications used to obscure the abuses and crimes committed during the plot against Trump.

Yet the Objective Medusa team finished the job it had set out to do. "We just can't show it yet," Patel says. "But we cut off the head."

ACKNOWLEDGMENTS

THANKS TO the publications and staff where some of this material first appeared in different form:

Alana Newhouse, David Samuels, Liel Leibovitz, Matthew Fishbane, and Jacob Siegel at *Tablet*; David DesRosiers, Tom Kuntz, Peder Zane, and Liz Sheld at *Real Clear Investigations*; Sean Davis, Ben Domenech, and Mollie Hemingway at the *Federalist*; James Taranto at the *Wall Street Journal*; Chris Buskirk, Julie Kelly, and Ben Boychuk at *American Greatness*. Thanks to Chris Blackburn, Chris Farrell, Svetlana Lokhova, and Mark Wauck for their generous insight. Thanks to my agent Keith Urbahn and his colleagues at Javelin. Thanks to my editor Kate Hartson and her staff at Center Street, especially Sean McGowan. Thanks to Allen Roth and Steven Schneier for their great support and encouragement. Thanks to Members of the House Permanent Select Committee on Intelligence, Congressmen Mike Conaway, Chris Stewart, Mike Turner, Brad Wenstrup, former congressman Tom Rooney, and their staff who shared their time and insights with me. Thanks to Congressman Mark Meadows and his staff, especially Mary Doocy and Ben Williamson. Thanks to Patrick Davis and Jason Foster. Thanks to friends and colleagues, especially Tony Badran and Mike Doran. Thanks to Mrs. Elizabeth Nunes, and Evelyn, Julia, and Margaret for their patience and generosity. Thanks to Congressman Nunes' staff. Thanks to Jack Langer and Kash Patel, and the entire Objective Medusa team. Thanks most of all to Devin Nunes. Thanks for fighting.

NOTES

Following are sources not identified in the text.

Page 1: **Welcome:** "Devin Nunes Opening Statement for Mueller Hearing," July 24, 2019.

2: **Mueller brushed:** Transcript of Robert S. Mueller III's testimony before the House Intelligence Committee, July 24, 2019.

2: **After spending:** *Report on the Investigation into Russian Interference in the 2016 Presidential Election*, p. 13.

3: **prepared statement:** "Representative Nunes on Russian Election Interference." March 22, 2017. C-Span.

16: **Their business concerns:** "Emails show 2016 links among Steele, Ohr, Simpson—with Russian oligarch in background," Byron York, *Washington Examiner*, August 08, 2018. York's carefully reported and well-sourced columns made him one of the most important of the handful of journalists covering the anti-Trump operation.

17: **Ohr's wife:** US House of Representatives, Committee on the Judiciary, Joint with the Committee on Government Reform and Oversight, Interview of Nellie Ohr, October 19, 2018, p. 8

25: **Halper . . . campaign war-room:** "Reagan aides describe operation to gather inside data on Carter," by Leslie H. Gelb, *New York Times*, July 7, 1983. "John McCain and the October Surprise," by Steve Kornacki, *New York Observer*, October 9, 2008.

26: **Halper . . . drew income:** "Trump-supporting Pentagon analyst stripped of security clearance after Stefan Halper complaints," by Rowan Scarborough, *Washington Times*. August 15, 2018. "FBI spy Stefan Halper's $240,000 Pentagon study disavowed by high-profile experts," by Rowan Scarborough, *Washington Times*. October 1, 2018. Letter from Office of Inspector General, Department of Defense to Sen. Charles Grassley regarding "DoD ONA contracts with Professor Stefan Halper," July 2, 2019. Scarborough's articles, particularly on Halper's interactions with Office of Net Assessment, were among the most significant reports highlighting central issues in the anti-Trump operation.

29: **February 26, 2016 Reuters:** A January 2, 2019 John Solomon article in *The Hill*—"Exculpatory Russia evidence about Mike Flynn that US intel kept secret"—showed conclusively that Flynn had notified his former agency before his trip, receiving a defensive briefing beforehand and providing one to former colleagues on his return. However, information about Flynn's trip was in the public record before his exit from the White House—"Trump Embraces Ex-Top Obama Intel Official," by Shane Harris, Daily Beast, March 9, 2016; "Top Trump adviser defends payment for Russian speaking engagement," Michael Isikoff, Yahoo! News, July 18, 2016; "Trump adviser Michael T. Flynn on his dinner with Putin and why Russia Today is just like CNN," Dana Priest, *Washington Post*, August 15, 2016. Nonetheless, the press routinely ignored Flynn's published remarks in order to prosecute a campaign against the retired general.

31: **He wrote an op-ed:** "The bear out there," by Devin Nunes, *Washington Times*, August 29, 2014.

32: **July 2009 trip to Moscow:** "Text: Obama's Speech at the New Economic School," *New York Times*, July 7, 2009.

32: **we could be doing economically to Russia:** "80 times Trump talked about Putin," by Andrew Kaczynski, Chris Massie, and Nathan McDermott, CNN, March 2017.

36: **Fred Ryan:** Audio recording of Donald Trump's meeting with *Washington Post* editorial board, March 21, 2016.

37: **Papadopoulos hit the press:** "Say sorry to Trump or risk special relationship, Cameron told," by Francis Elliott, *Times of London*, May 4, 2016.

336

38: **Robert Baer**: "Unpacking the Other Clinton-Linked Russia Dossier," by Lee Smith, Real Clear Investigations, April 26, 2018.

39: **Simpson was already familiar**: "How Lobbyists Help Ex-Soviets Woo Washington," by Glenn Simpson and Mary Jacoby, Wall Street Journal, April 17, 2007. "McCain Consultant Is Tied To Work for Ukraine Party," by Mary Jacoby and Glenn Simpson, *Wall Street Journal*, May 14, 2008

40: **The biggest intelligence failure**: "Intel chair: Russian moves biggest intel failure since 9/11," CNN, April 11, 2016.

42: **Hillary for America**: According to the Clinton campaign's law firm, Fusion GPS approached the campaign in early March 2016 and was hired in April. Letter from Matthew Gehringer, General Counsel, Perkins Coie LLP, to William W. Taylor, Zuckerman Spaeder LLP, October 24, 2017.

42: **Founded in 2010**: US Senate, Judiciary Committee, Interview of Glenn Simpson, August 22, 2017, p. 25.

42: **smear Romney**: "The President's Hit List," *Wall Street Journal*, May 11, 2012.

43: **several separate dossiers**: A spreadsheet, "WhosWho19Sept2016.xlsx," produced by Nellie Ohr cites numerous reports (from November 2015 to September 2016), suggesting that Fusion GPS compiled voluminous Trump-Russia and updated it frequently. Many of the dozens names on the spreadsheet appear in the May 20 and three other protodossiers. "Bruce Ohr Gave His Wife's Fusion GPS Research To The FBI. Here Are The Documents," by Chuck Ross, Daily Caller, August 14, 2019.

44: **Ohr was hired**: US House of Representatives, Committee on the Judiciary, Joint with the Committee on Government Reform and Oversight, Interview of Nellie Ohr, October 19, 2018, p. 10

50: **Byron York**: York wrote two *Washington Examiner* articles detailing events on the convention floor. "How pundits got key part of Trump-Russia story all wrong," March 18, 2017; and "What really happened with the GOP platform and Russia," November 26, 2017. The House Intelligence Committee's *Report on Russian Active Measures*, March 22, 2018, goes into great detail regarding the RNC platform issue, p. 68–70.

55: **Kristol and Stephen Hayes**: "Demand the Documents," by Stephen F. Hayes and William Kristol, *Weekly Standard,* August 10, 2015.

55: **Rhodes told the *New York Times Magazine***: "The Aspiring Novelist Who Became Obama's Foreign-Policy Guru," by David Samuels, *New York Times Magazine*, May 5, 2016.

59: **Mifsud taught intelligence**: "The Maltese Phantom of Russiagate" Lee Smith, Real Clear Investigations. My reporting on Mifsud's background and sensibility is indebted to information and insight provided by Stephan C. Roh, Mifsud's lawyer, and Thierry Pastor, who together authored a 2018 book, *The Faking of Russia-gate, The Papadopoulos Case: An Investigative Analysis.*

60: **Stephen Miller and Carter Page**: "Another Trump Campaign Aide Was Invited To Cambridge Event Where 'Spygate' Started," by Chuck Ross, Daily Caller, June 5, 2018. A tireless reporter who covered virtually every component of the anti-Trump operation, Ross broke several major stories, particularly regarding the role of Stefan Halper.

60: **Halper and Downer**: "An Email Referring To 'Collusion' Sheds Light On Cambridge Prof's Interactions With Trump Aide," by Chuck Ross, Daily Caller, May 20, 2018. A source confirms that Downer also approached Page.

60: **Henry Greenberg**: "Trump associate Roger Stone reveals new contact with Russian national during 2016 campaign," by Manuel Roig-Franzia and Rosalind S. Helderman, *Washington Post*, June 17, 2018

61: **remarkable episode**: "2016 Trump Tower Meeting Looks Increasingly Like a Setup by Russian and Clinton Operatives," by Lee Smith, Real Clear Investigations, August 13, 2018.

62: **Simpson had distinguished**: "Controversy Erupts Over Steward's Testimony Before Grand Jury," Brian Duffy and Glenn Simpson, *Wall Street Journal*, February 5, 1998. "Wall Street Journal Story Reflects Fast News Cycle," by Howard Kurtz, *Washington Post*, February 5, 1998

63: **Yanukovych was poised to sign**: "Ukraine suspends talks on EU trade pact as Putin wins tug of war," by Ian Traynor and Oksana Grytsenko, *Guardian*, November 21, 2013

65: **Derwick Associates**: "News-For-Hire Scandal Deepens: 'Fusion GPS' Sleazy Venezuela Links Shed New Light on Trump Dossier," by Lee Smith, Tablet, July 27, 2017.

66: **Thor Halvorssen . . . says Fusion GPS**: Halvorssen's allegations appear in his May 10, 2018 complaint against Simpson, Fritsch and others filed in the Eastern District of New York.

66: **Halvorssen filed a civil RICO lawsuit**: "Testimony of Thor Halvorssen to the Senate Committee on the Judiciary," July 26, 2017.

67: **Fusion GPS targeted**: Does U.S. Media Help Russia Destabilize The United States?" by Lee Smith, The Federalist, October 10, 2017

69: **Akhmetshin . . . former Soviet intelligence officer**: "Former Soviet Counterintelligence Officer at Meeting With Donald Trump Jr. and Russian Lawyer," by Ken Dilanian, Natasha Lebedeva and Hallie Jackson, NBC News, July 14, 2017.

70: **Simpson met with Veselnitskaya**: US Senate, Judiciary Committee, Interview of Glenn Simpson, August 22, 2017, p. 117.

71: **Project Charlemagne**: "Christopher Steele: The Man Behind the Trump Dossier," by Jane Mayer. *The New Yorker*, March 12, 2018.

71: **Admonished**: "FBI releases documents showing payments to Trump dossier author Steele," by Tom Winter, NBC News, Aug. 3, 2018.

72: **Fusion GPS hired a specialist**: Simpson testified that he believed Fusion GPS hired Steele in June, or late May. US House of Representatives, Permanent Select Committee on Intelligence, Interview of Glenn Simpson, November 14, 2017, p. 66. Simpson explained that after Fusion GPS exhausted its open-source material, it brought on Steele. US Senate, Judiciary Committee, Interview of Glenn Simpson, August 22, 2017, p. 143.

74: **Fusion pay Steele**: "Ex-British spy paid $168,000 for Trump dossier, U.S. firm discloses," by Mark Hosenball, Reuters, November 1, 2017.

75: **Sater . . . missing**: Sater was widely reported to have worked with numerous US agencies, see for instance, "Ex-Trump Affiliate Secretly Worked With Prosecutors, FBI and CIA for Years," By Michael Rothfeld, *Wall Street Journal*, August 23, 2019; and "The Asset," by Anthony Cormier and Jason Leopold. BuzzFeed, March 12, 2018.

76: **Julian Assange**: "WikiLeaks to publish more Hillary Clinton emails - Julian Assange," by Mark Tran, *Guardian*, June 12, 2016.

77: **Clinton claimed**: "Transcript: Everything Hillary Clinton Said on the Email Controversy," by Zeke J. Miller, *Time*, March 10, 2015

77: **In July 2015**: "Clinton–Obama Emails: The Key to Understanding Why Hillary Wasn't Indicted," By Andrew McCarthy, *National Review*, January 23, 2018. McCarthy, a former Justice Department official, was one of the first columnists who recognized irregularities in the FBI's Russia probe. His many articles explaining the inner-workings of the FBI and DOJ are vital resources in understanding the anti-Trump plot.

77: **McCabe had a conflict of interest**: *A Review of Various Actions by the Federal Bureau of Investigation and Department of Justice in Advance of the 2016 Election*, Department of Justice, Office of Inspector General, June 2018, p. 431.

78: **Clinton had sent an email to Obama**: Clinton's itinerary (https://history.state.gov/ departmenthistory/travels/secretary/clinton-hillary-rodham) as Secretary of State shows that from June 28 to 29, 2012 she was in St. Petersburg, Russia for the APEC Women and the Economy Forum. According to a response (http://www.judicialwatch.org/wp-content/ uploads/2016/09/JW-v-State-Presidential-Vaughn-00687.pdf) to a Freedom of Information Act application from Judicial Watch, on June 28, Clinton emailed Obama, who replied the same date. In Clinton's July 2, 2016 FBI interview, the interviewing agents noted that the email was sent from Russia. Her email and Obama's are being withheld by the State Department "pursuant to the presidential communications privilege."

78: **Reasonably likely**: *A Review of Various Actions by the Federal Bureau of Investigation and Department of Justice in Advance of the 2016 Election*, Department of Justice, Office of Inspector General, June 2018, p. 190.

78: **Comey . . . cleared Clinton:** "Statement by FBI Director James B. Comey on the Investigation of Secretary Hillary Clinton's Use of a Personal E-Mail System," July 5, 2016.

79: **Michael Gaeta visited Steele:** *Russian Roulette: The Inside Story of Putin's War on America and the Election of Donald Trump* (Hachette, 2018), by Michael Isikoff and David Corn, p. 153.

80: **Steele . . . Russian organized crime:** United States House of Representatives: Committee on the Judiciary, Joint with Committee on Government Reform and Oversight, Interview with Bruce Ohr, p. 63.

81: **Steele invited Jennings:** According to his House testimony, Ohr was head of the Organized Crime and Racketeering Section from 1999-2011. Two books on the FIFA scandal—Ken Bensinger's *Red Card* and Bonita Mersiades's *Whatever it Takes*—report that the Chief of the DOJ's Organized Crime and Racketeering Section, not named, met with Jennings in 2010 along with Steele. Ohr has not publicly acknowledged that he worked closely with Steele on the FIFA case.

82: **British Parliament:** "Written evidence submitted by The *Sunday Times* Insight Investigations Team," by Heidi Blake and Jonathan Calvert, November 2014. http://data.parliament.uk/writtenevidence/committeeevidence.svc/evidencedocument/culture-media-and-sport-committee/the-2022-world-cup-bidding-process/written/15880.html. The report submitted to Parliament does not name Steele. However, remarks attributed in the report to "MI6 source" are identical to those attributed to Steele in Luke Harding's 2017 book *Collusion*, e.g., p. 25: "Nothing was written down. Don't expect me..." etc.

84: **cybersecurity firm hired by the campaign:** Clinton campaign manager Robby Mook: "Clinton campaign manager: Russians leaked Democrats' emails to help Donald Trump," by Amber Phillips, *Washington Post*, July 24, 2016.

84: **Clinton campaign's communications director:** "The Clinton campaign warned you about Russia. But nobody listened to us," by Jennifer Palmieri, *Washington Post*, March 24, 2017.

85: **Anderson Cooper:** Transcript from "Anderson Cooper: 360 Degrees," July 29, 2016

85: **Steele was in Washington:** "McCabe's FBI Tried to Re-engage Christopher Steele After Comey Was Fired," by Jeff Carlson, *Epoch Times*, January 14, 2019.

87: **Strzok was lonely:** All exchanges from text messages between Peter Strzok and Lisa Page. See appendix to "Chairman Johnson Releases Interim Report Including Strzok-Page FBI Text Messages," Senator Ron Johnson, February 7, 2018.

88: **Glenn Simpson was introducing Steele:** "Meet the reporters behind the Trump dossier," by Steve Levine. *Axios*. October 29, 2017. "Hero or hired gun? How a British former spy became a flash point in the Russia investigation," by Tom Hamburger and Rosalind Hederman, *Washington Post*, February 6, 2018. "Isikoff Stunned That His Carter Page Article Was Used To Justify Spy Warrant," by Chuck Ross, Daily Caller, February 2, 2018. "Christopher Steele: The Man Behind the Trump Dossier," by Jane Mayer, *The New Yorker*, March 5, 2018.

91: **Strzok returned from London:** "Hey call me re D brief," Strzok to Page, August 10, 2016.

92: **He later testified before Congress:** US House of Representatives, Permanent Select Committee on Intelligence, Interview with John Brennan, May 23, 2017, p. 22

92: **Brenann took credit:** "How CIA Director John Brennan Targeted James Comey," by Lee Smith, Tablet, February 9, 2018.

94: **Damian Paletta:** https://twitter.com/carterwpage/status/1067793120 560058368

96: **Anthony Weiner:** "Despite Comey Assurances, Vast Bulk of Weiner Laptop Emails Were Never Examined," by Paul Sperry, Real Clear Investigations, August 23, 2018

97: **FISA . . . denied:** In, among other reports, "Trump 'compromising' claims: How and why did we get here?" by Paul Wood, BBC, January 12, 2017.

103: **Clinton's communications team:** "How the Russian collusion myth was hatched by Team Hillary immediately after her loss," by Larry O'Connor, *Washington Times*, May 4, 2018.

103: **Susan Rice:** "Grassley, Graham Uncover 'Unusual Email' Sent by Susan Rice to Herself on President Trump's Inauguration Day." Website of Senator Chuck Grassley, February 12, 2018.

105: **Obama added his voice:** "Obama, With Angela Merkel in Berlin, Assails Spread of Fake News," by Gardiner Harris and Melissa Eddy, *New York Times*, November 17, 2016.

105: **Obama partisans:** "Obama's secret struggle to punish Russia for Putin's election assault," by Greg Miller, Ellen Nakashima and Adam Entous, *Washington Post*, June 23, 2017.

106: **Evelyn Farkas:** "Former Obama official discloses rush to get intelligence on Trump team." Fox News, March 29, 2017.

106: **Brennan's handpicked team:** Senate Committee on the Judiciary, subcommittee on Crime and Terrorism. Statement of James R. Clapper, former Director of National Intelligence, concerning Russian interference in the 2016 United States Elections, May 8, 2018. US House of Representatives, Permanent Select Committee on Intelligence, Interview with John Brennan, May 23, 2017, p 17.

106: **Alexander Bortnikov:** Brennan testimony, May 23, 2017, p 11-12.

106: **"bombshell" report:** "Obama's secret struggle to punish Russia for Putin's election assault," by Greg Miller, Ellen Nakashima and Adam Entous, *Washington Post*, June 23, 2017.

111: **The assessment's methodological flaws:** *Assessing Russian Activities and Intentions in Recent US Elections*, Office of the Director of National Intelligence. January 6, 2017.

114: **Stefan Halper told the Kremlin-directed media outlet:** "Clinton Best Option for US-UK 'Special Relationship'—Ex-White House Official," Sputnik. November 3, 2016.

114: **Adam Schiff . . . RT:** "Schiff Appeared on Kremlin-Backed RT in 2013 to Discuss Push for Greater FISA Transparency," by David Rutz, Washington Free Beacon, February 6, 2018

114: *Russia Beyond* . . . American homes: "U.S. Media Long Carried Putin's Water - Odd, Given Facebook Uproar," Lee Smith, Real Clear Investigations, March 9, 2018

115: **RT's US market share:** "Just How Effective Is Russia's RT?" by Damir Marusic, *The American Interest*, January 21, 2017.

118: **CNN is . . . going forward:** "E-mails Show FBI Brass Discussed Dossier Briefing Details With CNN," by Sean Davis, The Federalist, May 21, 2018. A former Senate investigator, Davis was one of the most knowledgeable journalists covering the anti-Trump operation and broke several key stories.

119: **Prior to meeting with the president-elect:** *Report of Investigation of Former Federal Bureau of Investigation Director James Comey's Disclosure of Sensitive Investigative Information and Handling of Certain Memoranda*, August 2019, p. 22

119: **Tapper emailed *BuzzFeed*:** "Emails: Jake Tapper Tore Into 'Irresponsible' BuzzFeed Editor For Publishing The Steele Dossier," by Chuck Ross, Daily Caller, February 8, 2019.

120: **CNN did not disclose:** "CNN's Undisclosed Ties To Fusion GPS," Chuck Ross and Peter Hasson, October 28, 2017, Daily Caller.

120: **Steele had authored the memos:** "Christopher Steele, Ex-British Intelligence Officer, Said to Have Prepared Dossier on Trump," by Bradley Hope, Michael Rothfeld and Alan Cullison, *Wall Street Journal*, January 11, 2017.

125: **Felix Sater had directed . . . Michael Cohen:** "Trump Associate Boasted That Moscow Business Deal 'Will Get Donald Elected,'" by Matt Apuzzo and Maggie Haberman, *New York Times*, August 28, 2017. *Report on the Investigation into Russian Interference in the 2016 Presidential Election*, p. 74.

126: **Obama . . . press release:** "FACT SHEET: Actions in Response to Russian Malicious Cyber Activity and Harassment," The White House, Office of the Press Secretary. December 29, 2016.

126: **WikiLeaks . . . foreign intelligence services:** "How did WikiLeaks become associated with Russia?" Cathryn Watson, CBS News, November 15, 2017.

129: **Putin . . . visited Volgograd:** President of Russia, English-language website, Trip to Volgograd. August 15, 2016. http://en.kremlin.ru/events/president/trips/52727. "Viktor Yanukovych, Ukraine's fugitive ex-president, just sailed into Volgograd on a triple-decker yacht," Meduza, August 19, 2016.

130: **University of California:** Reporting on International Corruption (3rd Annual Logan Symposium 2009). https://www.youtube.com/watch?v=IQc4muYCl7Y&list=PLxKbSie2B cux5s9-Imj8eM60SroHqw6c9&index=3&t=0s

131: *Times* **more than a decade:** "The Times Announces Digital Subscription Plan," by Jeremy W. Peters, *New York Times*, March 17, 2011

132: **All these newspapers:** "The Aspiring Novelist Who Became Obama's Foreign-Policy Guru," by David Samuels. *New York Times Magazine*, May 5, 2016.

135: **Obama . . . warned Trump:** "Obama Warned Trump About Hiring Flynn, Officials Say," by Michael D. Shear, *New York Times*, May 8, 2017

135: **The president-elect was bewildered:** Committee on the Judiciary, US House of Representatives, June 19, 2019 "Interview of Hope Hicks," p. 191

136: **Strzok . . . worried:** Committee on the Judiciary, US House of Representatives, June 27, 2018. Interview of Peter Strzok, p. 44.

138: **Nick Hopkins:** Michael Flynn: Hopkins was one of three bylines, with Luke Harding and Stephanie Kirchgaessner, on a March 31, 2017 Guardian story about Flynn and Lokhova, "New evidence spy chiefs had concerns about Russian ties."

142: **Either Flynn had misled Pence:** "National security adviser Flynn discussed sanctions with Russian ambassador, despite denials, officials say," by Greg Miller, Adam Entous, and Ellen Nakashima, *Washington Post*, February 9, 2017.

142: **December 28:** Mueller Report, vol. 1, p. 169.

144: **The FBI director admitted:** "Ex-FBI Director Comey Explains How He Took Advantage of Fledgling Trump Administration," by Susan Jones, CNS News, December 14, 2018

145: **McCabe called Flynn:** The Threat: How the F.B.I. Protects America in the Age of Terror and Trump (St. Martin's Press, New York, 2019), by Andrew McCabe, p. 200

145: **Strzok and another FBI agent:** FBI Interview with Michael Flynn, January 24, 2017, entered February 15, 2017. "Why Is The FBI Muzzling The Only Person With Credibility Left in The Flynn Investigation: FBI SSA Joe Pientka III," by Sara Carter, SaraCarter.com, December 17, 2018. Carter's reporting, print and broadcast, was invaluable in uncovering details of the anti-Trump operation.

145: **Sally Yates:** "Justice Department warned White House that Flynn could be vulnerable to Russian blackmail, officials say," by Adam Entous, Ellen Nakashima and Philip Rucker, *Washington Post*, February 13, 2017.

146: **This is totally opposite:** *The Threat*, McCabe, p. 203

147: **New Jersey governor:** "Trump Thought Firing Flynn Would End 'Russia Thing,' Chris Christie Writes in Book," by Maggie Haberman, *New York Times*, January 27, 2019.

155: *Post* **adopted a new motto:** "The Washington Post's new slogan turns out to be an old saying," by Paul Farhi, *Washington Post*, February 24, 2017.

156: **Howard Kurtz at Fox News:** "The Media Backlash Against Howard Kurtz's Media Madness," by Lloyd Grove, Daily Beast, February 9, 2018.

161: **Trump's January conversations:** "'This was the worst call by far': Trump badgered, bragged and abruptly ended phone call with Australian leader," by Greg Miller and Philip Rucker, *Washington Post*, February 2, 2017. "After testy call with Trump over border wall, Mexican president shelves plan to visit White House," by Philip Rucker, Joshua Partlow and Nick Miroff, *Washington Post*, February 24, 2018.

164: **Her testimony was leaked:** "Rice told House investigators why she unmasked senior Trump officials," by Manu Raju, CNN, September 18, 2017.

167: **Nunes went on CNN:** Interview with Wolf Blitzer. "Rep. Devin Nunes' entire CNN interview," March 27, 2017

167: **Another story that sticks out in Langer's mind:** "2 White House Officials Helped Give Nunes Intelligence Reports," by Matthew Rosenberg, Maggie Haberman and Adam Goldman, *New York Times*, March 30, 2017.

168: Langer fired back: "Nunes mocks furor over 'secret tape' comments as 'left-wing media spin,'" Brooke Singman, Fox News, August 9, 2018.

171: **John Batchelor:** Adam "Pathfinder" Schiff: Stalking the Kremlin or the Chupacabra?" By Thaddeus G. McCotter, American Greatness, July 11, 2017

182: **Adam Schiff and media pundits:** "Full transcript: FBI Director James Comey testifies on Russian interference in 2016 election," *Washington Post*, March 20, 2017.

184: **Nunes's committee interviewed officials:** Even though HPSCI voted in September 2018 to publish all its interview transcripts from the Russia investigation after a declassification review by the DNI, as of this writing DNI continues to hold the bulk of them.

194: **Dianne Feinstein:** "Democrats Seek Special Counsel to Investigate Russian Election Interference," by Charlie Savage and Eric Lichtblau, *New York Times*, March 7, 2017.

194: **Trump had asked Comey about his testimony**: "Comey Memos Full Text: Trump Allegedly Discussed Putin, Russian Prostitutes, Clinton Investigation," by Nicole Goodkind, April 19, 2018, *Newsweek*.

195: **Rosenstein wrote a memo**: "'Shaken' Rosenstein Felt Used by White House in Comey Firing," by Michael S. Schmidt and Adam Goldman, *New York Times*, June 29, 2018.

196: **Rosenstein . . . raised with McCabe**: "Rod Rosenstein Suggested Secretly Recording Trump and Discussed 25th Amendment," by Adam Goldman and Michael S. Schmidt, *New York Times*, September 21, 2018. *Washington Post*'s Devlin Barrett and Matt Zapotosky published what amounted to a Rosenstein rebuttal hours later in "McCabe memos say Rosenstein considered secretly recording Trump."

197: **The acting FBI director said he was worried**: McCabe, *The Threat*, p.225

202: **Andrew McCabe called for a . . . briefing**: "McCabe told Congress 'Gang of 8' leaders about FBI probe into Trump. They had no objection," by Allan Smith, Alex Moe and Frank Thorp V, NBC News, February 19, 2019.

202: **The acting FBI director wanted the chairman**: McCabe, *The Threat*, p 244, 5.

205: **new funding source**: "Former Feinstein Staffer Raised $50 Million, Hired Fusion GPS And Christopher Steele After 2016 Election," by Sean Davis, Federalist, April 27, 2018. "Dark Money Org Gave $2 Million To Group Working With Fusion GPS, Steele," Chuck Ross, Daily Caller, March 10, 2019.

205: **Weissmann**: "Mueller deputy praised DOJ official after she defied Trump travel ban order: 'I am so proud,'" by Catherine Herridge, Fox News, December 5, 2017.

206: **hunting party**: "Mueller probe: Meet the lawyers who gave $$ to Hillary, now investigating team Trump," by Brooke Singman, Fox News, July 24, 2017. "Judicial Watch Obtains DOJ Documents Showing Andrew Weissmann Leading Hiring Effort for Mueller Special Counsel," May 14, 2019. The work of Judicial Watch and Tom Fitton in obtaining, and explaining, documents related to the anti-Trump operation, was instrumental in revealing the nature and scope of the extra-constitutional methods US law enforcement employed to overturn an election.

207: **Kevin Clinesmith**: Multiple sources identified Clinesmith as Attorney 2 in the Office of the Inspector General, Department of Justice, *A Review of Various Actions by the Federal Bureau of Investigation and Department of Justice in Advance of the 2016 Election*, June 11, 2018, p. 417 ff. "FBI Lawyer Who Sent Anti-Trump 'Resistance' Text Message Interviewed George Papadopoulos," by Chuck Ross, Daily Caller, June 25, 2018. "The Late, Not-So-Great Mueller Investigation," by Victor Davis Hanson, *National Review*, March 26, 2019.

208: **The post-9/11 FBI**: "A New Era of National Security, 2001-2008." https://www.fbi.gov/history/brief-history/a-new-era-of-national-security

209: **anthrax mailed**: "When Comey and Mueller Bungled the Anthrax Case," by Carl M. Cannon, Real Clear Politics, May 21, 2017.

210: **dirty FBI agents**: "Mueller's hands dirty in old FBI frame-up," By Howie Carr, *Boston Herald*, January 30, 2019.

210: **I like putting people in jail**: "Mueller in 2014: 'I Became A Prosecutor Because I Like Putting People In Jail,'" Patrick Hawley, Big League Politics, December 18, 2017.

218: **Eric Swalwell . . . Fusion GPS's lawyer**: "Nunes signs off on new subpoenas to firm behind Trump-Russia dossier," by Evan Perez, Manu Raju, and Jeremy Herb, CNN, October 11, 2017

219: **Elias had briefed . . . Robby Mook**: "Elias broadly summarized some of the information to top campaign officials, including the campaign manager, Robby Mook," Mayer, *The New Yorker*, March 5, 2018.

219: **September 23**: "Hillary for America Statement on Bombshell Report About Trump Aide's Chilling Ties To Kremlin," archived at The American Presidency Project. https://www.presidency.ucsb.edu/documents/hillary-for-america-statement-bombshell-report-about-trump-aides-chilling-ties-kremlin

219: **October 19**: "15 Facts About Donald Trump's Deeply Unsetting Russia Problem And WikiLeaks," Hillary for America Press, October 19, 2016.

220: **Maggie Haberman . . . Kenneth Vogel**: https://twitter.com/maggienyt/status/92296288 0206647297?lang=en; https://twitter.com/kenvogel/status/922955410327425027?lang=en

220: **Bank records showed**: "Fusion GPS Bank Records Show Russia-Related Payments," by Chuck Ross, Daily Caller, November 21, 2017.

221: **Nellie Ohr . . . was employed**: US House of Representatives, Committee on the Judiciary, Joint with the Committee on Government Reform and Oversight, Interview of Nellie Ohr, October 19, 2018, August 28, 2018, p. 8-9. US House of Representatives, Committee on the Judiciary, Joint with the Committee on Government Reform and Oversight, Interview of Bruce Ohr, p. 113.

224: **The twelve 302s**: Heavily redacted versions of the FBI interviews were released August 8, 2019 to Judicial Watch.

227: **Russia community**: US House of Representatives, Committee on the Judiciary, Joint with the Committee on Government Reform and Oversight, Interview of Nellie Ohr, October 18, 2018, p. 24

228: **David Kramer:** "John McCain Associate Had Contact With A Dozen Reporters Regarding Steele Dossier," Chuck Ross, Daily Caller, March 14, 2019

228: **Kathleen Kavalec:** "Citizens United FOIA Document Release – CU Releases Kavalec Memo & Related Records," May 10, 2019.

229: **Nuland and Winer's stories didn't match**: "Victoria Nuland says Obama State Dept. informed FBI of reporting from Steele dossier," by Emily Tillett, CBS News, February 4, 2018.

230: **Anne Applebaum:** Few opinion writers used their perch to push the "collusion" narrative as prolifically as Applebaum. In addition to the two July 2016 columns discussed earlier, among her *Washington Post* columns devoted to the Trump-Russia narrative are: "Stop obsessing over 'secrets' about Trump and Russia. What we already know is bad enough," January 13, 2017. "The critical questions on Russia," March 26, 2017. "Don't forget those smiling images of Trump and the Russians," May 11, 2017. "The Russian-American relationship is no longer about Russia or America," July 7, 2017. "This law might explain why a Russian lawyer wanted to meet with Trump," July 11, 2017. "The ugly way Trump's rise and Putin's are connected," July 25, 2017. "The case for Trump-Russia collusion: We're getting very, very close," September 8, 2017. "Did Russia teach Paul Manafort all its dirty tricks?" October 30, 2017. "It's not just Russia anymore," April 6, 2018. "This is how Putin buys influence in the West," June 15, 2018. "Trump is hinting at concessions to Putin. So what do we get back?" July 6, 2018. "Did Putin share stolen election data with Trump?" July 20, 2018. "The Trump-Putin revelations tell us what we knew all along," January 13, 2019. "Why was Trump so afraid of the Mueller investigation? We may never know," April 19, 2019.

230: Facebook post: "Did President Obama Read the 'Steele Dossier' in the White House Last August?" Lee Smith, Tablet, December 20, 2017.

231: **Simpson had committed a felony**: US House of Representatives, Permanent Select Committee on Intelligence, Interview of Glenn Simpson, November 14, 2017, p. 78.

233: **McCabe . . . testified before the committee**: US House of Representatives, Committee on the Judiciary, Joint with Committee on Government Reform and Oversight, Interview with Andrew McCabe, December 17, 2017.

235: **Downer was... an ally of the Clintons**: "Australian diplomat whose tip prompted FBI's Russia-probe has tie to Clintons," John Solomon and Alison Spann, *The Hill*, March 5, 2018.

236: **The story also omitted a key detail:** "The Curious Case of Mr. Downer: His story about the Papadopoulos meeting calls the FBI's into question," Kimberley A. Strassel, *Wall Street Journal*, May 31, 2018. I'm indebted here and elsewhere to Strassel's detailed reporting and strong voice. She was one of the first journalists to unravel the relationship between law enforcement officials, the press, and Fusion GPS.

237: **statement of the offense:** "United States of America v George Papadopoulos." US District Court for the District of Columbia. October 5, 2017

238: **Adam Schiff:** House Permanent Select Committee on Intelligence: Minority Views. March 26, 2018, p. 20

238: **mysterious professor's closest public links:** "The Maltese Phantom of Russiagate" Lee Smith, Real Clear Investigations. May 30, 2018.

239: **Mifsud had chaired a panel**: Devin Nunes letter to Michael Pompeo, Gina Haspel, Paul Nakasone, and Christopher Wray. May 3, 2019

241: **I never heard the words DNC**: Executive Session. Committee on the Judiciary, joint with the Committee on Government Reform and Oversight, US House of Representatives, October 25, 2018 Interview of George Papadopoulos, p. 21.

242: **Halper met with the Trump adviser**: "A London Meeting Before The Election Aroused George Papadopoulos's Suspicions," By Chuck Ross Daily Caller. March 25, 2018. "F.B.I. Sent Investigator Posing as Assistant to Meet With Trump Aide in 2016." *New York Times* May 2, 2019. Adam Goldman, Michael S. Schmidt, and Mark Mazzetti.

 For Papadopoulos' account, listen to Dan Bongino's podcast interview with Papadopoulos linked at "The Papadopoulos Interview—Explosive Revelations You Need to Know," by Matt Palumbo, bongino.com, November 3, 2018. A former New York City Policeman and Secret Service officer, Bongino provided outstanding analysis of the anti-Trump operation, especially regarding law enforcement issues.

242: **The pair asked Papadopoulos**: "The damning proof of innocence that FBI likely withheld in Russian probe," by John Solomon, *The Hill*, March 4, 2019. Solomon's deeply sourced reporting uncovering countless details of the anti-Trump operation make him one of the indispensable journalists covering the story.

242: **FBI agents interviewed Papadopoulos**: "United States of America v George Papadopoulos," United States District Court for the District of Columbia. Government's Sentencing Memorandum, page 4, footnote 2.

243: **Mifsud was in Washington, DC**: The FBI interviewed Mifsud in his hotel lobby February 10, 2017. Mueller Report, p 193.

251: **Hamilton 68**: Key Democrats urge social media companies to investigate Russia-linked accounts, Patricia Zengerle, Reuters, January 23, 2018

251: **Articles in the *Washington Post* and on the *Daily Beast***: "How a classified four-page Russia memo triggered a political firestorm," *Washington Post*, January 29, 2018 By Matt Zapotosky, Karoun Demirjian, Robert Costa and Ellen Nakashima. "The 'Nunes Memo' Ripping the Justice Department Was Written by Former Justice Department Lawyer," The Daily Beast, Betsy Woodruff. February 2, 2018

254: **Wittes**: "Thoughts on the Nunes Memo: We Need to Talk About Devin," Quinta Jurecic, Shannon Togawa Mercer, Benjamin Wittes, Lawfare, February 2, 2018

258: **HPSCI voted to release**: "Redacted Democratic Response to Nunes Memo Defends FBI Surveillance Of Trump Aide," by Martina Stewart NPR, February 24, 2018

260: **According to Strzok**: Committee on the Judiciary, US House of Representatives, June 27, 2018, Interview of Peter Strzok, pages 44-45.

260: **Lisa Page corroborated Strzok's explanation**: Committee on the Judiciary, US House of Representatives, July 13, 2018. Interview of Lisa Page, P. 44. "Transcripts of Lisa Page's Closed-Door Testimonies Provide New Revelations in Spygate Scandal," by Jeff Carlson, *Epoch Times*, January 11, 2019. Carlson contributed numerous important articles detailing the anti-Trump operation, as did several of his Epoch Times colleagues, such as Brian Cates.

260: **Nunes' public statements:** eg. "Nunes: Trump's Declassification Order Will Help Explain the Strzok-Page 'Insurance Policy,'" Susan Jones, CNS News, September 18, 2018.

263: **Memo was further reinforced:** "Criminal Referral Confirms Nunes Memo's Explosive Claims Of FISA Abuse," by Mollie Hemingway, The Federalist, February 7, 2018.

264: **The second significant document:** House Permanent Select Committee on Intelligence, *Report on Russian Active Measures*, March 22, 2018.

265: **Glenn Kessler:** "The unsupported claim that James Clapper tipped Jake Tapper about the dossier," by Glenn Kessler, *Washington Post*, May 3, 2018. According to Kessler, Clapper told him the Republican report "'deliberately conflated' his interview to make it appear he had spoken to Tapper in January, but he insisted that was not the case." However, Sean Davis noted in The Federalist (May 3, 2018) that the report filed by HPSCI Democrats ("Minority Views," March 26, 2018, p. 61) made the same assessment. An unnamed "spokesman for the Democrats" told Kessler to ignore the documentary record and take his anonymous word for it. "Having now read that section again," said the Democratic spokesman, "I can see how you think the Minority in its Views is referring to [Clapper's] time as DNI; but that would be an incorrect reading."

273: **HPSCI sent a classified letter:** "Secret intelligence source who aided Mueller probe is at center of latest clash between Nunes and Justice Dept.," by Robert Costa, Carol D. Leonnig, Devlin Barrett and Shane Harris, *Washington Post*, May 8, 2018

274: **Pulitzer:** https://www.pulitzer.org/winners/staffs-new-york-times-and-washington-post

276: **Costa tweeted:** https://twitter.com/costareports/status/998722625227587584?lang=en

277: **Halper invites Page:** "Cambridge Prof With CIA, MI6 Ties Met With Trump Adviser During Campaign, Beyond," Chuck Ross, Daily Caller, May 17, 2018.

278: **Dearlove . . . meets with Steele:** "Hero or hired gun? How a British former spy became a flash point in the Russia investigation," by Tom Hamburger and Rosalind S. Helderman, *Washington Post*, February 6, 2018

279: **denounced Putin:** "Alexander Litvinenko accused Vladimir Putin of being a paedophile four months before he was poisoned," by Lizzie Dearden, *Independent*, January 21, 2016.

279: **£2000 MI6:** "Alexander Litvinenko was 'a paid consultant' for MI6," BBC, February 2, 2015.

279: **Italians had set up a commission:** "The Litvinenko murder: Scaramella : The Italian Connection," by Lauren Veevers, *Independent*, December 3, 2006.

280: **Litvinenko . . . Prodi:** "Why a spy was killed," by Cathy Scott-Clark and Adrian Levy, *Guardian*, January 26, 2008

280: **Litvinenko's information:** ibid

280: **Litvinenko's murder was a Russian state operation:** "Donald Trump dossier: intelligence sources vouch for author's credibility," by Nick Hopkins and Luke Harding, *Guardian*, January 12, 2017. In July 2008, a senior British security official leaked to media sources that "we very strongly believe the Litvinenko case to have had some state involvement; there are very strong indications that it was a state action." "Litvinenko killing 'had state involvement,'" by Mark Urban, BBC July 7, 2008. The leak was unauthorized: "No intelligence or security officials were authorized to comment on the Litvinenko case," a British government spokesman said at the time. "Britain seeks to defuse row with Russia over Alexander Litvinenko murder," by Jon Swaine, *Telegraph*, July 11, 2008.

280: **Steele left MI6:** According to Mayer's March 2018 *New Yorker* profile: "In 2008, Steele informed M.I.6 that he planned to leave the service and open a commercial intelligence firm . . . He left in good standing, but his exit was hastened, because M.I.6 regarded his plans as a potential conflict of interest." Intelligence sources I interviewed cannot explain what conflict of interest would be resolved with an early departure from active service.

281: **Steele . . . shared these memos:** "Devin Nunes is investigating me. Here's the truth," by Jonathan Winer, *Washington Post*, February 8, 2018.

282: **Jonathan Winer introduced Steele:** "Citizens United FOIA Document Release – CU Releases Kavalec Memo & Related Records," May 10, 2019.

284: **Surkov was a well-known figure:** "Ex-rebel leaders detail role played by Putin aide in east Ukraine," by Anton Zverev, Reuters, May 11, 2017.

284: **Bruce Ohr . . . confirmed:** United States House of Representatives: Committee on the Judiciary, Joint with Committee on Government Reform and Oversight, Interview with Bruce Ohr, p. 27

284: **Pentagon-funded project:** "The Russia-China Relationship: The Impact on the United States' Security Interests," Project Director Professor Stefan Halper, p. 8.

286: **The evidence points:** Sources told *Washington Post* reporters Tom Hamburger, Robert Costa, and Ellen Nakashima for a June 5, 2018 article ("How the Trump echo chamber pushes bit players like Stefan Halper to center stage") that "Halper and Steele are not acquainted and did not work together during the 2016 campaign season." That is no more believable than the Ohrs' claim they didn't know Steele was working on Trump-Russia reporting until he told them in July 2016.

287: **Rowan Scarborough:** "FBI spy Stefan Halper's $240,000 Pentagon study disavowed by high-profile experts," by Rowan Scarborough, *Washington Times*. October 1, 2018.

289: **John Heileman:** "MSNBC analyst suggests Devin Nunes is a Russian agent for penning secret FBI memo." Rowan Scarborough, *Washington Times*, January 30, 2018

291: **Ryan Lizza:** Ryan Lizza's Hit Piece On Devin Nunes' Extended Family Is Deeply Flawed, Mollie Hemingway, The Federalist, October 2, 2018. Hemingway was among the fiercest critics: in her articles, as well as on social media, and television: of the establishment media's advocacy of the Russiagate conspiracy theory.

302: **special counsel was based on the dossier**: "The Scope of Investigation and Definition of Authority," August 2, 2017 memorandum from Deputy Attorney General Rod J. Rosenstein to Special Counsel Robert S. Mueller III.

303: **Weissmann announces:** "Top Mueller Prosecutor Stepping Down In Latest Clue Russia Inquiry May Be Ending," Carrie Johnson. NPR, March 14, 2019

305: **William Barr**: My understanding of Barr's memo is informed by pseudonymous twitter user Undercover Huber, in particular an April 17, 2019 thread: https://twitter.com/JohnWHuber/status/1118643987487887361. Undercover Huber was one of a number of independent researchers whose work proved invaluable in discovering and deciphering documents. Others important researchers working pseudonymously include Twitter users like Techno Fog, Last Refuge, RosieMemos, TracyBeanz—there are too many to include here but I am indebted to them all, evidence that the American public not only wants accurate and detailed news and reporting but can produce it as well.

306: **Mueller's tactics**: "The False Evidence Against Scooter Libby," by Peter Berkowitz, *Wall Street Journal*, April 6, 2015.

309: **Rosenstein had announced**: "Rod Rosenstein to leave DOJ in mid-March," David Mark and Daniel Chaitin, *Washington Examiner*. February 18, 2019.

312: **Mueller . . . TV appearance:** "Special Counsel Robert Mueller Statement on Russia Investigation," C-Span. May 29, 2019

312: **Schiff conducted a public hearing:** "2 Former FBI Officials Appear At Latest Hearing On Russian Political Interference," Mary Louis Kelly. NPR, June 12, 2019. Andrew McCarthy also appeared at the invitation of the HPSCI minority.

315: **I'm coming to clean up the mess.** "Nunes sues Twitter, some users, seeks over $250M alleging anti-conservative 'shadow bans,' smears," Gregg Re and Catherine Herridge. Fox News. March 18, 2019. Nunes files $150M lawsuit against McClatchy, alleging conspiracy to derail Clinton, Russia probes," Gregg Re. Fox News. April 8, 2019.

318: **Steven Biss:** Biss also represented Svetlana Lokhova in her May 23, 2019 defamation suit filed against Stefan Halper, Dow Jones & Co (owner of *Wall Street Journal*; *New York Times*; *Washington Post*; and NBC.

321: **Cleta Mitchell:** "Bruce Ohr Revealed Political Operatives Got The FBI To Investigate The NRA, by Margot Cleveland, The Federalist, March 14, 2019. Cleveland's prescient articles illuminated many of the legal issues underlying the anti-Trump operation.

324: **Davidson followed up:** "Senators Ask for an Investigation into Trump Dealings in Azerbaijan," Adam Davidson, *The New Yorker*, March 30, 2017.

326: **Dean Baquet:** "The New York Times Unites vs. Twitter," by Ashley Feinberg, Slate, August 15, 2019. "From Russian Collusion Hoaxing to White Supremacy Hysteria," Julie Kelly, American Greatness, August 8, 2019. I'm indebted to Kelly's sharp reporting—and even sharper criticism of the hypocrisies of Left and Never Trump Republican media.

327: **eight criminal referrals:** "Nunes to send eight criminal referrals to DOJ concerning leaks, conspiracy amid Russia probe," Gregg Re. Fox News. April 7, 2019.

INDEX